Philanthropy, Fundraising, and the Capital Campaign

A PRACTICAL GUIDE

G. David Gearhart

UBO

With editorial assistance by Judy Gregson Schwab
With research assistance by Brenda Brugger

Library of Congress Cataloging-in-Publication Data

Gearhart, G. David.
Philanthropy, fundraising, and the capital campaign : a practical guide / by
G. David Gearhart.
    p. cm.
 Includes bibliographical references.
 ISBN 1-56972-034-7
1. Educational fund raising--United States. 2. Universities and
colleges--United States--Finance. I. Title.
 LB2336.G435 2006
 378.1'06--dc22

                    2005017022

National Association of College and University Business Officers
Washington, DC
www.nacubo.org

Printed in the United States of America

Contents

Dedication

This book is dedicated to six outstanding gentlemen who have had an impact on my life:

William A. Schreyer, Chairman, Emeritus, Merrill Lynch, New York City and Princeton. Mr. Schreyer is one of the finest gentlemen with whom I have had the privilege of working. He was the chairman of the Campaign for Penn State from 1985 to 1990. His loyalty to his friends and devotion to any task before him made him one of America's most admired captains of industry. He is respected worldwide as a significant leader in business, education, philanthropy, and world financial markets. It was my absolute privilege to work with him in his capacity as chair of the campaign at Penn State as well as chairman of the Penn State University Board of Trustees. He and his wife, Joan, are among America's most generous benefactors, having created and endowed the Schreyer Honors College at Penn State. His generosity to many, many endeavors worldwide is well known and respected. He remains a dear friend to this day and has been a major influence on my life and career. He has taught me much, but in particular, that "life is a journey, not a destination."

John A. White, Chancellor of the University of Arkansas. Dr. White afforded me and my family the opportunity to return to Arkansas after living in Pennsylvania for 14 years. Arkansas is home. I was born and raised in Fayetteville, and my wife, Jane, lived in the state most of her life. Both of our children, Katy and Brock, were born in Arkansas. Our roots run deep here. Chancellor White has been an agent for change in the university. Change always brings adversity, but I know of no one in my life who has met adversity with such courage, determination, hard work, and absolute, laser-like focus on building a great university. He simply would not be deterred in changing the institution for the better. His leadership will be felt by this university and Arkansans everywhere for years into the future. Chancellor White has provided incredible leadership to the University of Arkansas, and it has been my privilege to serve alongside him and be a part of the "Arkansas Miracle."

Dr. B. Alan Sugg, President, the University of Arkansas System. Dr. Sugg is one of the finest gentlemen I have ever met. He is a collegial leader of all of the university's multiple campuses and has been incredibly supportive and extremely helpful to Chancellor John A. White as well as to me in our advancement program. There would be no "Arkansas Miracle" without his steady hand, synergistic spirit, and genuine nature. He has, almost single-handedly, held together and moved forward a huge university organization with 11 campuses and more than 42,000 students. He has a massive job, and no one has ever done it better. He is highly respected by faculty, alumni, students, legislators, and university constituents.

Coach Frank Broyles, Director of Men's Athletics at the University of Arkansas. Coach Broyles is not only a phenomenal leader of people, who won a national championship for the university years ago, but also has built one of the best athletic programs in the country. He is also a phenomenal fund raiser. Practically everything that has happened in building facilities and programs in the Athletic Department at the University of Arkansas is because of his fund-raising prowess. He is a towering figure, who never accepts anything but the best in everything he does. He has been a marvelous volunteer, mentor, teacher, and role model for our entire staff in University Advancement. Recently he lost his beloved wife, Barbara, to Alzheimer's disease after 59 years of marriage. The love and devotion that he expressed during her years of illness was and is a constant reminder to all of us of dignity, duty, love, and devotion. He is an Arkansas icon.

Dr. Roy B. Shilling Jr., President, Emeritus, Southwestern University, Georgetown, Texas. Dr. Shilling took a chance on hiring a 25-year-old development officer with little experience as his vice president of development in 1978. Why he took that chance is still a mystery to me, although I suspect it was because I came "cheap." Dr. Shilling's act of faith in me changed my life. He was a college president for more than 30 years at two extraordinarily prestigious institutions—Hendrix College and Southwestern University. Whether it was divine providence or my good fortune, his leadership and guidance in my early career made all the difference for me. We have stayed in close touch for over 25 years of friendship, and I'm grateful to him for being a phenomenal teacher, mentor, and dear friend.

John J. Glier, President and Chief Executive Officer, Grenzebach Glier and Associates. John Glier heads one of America's most distinguished international consulting firms. He has, most likely, provided consulting services to more multimillion-dollar capital campaigns than anyone else in the history of philanthropy, and I have learned a great deal through the years from him and his colleagues at GGA. John and his partner and firm chairman, **Martin Grenzebach,** have built an internationally respected company, providing services to clients with cumulative goals in excess of $27 billion. John is a hard driver with a rare tenacity for doing things right the first time. He is a mentor, a teacher, and a dear friend.

Foreword

In 1997 private gift support at the University of Arkansas totaled approximately $20 million per year. A year earlier, the university had successfully completed its first comprehensive capital campaign, raising $178 million.

After the retirement of a highly popular chancellor and vice chancellor for advancement, the challenge was to take a good program to greatness. The university had reached a point in its development program where growth and the infusion of capital were essential for fund raising to grow and prosper. Seven years later, the University of Arkansas is approaching $100 million in annual gift receipts and is in the final stages of a capital campaign that approaches $1 billion.

In a world of uncertainties, particularly in higher education, one thing is certain: fund raising, development, advancement, and capital campaigns are critically important to the operation, and even survival, of universities—private and public! Ninety-nine point nine percent of colleges and universities in America—both public and private—have a fund-raising or development function. Higher education leaders realize tuition revenue and legislative support alone will not build a great university. It is only private gift support that builds a substantial endowment and provides scholarships for students, endowed faculty chairs and professorships, and capital support for bricks and mortar—not to mention the acute importance of annual giving to provide unrestricted support for an institution. Private gift support is essential for any institution to advance in today's highly constrained resource environment.

At public universities, the decline of state support in recent years has been dramatic. Many major public research universities—highly prestigious ones—now receive less than 15 percent of their total support from the state tax dollar. Attempting to finance an institution "on the backs of students" through double-digit increases in tuition and "on the backs of faculty and staff," who may not receive even cost-of-living increases will ultimately be the demise of higher education. Sooner or later (and hopefully sooner) state governments will realize that continued cuts in higher education appropriations or, in the alternative, simply maintaining the status quo of an institution's budget diminishes a state's economic and cultural future. All citizens pay a significant price when a state fails to provide adequate support for public higher education; underfunding public universities erodes their ability to educate the sons and daughters of our great republic.

Fortunately, successful capital campaigns can fundamentally transform an institution of higher learning. Entire campuses, colleges, faculty, and students can be changed for the better because of private gift support. Few presidents or chancellors would disagree that private gift support is the critical factor in making the proverbial quantum leap to greatness. There is simply no other way to move a university forward dramatically.

Unfortunately, there is a shortage of seasoned development professionals who can provide leadership to our nation's philanthropic organizations. The number of 501(c)(3) organizations in this country has increased dramatically in the last 10 years. There are now literally millions of organizations seeking private gifts. Unfortunately, there are few places where a person can be taught fund raising. The best place to learn the profession is in the workplace, gaining valuable experience alongside seasoned veterans.

This book, written by a distinguished university administrator and one of the nation's most effective fund-raising professionals, makes an important contribution to the field of philanthropy and capital campaigning. Dr. G. David Gearhart, vice chancellor for university advancement at the University of Arkansas, and former senior vice president of the Pennsylvania State University and senior vice president and managing director of an international consulting firm, has almost 30 years of experience to share with others who understand the importance of philanthropy to their organizations. Covering a variety of topics that are necessary and the most important components of any solid development program, this book will enable the practitioner to know the ins and outs of capital campaigning.

What a difference Dr. Gearhart has made in the life of the University of Arkansas! And, he had similar impacts at Penn State University, Hendrix College, and Westminster College, where he also led the development efforts. Since coming to the University of Arkansas in 1998, he and his colleagues have raised well over $1 billion for our institution. More money was raised during his first five years here than had been raised over the previous 127 years.

I recommend this book to anyone who wants to know the basics of philanthropy and the launching of a capital campaign. Studying this book carefully will help you lead your fund-raising program. It will help transition your university to a position of greatness that few would have thought possible. Private philanthropy has the power to make incredible dreams come true for a university; I've seen it happen.

Dr. John A. White, Chancellor
University of Arkansas
Fayetteville, Arkansas

Preface

In 1995 the National Association of College and University Business Officers published *The Capital Campaign in Higher Education; a Practical Guide for College and University Advancement.* At the time I wrote this book, I was the senior vice president for development and university relations at Pennsylvania State University. Penn State had completed a major capital campaign in 1990 and was in the planning stages for a $1 billion campaign to be launched in the next year or so.

The book attempted to lay out the ins and outs of capital campaigning at colleges and universities. It was meant to be a practical guide for presidents, chancellors, development officers, deans, and others planning a major philanthropic effort.

The book sold well and continues to sell 10 years later. However, I am amazed at how much was left out of the original book—or perhaps a better way to put it—how much I have learned in the intervening decade. Everything in life needs a little nip or tuck after 10 years, but sometimes things need, as one donor told me in regard to a building that needed renovating, "not just a facelift, but a whole body job." Therefore, I set out to add to, delete from, readjust, and recalibrate the 1995 book. What has been created is best described as an entirely new and different book. You will still find the same practical guide for capital campaigns, but this new book has been expanded to include many more topics relevant to philanthropic endeavors as well as a hefty dose of the proverbial paradigm shifts in our profession. Much has changed in 10 years to be sure. The intense competition among eleemosynary organizations is at an all-time high. Capital campaigns are being run by all types of organizations, including health agencies, arts centers, hospitals, primary and secondary schools, human service organizations, museums—the list goes on and on. It is my hope that this book will provide a practical summary of the major elements of planning and conducting a capital campaign for any organization, with special emphasis on colleges and universities.

As tuition rises faster than the consumer price index and legislative appropriations continue to dwindle in jurisdiction after jurisdiction, both public and private organizations are turning to gift support not only to strengthen their missions but also to maintain them.

The goal of this book, like the first one, is to present practical information in a simple, easy-to-absorb manner. It is, therefore, a practical guide for the development and capital campaign practitioner. It is intended for use by anyone who is interested in launching a capital program for their organization.

Chapter 1 begins with a short history of philanthropy and a discussion of the United States leading the way as the world's philanthropist. The capital campaign is discussed in terms of definition and purpose. This chapter also offers an overview of the current philanthropic landscape, trends in philanthropy the past 10 years, and some of the newer philanthropic thrusts, including diversity in our profession, women in philanthropy, and freedom of information issues.

Chapter 2 discusses institutional readiness for a major philanthropic effort, including the case statement, strategic objectives, goal setting, prospecting, feasibility study, and many other readiness issues.

The organization of a campaign is addressed in chapter 3, including use of campaign counsel, campaign phases, and various campaign components.

Chapter 4 discusses staffing requirements necessary for a major campaign. The chapter also explains corporate and foundation initiatives, opportunities, and challenges and concludes with the role of the CEO in the campaign environment.

Volunteers and the external campaign organization are depicted in chapter 5. An in-depth discussion of the use of volunteers and the various volunteer organizational models is presented. The role of the campaign officers is also discussed as well as the various campaign meetings.

Chapter 6 concentrates on a variety of campaign details, including the campaign budget, campaign financing, the gift range chart, campaign cash flow, and an in-depth discussion of campaign counting guidelines.

Chapter 7 is devoted primarily to strategic steps and critical factors in major gift solicitation and concludes with new paradigms in fund raising.

Chapter 8 addresses campaign communications, including creation of a communications plan and its basic elements. The various campaign publications are presented as well as a discussion of the campaign kickoff and concluding events.

Finally, chapter 9 presents the post-campaign plan and the inevitable planning for the next campaign.

A significant part of the book is the "Campaign Tools" section on CD-ROM, which is designed to give useful materials to the development professional on a variety of campaign issues and topics. It should be helpful to any practitioner who wants to conduct a capital campaign.

one

Campaigning in the 21st Century

Viewing the matter in retrospect, I can testify that it is nearly always easier to make $1 million honestly, than to dispose of it wisely.

Julius Rosenwald

These Americans are peculiar people. If, in a local community, a citizen becomes aware of a human need which is not being met, he thereupon discusses the situation with his neighbors. Suddenly, a committee comes into existence. The committee thereupon begins to operate on behalf of the need and a new community function is established. It is like watching a miracle, because these citizens perform this act without a single reverence to any bureaucracy, or any official agency.

Alexis De Tocqueville

Giving Money Away Has Become Big Business

The American people have been generous contributors to many causes, even before this country was formed and when those living in the new colonies were British citizens. We have always been a nation of givers, and philanthropy has grown steadily in the 230 years since our birth as a nation. In 1991 approximately $124 billion was given away in the United States. That figure surpassed $240 billion in 2003, and all experts believe the figure will continue to increase dramatically as we witness a major transfer of wealth over the next 10 to 20 years.[1]

Yes, not only is philanthropy big business in America, but it also has the capacity to transform institutions—be they colleges or universities, health agencies, hospitals, social service organizations, the arts, humanities programs, environmental concerns, high schools, grade schools, or preschools. America continues to maintain its place as the world's leader in philanthropic gifts and grants.

In the wake of the horrible terrorist attacks of September 11, 2001, the American public, as well as nonprofit and philanthropic organizations, responded courageously with disaster relief assistance. It is estimated that within a month's time of the terrorist attacks, the American public had responded with well over $1 billion in support.

According to Independent Sector, many others stepped forward to donate blood or give their time to help in the relief effort. Seven out of 10 Americans contributed something to the relief efforts—money, time, blood, property, articles of clothing, or food—to respond to the dramatic need. The outpouring of support following the recent devastating tsunami in Southeast Asia was nearly as remarkable. Within three months, Americans gave more than $1.2 billion in private donations. Americans are extremely generous, and our giving keeps alive many organizations that would have ceased to exist years ago were it not for philanthropic support.

According to the *Nonprofit Almanac*, America has 1.23 million charitable nonprofit organizations, all of which are looking for private gift support. For many of these organizations, particularly arts organizations, human service agencies, and religious congregations, private contributions may be the sole source of their support.

And it does not appear that American philanthropy will slow down soon. More than 13 million households in the United States have incomes exceeding $100,000 or net worth greater than $500,000, not including one's principal place of residence.

More than 240,000 households in this country have more than $5 million in net worth, and households that have met this threshold are growing at a rate of 4 percent per year.

Millionaires represent 2.5 million households and are growing at a rate of 7 percent per year. Baby Boomers, the population born generally between 1946 and 1964, are beginning to represent the single largest group of affluent households in the United States. As Baby Boomers age, they inherit resources from their parents. This country will experience the well-documented "intergenerational transfer of wealth," which could be as high as $40 trillion to $100 trillion, and could lead to a huge explosion of philanthropic potential.[2]

Additionally, statistically women tend to be more philanthropic than men, and they certainly live longer. Over three-quarters of affluent households are composed of married couples, with both spouses typically making investment decisions jointly. Not only do women have a profound impact on investment decisions, but they also have substantial resources in their own right. Research reveals one-third of businesses and more than one-third of all estates over $5 million are owned by women.[3]

It is now evident to all in the business of fund raising that philanthropy will continue in spite of war, recession, depression, and even the plague. Giving has been a part of human life throughout recorded history and probably before then. The United States of America has been characterized as the most charitable nation on earth, and this continues to be true in the 21st century as it was in the 20th, the 19th, and the 18th.

The word *philanthropy* is of Greek origin and means "love of mankind." We have evidence that the art or science of giving was evident thousands of years ago.[4]

According to Jon Van Til, in his book, *Critical Issues in American Philanthropy*, the philanthropic spirit was mentioned 4,000 years ago in the Egyptian Book of the Dead, which provides a good starting point. Dating from about 4000 B.C., it praises those who give bread to the hungry and water to the thirsty. The tombs of Harkhuf and Pepi-Nakht, dating from the Sixth Dynasty (2500 B.C.), offer this motivation for giving and doing good: "I desired that it might be well with me and the great god's presence."[5]

It is generally an accepted fact that American philanthropy was inherited from our British roots. Giving was primarily a religious function in the early days of the history of this continent. It did not always take the form of money or coins of the realm but rather goods, services, and personal property, or chattels.

Some of the earliest philanthropic endeavors were to support the founding of colonial colleges. In fact, Harvard, Princeton, Yale, Penn State, and many of the early Ivy League institutions were provided their sustenance from gifts. Michael Worth describes this phenomenon most accurately:

> In 1641, William Hibbens, Hugh Peter, and Thomas Weld set sail from Boston to London on a mission to solicit gifts for a young American college. Their stated purpose was to raise money enabling the college to "educate the heathen Indian," a cause apparently viewed as worthy by wealthy British citizens of the time.
>
> Weld remained in England, never to return to America. So too, in a manner of speaking, did Peter, who was hanged for crimes committed under British law. Only Hibbens returned to America, a year later, with 500 pounds to support the struggling institution—Harvard College.
>
> The adventures of Hibbens, Peter, and Weld are regarded as the first organized fund-raising activity undertaken for an American college. Throughout the 18th and 19th centuries, however, fund-raising methods were primitive by today's standards, mostly consisting of passing the church plate, staging church suppers or

bazaars, and writing "begging letters." The principal technique was the "begging mission," usually carried out by a trustee, the president of the institution, or a paid agent, who was often given a percentage of the funds raised.

Early colleges were often connected with a sponsoring church, and their fund raising reflected a religious zeal, with gifts being solicited for the purpose of advancing Christianity in a young and uncivilized nation.[6]

For those readers wishing a more complete history of philanthropy, there are several sources of particular note worth citing.

The first is Waldemar A. Nielsen's book, *The Golden Donors*.[7] In this book, Nielsen discusses philanthropy from the viewpoint of the formation of the great private foundations in America. It is an interesting account of the formation of the Ford, Rockefeller, MacArthur, and Robert Wood Johnson Foundations, and many others.

The second citation is a dissertation written in 1999 by Frank H. Oliver titled, "Fellow Beggars: The History of Fund Raising Campaigning in U. S. Higher Education." Dr. Oliver's dissertation was submitted in partial fulfillment of the requirements for the degree of doctor of education at Teacher's College at Columbia University. This exhaustive study of all facets of philanthropy in higher education provides more than 300 pages of information about college and university fund raising and campaigning from 1641 to 1999. It is recommended to anyone who is interested in an anthology of the history of such fund raising.[8]

A book by Dwight Burlingame at Indiana University that has just recently been published gives an extraordinarily comprehensive view of philanthropy in America. It is a three-volume reference work and relates philanthropy in America in an historical context from the early 1600s to the present day. Burlingame offers his work, *Philanthropy in America*, as being the first and only encyclopedia on philanthropy and as including contributions from more than 200 scholars in the world of philanthropy. [9]

Finally, mention is made of a book edited by Lawrence J. Friedman and Mark D. McGarvie titled, *Charity, Philanthropy, and Civility in American History*. The book is a series of essays on the history of American philanthropy. It examines philanthropy from the 17th century through the present, with chapters discussing legal court cases, important world philanthropic events, and the approaches to philanthropy by some of the wealthiest families in the United States.[10]

The Capital Campaign

Capital campaigns, as they exist today, appear to be a 20th-century phenomenon.

The last 10 years have seen an absolute explosion of capital campaigns across America. With goals ranging from a few hundred thousand dollars to multibillion dollars, eleemosynary organizations across the nation are either concluding capital campaigns, organizing to begin them, or in a temporary hiatus in-between campaigns. Indeed, few philanthropic organizations are not planning or engaged in some type of private fund-raising effort, some more formal than others. For an institution to ignore at least the discussion of a capital campaign is to risk being left behind amid intensifying competition.

A common thread that runs through the psyche of the American public is the need to be successful and financially secure. Bigger, grander, broader, bolder, and better are all adjectives that describe traditional American aspirations. The spirit of competition runs deep in every aspect of American society. Organizations realize that to remain financially viable and provide for the future success of their organizations, launching a capital fund-raising drive may be essential.

Capital campaigns are now being conducted by hundreds—perhaps thousands—of charities for a diverse range of purposes. Most of the capital campaigns in this country are conducted by nonprofit organizations such as the Boys Club of America, Girls Scouts, Boy Scouts, fraternities, sororities, hospitals, health agencies, historical societies, orchestras, synagogues, mosques, the American Heart Association, the American Cancer Society, Easter Seals, United Way, Special Olympics, symphonies, churches, temples, social service organizations—the list is endless.

In her book *Capital Campaign: Strategies that Work*, Andrea Kihlstedt analyzes both the opportunities and the challenges of capital campaigns. She writes that "a capital campaign is hard work—for staff, board members, and for volunteers. Yet, when well-planned and conducted, it enables an organization to expand and strengthen its leadership, its volunteer base, its family donors, and its visibility in the community, as well as its finances."[11]

A total of 37 separate capital fund-raising campaigns by local organizations currently exist in the metropolitan area of northwest Arkansas. The new Boys and Girls Club of America in Fayetteville was built because of a capital campaign. The new Washington Regional Medical Center—caring for the health needs of the community—was built primarily because of private gift support. The city library named in honor of a local philanthropist and teacher was built because half of the support was raised from private giving.

The recent transformation of the University of Arkansas is almost entirely the result of the generous support of alumni, friends, corporations, and foundations. Capital campaigning and the philanthropic spirit are alive and well in this small southwestern community in the corner of northwest Arkansas.

Many more kinds of organizations are engaged in capital campaigning today than even in 1995. In the past 10 years, we have seen new organizations moving forcefully into capital campaigning. Human service groups, public television stations, YMCAs, symphony orchestras, and secondary and primary schools are all launching capital campaigns. A kindergarten nursery school has even launched a campaign for new school equipment. While the competition for the private dollar was keen in the 1980s and 1990s, it has become absolutely acute and a necessary way of life for hundreds—if not thousands—of organizations. As one generous benefactor to the University of Arkansas related recently, "On the average, I get 20 solicitations a month asking for contributions, and I'm not talking about hundred-dollar contributions, but organizations that are looking for $5,000, $10,000, or $25,000 gifts, if not more. I've never seen anything like it."

And what about the explosion of fund raising and capital campaigns at higher education institutions?

The Chronicle of Higher Education maintains a database that shows at the latest count 41 public and private universities were conducting campaigns with billion-dollar-plus goals.

Several of the institutions are in multibillion-dollar campaigns, the largest being the University of California at Los Angeles, which is involved in a $2.4 billion campaign scheduled to end in 2005. As of July 31, 2004, UCLA had already raised $2.78 billion!

Public colleges and universities jumped aggressively in the fund-raising arena during the 1980s and today appear to be even more zealous than their private counterparts. While historically capital campaign fund raising was a creature of private institutions, that has dramatically changed. Today, many public organizations—from major public universities to public grade schools and secondary schools—are involved in capital campaign fund raising. This is a dramatic shift from the 1960s and even 1970s when many public institutions were not even considering private fund raising. Those that were more sophisticated and understood the importance of garnering private support may have had a staff of one, two, or three persons. Today, many of these public organizations have hundreds of persons on the staff and are raising millions of dollars annually from alumni, friends, foundations, and corporations. This dramatic shift, caused mainly by the drying up of public resources, is a trend that will only intensify as tax support for public organizations continues to decline.

What Is a Campaign?

The term "capital campaign" is probably one of the most confusing in the fund-raising vocabulary and conjures up all kinds of misconceptions. In fact, professionals in the business aren't always certain how to define what is and is not a capital campaign. William P. McGoldrick, former vice president of Rensselaer Polytechnic Institute, describes a campaign as "an organized and intense effort to secure extraordinary gift commitments during a defined period of time to meet specific needs that are crucial to the mission and goals of an institution."[12]

Today's capital campaign, however, has, in a sense, become a generic term that describes an intense effort to raise funds from the private sector through multiyear pledge commitments within a specified time period.

Generally, capital campaigns are comprehensive in nature and count all gift support that flows to the organization during that specified time period. In college and university capital campaigning, it is rare when the campaign does not include every gift that it has received during the life of the campaign. There are, however, a number of organizations, particularly noneducational institutions, that specify certain projects and programs within the context of their campaign and do not count all gift support.

A capital campaign essentially positions an institution to publicly proclaim its critical need for private gift support that will allow the continuation of current programs as well as the launching of important new initiatives. In a capital campaign, the organization declares that it is serious about philanthropy and that it is bringing together all constituents—internal and external—in an all-out effort to garner private financial support.

Kent E. Dove describes the capital campaign as "an organized, intensive, fund-raising effort on the part of the third-sector institution organization to secure extraordinary gifts and pledges for a specific purpose or purposes (such as building, construction, renovation, equipment, acquisition, or endowment funds) during a specified period of time."[13]

Whether the campaign is comprehensive or program specific, the term "capital campaign" has become the most widely accepted term for systematic, major gift, time-specific fund raising at any major philanthropic organization. The term has certainly weathered the test of time and likely will continue to be used to describe any major effort with a prescribed timeframe seeking financial support from the private sector. While there have been some attempts to describe and name campaigns as "major gift efforts," the term "capital campaign" is a part of the American language. It has become the rubric philanthropic organizations use to demonstrate that garnering private financial support will be a critical priority in the long term as well as in the short term. In the 21st century, the capital campaign can be best defined as a specific, tailored effort with a term of months or years that will conclude with a specific program, project, endowment, or effort being successfully funded.

Ten Years of Trends

Since my first book on capital campaigns, published in 1995, many events have had an impact on philanthropy, capital campaigns, and major gift fund raising. The terrorist attacks of 2001 had a monumental effect and continue to take a toll on the economic atmosphere of nonprofits.

In January 2004, the Association of Fundraising Professionals cited a report released by the Johns Hopkins Center for Civil Society Studies as part of its ongoing Nonprofit Listening Post Project. The report, titled "Stressed but Coping: Nonprofit Organizations and the Current Fiscal Crisis,"[14] is based on a survey of 236 senior development executives at nonprofit organizations conducted between October and December 2003.

Nearly 90 percent of the organizations surveyed reported stress in their organizations, with 51 percent reporting severe stress. The survey went on to show that nonprofits are tightening their belts dramatically and expanding their fund-raising efforts to include the launching of "major capital campaigns." More than half of those surveyed found it necessary to freeze salaries and cut benefits for staff members or postpone hiring of new personnel or eliminate altogether positions that were vacant. A total of 72 percent of those surveyed indicated that they are relying more on part-time help as they are continuously forced to cut their budgets.

While nonprofits have always been squeezed for revenue and many operate hand to mouth and month to month, the events of recent years and the increased competition for private dollars have placed severe stress on our nation's nonprofit organizations. This increased pressure on nonprofits has made the capital campaign vitally important for hundreds—if not thousands—of philanthropic organizations. For those nonprofit officials, particularly the ones who are not knowledgeable about the nature of capital campaigns, the capital campaign is openly discussed as being the salvation, the knight in shining armor on the white horse, the solution to all of the problems that will ultimately save the organization from despair. Of course, ignorance is bliss, and as we will see in the chapters ahead, there is never a quick fix to budgetary problems. The capital campaign is certainly no magic bullet.

It is evident to many professionals in the fund-raising arena that some of the old capital campaign rules have changed when working with certain potential benefactors. As the Baby Boomers secure their positions in business, industry, and professional life, they also secure their positions in the world of philanthropy. Ten to 20 years ago, the major philanthropists of America were still coming from the "greatest generation" as described by Tom Brokaw. They were born of the depression and grew up in difficult economic times, scarred by war and international turmoil.

Today's benefactor is quite different, and development professionals would be wise to accept the paradigm shift that has resulted from a new generation of donors.

As reported in *Professional Fundraising Magazine*, Marianne Briscoe, of the consultant organization the Briscoe Group, made the following comments in a workshop on venture philanthropy:

> New charitable investors have "little experience of philanthropy" and even "less respect" for the way nonprofits work. These people wear sneakers, khakis and don't wear a tie. They have a new board culture and one of their guiding principles is to step outside the box. Show them where your box is and they will immediately step outside it.
>
> You have a self-actualized, confident individual who has succeeded in an area where nine out of 10 businesses fail, walking into your nonprofit. You cannot ask these people to run a campaign for an endowment because they believe money is a tool, not a commodity, so you are just not speaking their language.[15]

Working with the new generation of benefactors may argue for some important changes in the way we run capital campaigns. The entrepreneurs may not be interested in tried and tested formulas. The use of committee structures and hierarchical organizational patterns may be anathema; they may prefer a more horizontal structure with shared committee assignments and roles.

These new philanthropists will not always accept the word of a professional but will expect professional development personnel to prove their theories of major gift fund raising as well as show hard evidence as to why certain fund-raising theories will indeed operate efficiently in today's environment.

Change in Corporate Giving

In recent years, there has been a change in corporate giving philosophy, brought on, in part, by the economic slump of recent years. Corporate America wants to be certain that its dollars are being spent appropriately and are finding their way to those programs and activities that can be of the most benefit to the most people. Corporate giving, while always conjoined with a certain quid pro quo benefit, has become even more concerned with giving to those programs and projects that show some direct benefit back to the company shareholders. Corporate fund raisers frequently are asked "How will this contribution help my company?" Ian Wilhelm points out that many corporate entities are becoming more selective in their philanthropy:

> One example: Wal-Mart Stores, in Bentonville, Arkansas, plans to be more selective in its giving. It is requiring its 3,000 plus store managers to seek suggestions from local government officials and community leaders, such as the heads of United Ways, to identify the most pressing needs in their areas, and then is focusing local donations on those two or three problems to the exclusion of other requests for money.[16]

Wilhelm cites a number of corporate entities that are changing or shifting their giving programs in what can only be called a new paradigm in corporate giving in America.

Sarbanes-Oxley Act

The corporate scandals of recent years, particularly those related to Enron, Arthur Andersen, and Global Crossing, prompted Congress to enact the American Competitiveness and Corporate Accountability Act of 2002. This act, generally referred to as the Sarbanes-Oxley Act, primarily broadens a governing board member's role in overseeing the financial transactions and auditing procedures of the company to which he or she is a member of the board.

Current law applies these provisions only to publicly traded corporations, but many in the profession believe that the government could very well extend the reach of the Sarbanes-Oxley Act to nonprofit organizations. In some jurisdictions, state legislators are calling for the act to apply to local nonprofits.

Most nonprofit organizations have outside audits. Nonprofit organizations would be well advised to create separate audit committees of the board. While there are no standard guidelines currently for nonprofit organizations, nonprofit boards should be aware of the new regulations and how they affect the corporate world. Their reach may well extend to the nonprofit sector within a matter of years.

International Competition

While major foundations have always supported international programs, a decided trend toward international fund raising has developed in the last 10 years. This has placed increased competition on programs in the United States, particularly those that are supported by this country's major philanthropic foundations. "International giving by private and community foundations—which includes grants to overseas recipients and funding for U.S.-based international programs—realized extraordinary growth through 2001, outpacing foundation giving overall," reported Highlights of the Foundation Center's 2004 Study International Grantmaking III. [17]

Not only has international giving grown at a faster rate than overall giving by our nation's foundations, but the number of funders is also up dramatically. Even community foundations, which used to account for less than 1 percent of international giving, reported a 360 percent increase this past year in international grantmaking.[18]

The Foundation Center reports that foundations are increasing their funding levels to international programs: "Since 2000, the international grantmaking environment has been buffeted by a series of tumultuous events, from the stock market slide, to the 9/11 attacks, to the 'war on terrorism.'"[19] There is a much greater urgency to address global issues, particularly issues having to do with the environment and health.

No doubt the world is a smaller place and the internationalization of American philanthropy will most certainly continue. This shrinkage has been spurred by broad access to technology and travel, Deborah Bongiorno writes in a 2003 *CASE Currents* article. "A growing number of educational institutions—from Botswana to Belgium to British Columbia—are employing advancement's functions to engage donors, serve alumni, recruit students, and communicate with other constituents," Bongiorno writes.[20]

In a 2003 article in *CASE Currents*, Deborah Bongiorno interviews five experienced professionals about how globalization is changing the way they engage donors and serve alumni of their institutions. Colleges and universities, in particular, are much more engaged in international programs. The Council for Advancement in Support of Education (CASE) has progressively pursued a high profile in international advancement matters.

Major consulting firms have expanded into international markets. The Grenzebach Glier firm has organized Grenzebach Glier Europe and is providing consulting services to a multitude of clients in Europe, Asia, and particularly the Pacific Rim.

Scholars interested in American philanthropy on the international scene would be well advised to review Holt Ruffin's paper on "The Globalization of American Philanthropy," written in 2003.[21]

Ruffin is the executive director of the Civil Society International. This society assists independent organizations working for democracy on the international scene. Ruffin believes the vigorous growth rates of international giving by U.S. foundations is likely to continue in the coming years.

> Signs of globalization can be found everywhere: in the number of items purchased by the American consumer that were manufactured abroad; in the modern multinational corporation on which "the sun never sets"; in the explosion of technology that has made possible the integrated capital, labor, and product markets the global corporation relies upon; and the internet, that has enabled routine communications around the world to individuals, families, and NGOs [nongovernmental organizations] to a degree never imagined. No matter where one looks, virtually nothing today is unaffected by the growing globalization of human activity. . . including American philanthropy.[22]

Ruffin gives a very interesting history of international giving by American foundations, indicating that international giving actually declined until the late 20th century. From 1968 to 1982, the percentage of support to international purposes declined 4 percentage points, from 9 percent in 1968 to 5 percent in 1982. Ruffin also states, "Over the past two decades international giving by U.S. foundations has risen at a much more rapid pace than giving overall. In just the three years from 1998 to 2001, international giving by American foundations more than doubled, from $1.6 billion to an estimated $3.3 billion (e.g., "Ruffin, 7")."[23]

The globalization of philanthropy was never more apparent than when a recent donor to many philanthropic endeavors in northwest Arkansas and the surrounding region indicated that much of his philanthropy would now be directed toward relief efforts in Ethiopia. The channeling of funds to this important relief effort has become a priority for his personal family foundation, and he plans to dedicate several million dollars to help relieve the crisis situation in that country despite the fact he has never set foot in Ethiopia or on the continent of Africa.

The competition for philanthropic funds from American foundations and corporations includes many worthy and important international objectives. A significant, sizeable philanthropy base is being expended on the international scene. This continued trend is bound to have an impact on American organizations seeking private support.

Increased Competition for Development Professionals

One only need look in *The Chronicle of Higher Education*, the *New York Times*, the *Wall Street Journal*, and other major publications that carry advertisements for nonprofit fund-raising positions to gain an appreciation of the philanthropy job market. There has been an absolute explosion the last 10 years. Cassie J. Moore states, "The number of Americans who work at nonprofit organizations now exceeds 12.5 million, and hiring by such groups has been rising faster than in business or government, according to a report by two Washington organizations that study charities."[24] This is particularly true in the health services and independent higher education.

Headhunter firms, while reporting some falloff in hiring activities in 2001 and 2002, appear now to be conducting a record number of searches for nonprofit organizations. It is almost as if it has become fashionable to be in the fund-raising business. The search for the "ultimate fund raiser" has become the number one imperative for many organizations.

No doubt a major shortage of development personnel who are experienced and seasoned in capital major gift fund raising exists. It used to be that colleges and universities would require several years of experience in hiring vice president-level advancement personnel. Today, a track record of two, three, or four years seems acceptable as the competition for personnel increases and the maddening rush to fill vacant fund-raising positions escalates.

This trend has put enormous pressure on the fund-raising industry and is driving up salaries to unheard of levels.

Twenty years ago, there was practically no place an individual could go to study how to become a fund raiser and work in the nonprofit sector. Programs in nonprofit management were nonexistent until the early 1980s, and many fund-raising jobs, particularly on college and university campuses, were filled by retiring coaches, retiring faculty, or in some cases, by persons who had been moved from another position under the assumption that anyone can raise money. It might be said that the profession of fund raising had not yet arrived and was still considered to be an art rather than a science, certainly not the blending of art and science as is the case today. As Heather Joslyn notes in "Young People Fuel Demand for Nonprofit Study," "Programs in nonprofit management began gathering momentum on campuses in the early 1980s, but their explosive growth in the past decade was triggered by changes in the philanthropic world as well as by trends rippling through American society. The rapid growth has not been without its costs. Such programs are not overseen by an accrediting body that can ensure a college's nonprofit curriculum meets certain basic academic standards. Now, however, as the field matures, new efforts are under way to make it easier to evaluate nonprofit-management programs."[25]

Penn State University began teaching a course in higher education advancement in the late 1980s. The course was rooted in the higher education curriculum and was offered primarily to masters- and Ph.D.-seeking students. Since those years, many colleges and universities throughout the country recognize the importance of curriculum in nonprofit management and are offering courses designed to teach the basics of fund raising to students interested in academic administration. No course currently exits at the University of Arkansas in this area, but discussions are under way to offer such a course in the future.

Programs on nonprofit management are not in the mainstream and don't always receive respect from the academic community. Katheryn W. Heidrich, president of a nonprofit consulting group says:

> Many of these programs are on the margins of their universities. They are often where the community can connect with the university, or they're on the margins of some academic field so they're not central to something like economics or law, some of the more traditional disciplines. And so since they're on the margins, they have great assets: They can be flexible, they can be responsive to the needs of the nonprofit sector. But they also pay a price by being on the margins, unless they're tightly connected to the missions of their universities.[26]

Only a few years ago, a $50,000-to-$75,000 salary for a senior development officer in a college or school at a major university was quite competitive. Today, many candidates for the same positions are expecting salaries of $80,000 to $120,000. Vice presidents' and associate vice presidents' salaries have also continued to push upward at a dramatic pace. To attract the best personnel possible, it has become necessary to offer perquisites that a few years ago were reserved for only the most senior officers of nonprofit organizations. Cars, car allowances, country club memberships, moving expenses, relocation expenses, and signing bonuses are all negotiable items when attracting and retaining top-level staff members. As one headhunter mentioned recently, it used to be that the promise of a car and $100,000-a-year salary would turn the heads of many a development officer. Today, it takes a lot more than that to get personnel to even consider relocating. In today's market, some vice presidents with considerable track records are making $250,000-to-$450,000 a year, a salary that was unheard of 7 to 10 years ago.

Paul C. Light, director of the Center for Public Service at the Brookings Institution, a Washington public policy think tank, says that, "The top three positions in the market are fund raising, fund raising, fund raising. If you know how to raise a dollar, you're imminently employable."[27]

As public agency budgets decline and state governments continue to shrink tax support to nonprofit organizations and as the competition for the private dollar continues to be keen, the shortage of good, solid, high-energy people will persist. The philanthropic market place has become extraordinarily competitive, particularly in colleges and universities. Hospital-affiliated organizations are also willing to spend top dollar to recruit and retain high producers.

Increased Scrutiny

The last 10 years have brought an increased degree of cynicism and mistrust in all walks of life. Philanthropy has not escaped the careful, watchdog eye of the American public.

Certainly, the cataclysmic events of the Vietnam War contributed greatly to the mistrust of the American people in our modern institutions. This heightened mistrust was again exacerbated as a result of the events of Watergate in the early-to-mid 1970s. People now give much more scrutiny to organizations and institutions they once accepted as being untouchable and always operating with good and proper intentions. Certainly, the misuse of funds by the National United Way organization heightened this basic mistrust among the American people. Donna Harrington-Lueker suggests that:

Nonprofits experienced their equivalent of the Watergate scandal in 1992, when William Aramony, then president and CEO of the United Way of America, was convicted of stealing $1.2 million from the organization, among other crimes.

Since then, the media have shone a spotlight on excessive salaries, conflicts of interest, abuses of funds, and other malfeasance in the fast-growing nonprofit sector. As they continue to do so, the higher education sector will face increasing scrutiny as well. Potential flashpoints include salary supplements that affiliated foundations provide to campus CEOs, multimillion-dollar salaries for endowment investment managers, operating agreements between campuses and their foundations, and any irregularities in gift procedures.[28]

Lester M. Salamon, director of the Center for Civil Society Studies at the John Hopkins Institute for Policy Studies, stated in his recent book, "America's charities have moved well beyond the quaint, Norman Rockwell stereotype of selfless volunteers ministering to the needy and supported largely by charitable gifts. Yet popular images remain rooted in this older image, and far too little attention has been given to bringing popular perceptions into better alignment with the realities that now exist."

Salamon goes on to say that, "As a consequence, nonprofit groups find themselves vulnerable when highly visible events, such as the September 11 tragedy, let alone instances of mismanagement or scandal, reveal them to be far more complex and commercially engaged institutions than the public suspects. The result is a growing threat to the public trust on which nonprofit organizations ultimately depend."[29]

In a nationwide random sample of 1,012 adults interviewed by telephone in July 2002, the Barna Research Group discovered an alarming trend: Confidence in most of our major social institutions and professions is declining, and donor confidence in nonprofit organizations is at a historic low. What is most notable about Barna's research is that nonprofits are rated low in the areas of integrity and trustworthiness, problem solving, financial efficiency, fast response, and effective leadership.[30]

Today, donors, benefactors, and volunteers want to witness for themselves that their time and resources are being used appropriately and are not being diverted to other purposes or squandered for personal rather than public gain. This has spawned a fresh round of freedom of information issues (discussed later in this chapter) that have made it very difficult for nonprofits to conduct business, or even receive gifts, without some public scrutiny. This trend is likely to continue and become even more acute in the future.

Stewardship reports to donors will become more important as we move into the 21st century. Stewardship used to be an add-on responsibility at nonprofit organizations, and the predominate number of nonprofits had no stewardship program whatsoever.

It is now becoming increasingly understood that colleges, universities, health agencies, hospitals, and nonprofit organizations in general must start to spend their resources, not just in garnering private support for their organizations, but also in keeping their benefactors completely informed of how they are spending private support.

Recently, a benefactor to the University of Arkansas was most upset because she received a stewardship report that indicated her endowment market value had declined. Even though we explained this resulted from the recent stock market declines, she felt that we should have notified her immediately upon learning that her endowment fund was under water. (Of course, she readily admitted that her personal portfolio had also declined because of the condition of the stock market!)

Headline-grabbing accounts of misuse of funds and malfeasance in office can greatly affect what donors think and do. In a 2004 *CASE Currents* article, Donna Harrington-Lueker notes that successful fund-raising programs are able to accommodate shifts in donor attitudes, such as the Baby Boom generation's skepticism of and weariness with authority.[31]

There is no substitute for good practices in the workplace. Nonprofit managers and development offers would be well advised to keep their programs above reproach as the demand for public accountability reaches heightened levels. Neither public nor private charities will be immune from the public's eye, and all professionals in the nonprofit business will have to get used to conducting their business under strict scrutiny. The Association of Fundraising Professionals (AFP) reported in September 2004 that American confidence in charitable organizations was 15 percent lower in 2004 than it was in the summer of 2001.[32] The findings by the AFP come from a random telephone survey of 1,417 Americans interviewed by Princeton Research.

The main areas of dissatisfaction have to do with how well and with how much wisdom nonprofit organizations are spending their funds. Unfortunately, only 11 percent of Americans believe that charitable organizations do a good job in spending their funds wisely. Only 15 percent of surveyed Americans expressed confidence in nonprofits, a level of satisfaction that places the nonprofit sector on par with organized labor, television news, corporate America, HMOs, Congress, the military, the U.S. Supreme Court, and the church.[33]

Brookings Institution's Paul C. Light, in his capacity as a professor at New York University, believes that "confidence will not improve without demonstrable action to improve actual performance. The decline was not only real," he argues, "but appears to be durable."

"The solution," Light believes, "will not come from telling more success stories, complaining about negative media coverage, or worrying about legislative change. Instead, organizations need to improve their core performance and police their poor performers."[34]

Donor-Advised Funds

Donor-advised funds have emerged over the past few years to play a significant role in capital campaigns at many colleges and universities. Once relegated primarily to the community foundation, donor-advised funds are increasingly offered by public charities, financial corporations, colleges, and universities as a way of providing an economically attractive and convenient alternative to the private foundation.

A donor-advised fund is a segregated fund held by a tax-exempt organization that allows a donor to receive a current charitable income tax deduction upon contributing to the fund, whether or not the fund makes a charitable grant during that same tax year. The charity controls investment of and distributions from the fund but may consider the advice or suggestions of the donor in determining grants to be made within the charity or to other charitable organizations (within parameters set by the charity). This aspect of the donor-advised fund makes it potentially attractive to donors considering the less economical and more administratively burdensome private foundation.

The donor-advised fund also has several tax advantages over the private foundation. It is not subject to charitable income tax deduction restrictions applicable to private foundations. As a result, an individual's cash gift to such a fund may be deducted up to 50 percent of adjusted gross income rather than the 30 percent rule applicable to private foundations. Donor-advised funds are not subject to private foundation excise taxes or restrictions on investments. Because the fund is controlled by the charity, earnings on the fund are tax exempt.

The principal benefits of such a fund to a capital campaign are essentially three-fold. First, this fund may increase the likelihood your institution will receive and benefit from major or mega gifts that would have traditionally gone to a private foundation. Second, although your organization will take on additional administrative responsibility, the donor-advised fund provides your organization the opportunity to maximize contact with and stewardship of high-wealth donors who are vital to the capital campaign. Finally, such funds allow your institution to stay competitive with the increasing number of organizations offering this giving option.

Women in Philanthropy

Fund raisers are beginning to realize that more women have more control over more money.

Women are realizing their own tremendous potential to apply their charitable dollars to shaping the future of society. And, of course, women statistically live longer than men. Philanthropy truly offers women an opportunity to make a significant difference in their personal and professional lives. Women are making a huge difference in nonprofit organizations and are helping to reshape entire organizations through their generous giving.

The Independent Sector indicates that 62 percent of women and 49 percent of men volunteered in 2001.[35] Some 85 to 90 percent of women are left in charge of family financial affairs because they outlive their husbands by an average of seven years. Women, in fact, control much of philanthropy in this country.

Twenty years ago women were taken for granted in the philanthropic decision making of families. This was almost the exclusive province of the male. Development officers tended to gravitate toward the "head of the household" and exclude women from the cultivation process. Much has changed in the last 20 years, particularly with a strong focus on women's giving in the last 10 years. Lilya Wagner suggests that "Women have always been involved in philanthropy, but only since the early 1990s has much attention been paid to women's preferences for giving and for being asked.

Most Americans don't know that women over 70 control most of the wealth in this country. Yet institutions still fail to address their interests, needs for giving, preferences for how they are asked, and how they want their money used. Therefore, it's vital that the knowledge about women as donors be researched on an ongoing basis and that both donors and organizations (especially fund raisers) be educated on women as donors."[36]

The most recent example of a women's impact on a philanthropic organization was the $1.5 billion bequest Joan Kroc made to the Salvation Army. The widow of Ray Kroc, of the McDonald's restaurant chain, helped many nonprofit organizations during her lifetime, and her philanthropy will live on for years to come. Dr. Wagner summed it up as follows: "Women are not small men! Women want involvement in causes to which they give. They ask more questions and demand more outcomes than do men. They don't seek as much recognition, they value connections, they like new initiatives, and they are more likely to volunteer."[37]

An incredible shift in the gender balance has occurred among advancement professionals. In 1982, 61 percent of advancement professionals were men. In 2002 the gender balance had shifted so that 65 percent in the advancement profession were women. The majority of practitioners for most of the advancement profession's history were male professionals. With two-thirds of the practitioners now being women, women's issues in philanthropy will certainly take center stage.[38]

Diversity in the Nonprofit Sector

A major disappointment in the nonprofit sector has been the inability to increase diversity among the professional ranks. According to the National Society of Fundraising Executives, African-Americans make up just under 2 percent of the organization's members, despite the fact that the organization has grown from 10,000 to 23,000 members in the last decade. Hispanics (1.1 percent), Asians (0.4 percent), and Native Americans (0.4 percent) have also remained at those levels for well over 10 years.[39]

According to a 1995 CASE Survey of Institutional Advancement, minority advancement professionals comprise 5.6 percent of the profession, up slightly from 4.5 percent in 1990.

A distressing anomaly, however, of this five-year span was a decrease in the number of African-American advancement professionals, from 3.3 percent in 1990 to 2.5 percent in 1995. During this same time, Native Americans showed the biggest increase, from 0.2 to 1.5 percent of the profession. Hispanics rose from 0.3 to 1.1 percent, while Asian-Americans declined slightly from 0.7 to 0.5 percent.

Gender wise, nonprofits, as pointed out previously, are doing quite well. Any aggressive movement to involve people of color in the profession, however, has been met with a dismal defeat.[40]

A few organizations are making the diversification of their staff a top priority. At the University of Arkansas, Chancellor John A. White declared diversity as the number one priority. In his state of the university address in 2004, Chancellor White described the reasons why building a more inclusive community are important.

> As you know, there have been questions by a few regarding our commitment to diversity. Let me be very clear on this subject: Increasing the diversity of the staff, faculty, and student body is the very highest priority of this administration.
>
> We are absolutely committed to building a diverse, inclusive campus. Not because it sounds like an appropriate thing to do. Not because someone told us we had to. Not even because it's the "right" thing—the correct, moral thing to do—though, of course, it is.
>
> No, diversity matters most because it is integral to building the quality and strength this institution must have to compete on a national and international level. Because the things that power the highest achievements of universities—things like intellectual muscle, mental energy, and intestinal fortitude—do not have a skin color or come in only one kind of human package. Because learning absolutely requires the willingness to tolerate change and to embrace not only the established and venerable cannon but also the new and different discovery, the cutting edge, the unknown.
>
> We must prepare our students to enter a world that is changing rapidly—one that is increasingly diverse. We must prepare them to work with and for people who do not look like themselves, sound like themselves, think like they do, or believe as they do.
>
> Diversity is a strength to be pursued, not a requirement to be met.[41]

The Schusterman Foundation in Tulsa, Oklahoma, generally supports programs that are Jewish affiliated. However, the foundation has worked at diversifying its staff and employs well over one-third of its staff from non-Jewish backgrounds. Sandy Cardin, the executive director of the foundation explains it this way, "Jewish life does not occur in a vacuum. We live within a larger world, one to which we owe a responsibility to help repair and perfect. Not only do the non-Jewish members of our team help us avoid myopia, they also provide invaluable assistance in the implementation of our secular agenda in the community in which we all work and live."[42]

Not only are the numbers of minority personnel in the nonprofit sector quite low, abysmally so, but recent surveys note that men outnumber women markedly as the chief development officers, particularly at colleges and universities. Paula Carabelli, an executive search consultant, points out that organizational leadership must "take responsibility for mentoring underrepresented groups and ensure that women and minorities have access to the opportunity pipeline that leads to executive leadership roles."[43]

The National Center for Black Philanthropy (NCBP) was established in 2000 in Washington, D.C., to ensure there is some movement in the profession to increase the number of minorities in the field. The mission of this center is to promote giving and volunteerism among African-Americans. NCBP conducts a number of national programs on Black philanthropy.

Both CASE and AFP continue to support programs that call for diversifying the workplace.

A few other regional and national organizations worth mentioning are:

Bay Area Blacks in Philanthropy (BABIP)
BABIP is a regional nonprofit-membership organization which seeks to advance the interests of African-Americans in philanthropy and address the impact of race and diversity within Bay Area philanthropic institutions.

Hispanics in Philanthropy (HIP)
Promoting stronger partnerships between organized philanthropy and Latino communities, HIP is a transnational association of grant makers with more than 450 members representing corporate, public, and private philanthropies, nonprofit leaders, and academia.[44]

Native Americans in Philanthropy (NAP)
NAP is made up of individuals who seek to enrich the lives of native people through bridging organized philanthropy and indigenous communities in order to foster understanding and increase effectiveness.[45]

The University of Arkansas has made a strong attempt to attract minority professionals. This attempt has been met with some early success.

Some of Arkansas' strategies to attract minority staff members are as follows:

1. Identify promising minority students on campus and offer them internships and other work-study opportunities in the division.

   This "growing your own" strategy is designed to attract persons of color to the advancement profession. The challenge is to create internships, fellowships, and other work-study opportunities that will attract minority students to the Division of University Advancement.

   This allows the division to identify promising persons of color as candidates for entry-level professional employment.

   To make the effort successful, the university has worked with African-Americans and other minority students and their social organizations to create awareness of and interest in these opportunities. The university has also worked with African-American faculty and staff members across the university, making them aware of the internships and fellowships in the division.

2. Recruit a higher number of minority students to serve on the student alumni board of the alumni association. Like many university alumni associations, our institution has formed a student alumni ambassador corps to involve students in the life of the university and the alumni association and provide opportunities for them to assist with special events, programs, and other outreach and service initiatives.

   As such, this organization serves as a gateway to the advancement profession for many college students, and also provides high-profile opportunities for them to attend events and be seen as university representatives. We hope this effort will expose talented minority students to the nonprofit profession and allow the division to identify promising candidates for entry-level professional employment, enabling us to visibly demonstrate our commitment to diversity before key external constituencies.

3. Forge stronger relationships with historically black colleges and universities (HBCU) in the region to create opportunities for identifying advancement professionals who might be interested in joining the staff. This initiative could take several forms, such as visiting historically black colleges throughout the region in an effort to "get acquainted," learning more about them, and scouting for promising advancement professionals who might be interested in employment.

Stage professional development workshops specifically for advancement professionals at regional HBCUs and cultivate relationships with those who attend.

Offer "advancement fellowships" or "professional development semesters" and other enticing professional development opportunities on a competitive basis to African-American advancement officers. This initiative allows advancement professionals to work in the division for a semester or academic year and then return to their campus with enhanced capabilities. The most promising of these candidates might be identified for eventual recruitment.

Make special efforts to identify graduate students at HBCUs who might be interested in advancement work.

4. Use the resources of Black alumni to help identify promising candidates for employment and create an African-American prospective employee pool. The division works aggressively with Black alumni to explore ways in which its network of contacts might be tapped for employment purposes. Although our initial aim would be to elicit names of African-Americans with professional backgrounds relevant to advancement work, the pool of prospective employees could be enlarged for the entire university. This activity is carried out with collaboration with the office of career services.

5. Identify new positions and vacancies to be filled by African-Americans or minority candidates.

Sometimes it is necessary to move "outside the box" of standard employment procedures and identify positions that should be filled by minority candidates.

6. Send a signal to the national community of minority advancement professionals that this institution is interested in recruiting minority talent.

This can be accomplished through regional and national meetings of professional associations. Notice of our intention to seek out and interview minority professionals can be set before these meetings take place, and interviews of prospective candidates can be done on the spot at these conventions.

Make a point to advertise staff vacancies in *Black Issues in Higher Education*, a monthly publication that targets specifically African-American faculty and staff members, as well as in key Hispanic publications.

7. Create a pool of funds to help recruit minority staff members to the nonprofit sector.

Talented minority nonprofit professionals are expensive to recruit. They are often juggling recruitment offers from competing institutions and remuneration packages that can be most competitive.

It may be difficult to recruit minority advancement talent without additional financial incentives. The creation of a pool of funds to be used when an additional financial incentive will make the difference between hiring or losing a prospective minority staff member might be necessary. This same pool might be used to help retain a minority staff member being lured elsewhere.

Finally, although the main concern of this section has been a call for diversity of the nonprofit sector within the confines of race, color, and ethnicity, it is important that we not forget that diversity also can involve sexual orientation.

Recognizing that homophobia still exists, particularly in certain regions of the country, it is nonetheless important to keep an open mind when hiring persons who are open and public about their sexuality.

Many organizations have opted for domestic partner benefits while others have decided that their conservative benefactors may be opposed to such a move. It is a national debate that will continue to rage in the months and years ahead, and there are certainly no easy answers. What is important, however, is to treat all people equally regardless of what their political, social, religious, or sexual orientation might be.

Privacy Issues and Freedom of Information

The last 10 years have brought heated national debate on the issue of privacy of donor records. This debate affects both public and private philanthropic organizations and causes much angst among development professionals in an attempt to balance the public's right to know and the donor's right to privacy.

The issue not only affects donor records, but it also affects biographical information that may be contained in donor files. The issue can cause embarrassment to organizations and consternation to their benefactors. News organizations today will stretch freedom of information laws to the absolute limit to gain access to donor information. Some reporters will push hard for copies of correspondence related to a benefactor as well as proposals, working papers, research reports, and other data that henceforth have been considered classified and off limits.

To be sure, there are two definitive sides to this issue of right to know and right to privacy. Not only is the issue rampant in the United States, but it has also affected several companies around the globe. Within the last 10 years, close to 30 countries have enacted legislation that affords their citizens unprecedented access to government information. Thomas Blanton, director of the National Security Archive at George Washington University, explains it this way: "The concept of freedom of information is evolving from a moral indictment of secrecy to a tool for market regulation, more efficient government, and economic and technological growth. In 2000, the U.S. federal government received more than 2 million FOIA [Freedom of Information Act] requests from citizens, corporations, and foreigners."[46]

Although some suggest there has been a tightening of information flow, particularly on the federal level, since the terrorist events of 9/11, it doesn't appear that laws meant to protect against terrorism have slowed the public's desire to obtain government information. The Internet is rife with chat rooms and electronic discussion about freedom of information issues.

About four years ago, George Soros funded a major Internet program called Freedom Info.org, which provides a survey of rules, regulations, and statutes worldwide that affect freedom of information.

Don't think for a moment that the issue involves only public universities, colleges, and public agencies in the nonprofit sector. The long arm of the law has found a way to encroach on private organizations, particularly those that are considered to be support organizations to public agencies. There are arguments on both sides of the equation, and much has been written during the last 10 years about the encroachment of FOIA laws into the private sector.

Rick Cohen, with the National Committee for Responsive Philanthropy, views the issue this way:

> Freedom of information is under siege. In the wake of the Enron scandals, corporations still oppose demands to fully disclose their grant making. Crafty congressmen are circumventing campaign-finance regulations by using charities as vehicles for donors to purchase influence without having to reveal their identities or the specific gifts and benefits to the politicians. More recently, federal agencies like the Treasury Department, the Environmental Protection Agency, and the National Archives and Records Administration have used the Patriot Act and antiterrorism fears to restrict access to significant amounts of information with questionable relevance to the nation's security.
>
> Questions are arising about whether the public has a right to know the financial aspects of the "independent" fund-raising

foundations connected to state universities. In past months, courts in Iowa, Kentucky, and other states have issued different decisions on the matter, with several judges in Kentucky ruling that a foundation must reveal its donors, and one in Iowa allowing a foundation to keep its records private.[47]

But issues regarding how far open-records laws should extend into what arguably can be considered an individual's privacy (e.g., should the law extend to a person's own e-mail?) are being debated on every front.

In September 2003, Iowa State University narrowly escaped having to turn over its donor records for public scrutiny. David Bass writes in a 2004 article in *The Chronicle of Higher Education*, "A judge in Iowa dismissed a lawsuit against Iowa State University Foundation in which the plaintiffs have sought its list of donors and meeting minutes on the grounds that it was not a public organization. Most recently, the Iowa Supreme Court reversed the lower court. Also in September 2003, a Kentucky judge ruled that the University of Louisville Foundation could not withhold the names of donors except for a few who had specifically required anonymity, thus reaffirming that the foundation is a state agency subject to open-record laws. These rulings illustrate the difficulty of authoritatively distinguishing public from private agencies."[48]

The State of Arkansas has one of the most stringent freedom of information laws in the United States. The law is written and has been interpreted by a number of courts as granting wide access to public records, e-mails, and a host of other information.

When the law was enacted in 1967, it broke new ground in the area of freedom of information. The law does entertain a number of exceptions, including the withholding of information if the information contains sensitive personal information that would be harmful or embarrassing to a reasonable person if disclosed, unless this right to privacy is outweighed by the government's interest in making the information public. The law requires a case-by-case determination.

In the fall of 2001, the *Arkansas Times*, a weekly newspaper headquartered in Little Rock, Arkansas, filed a complaint against the University of Arkansas pursuant to the Arkansas Freedom of Information Act. The case revolved around the release of a proposal that had been submitted to the Walton Family Charitable Support Foundation, which resulted in a $300 million gift to The University of Arkansas Foundation, Incorporated. The *Arkansas Times* characterized the university as concealing information and operating in secret against the state's freedom of information act.

The lawsuit and subsequent ruling in favor of the university received national attention, but much was written on both sides of the argument that was inaccurate and filled with misinformation.

The major point of contention was the *Arkansas Times'* request for a copy of the proposal that was used to secure the $300 million gift to the university. The university had already fully complied by giving all gift agreements to the *Arkansas Times* or promising those gift agreements once they had been completed.

The university refused to give the proposal to the *Times*, because they claimed the proposal reflected the prudent strategies, business methods, practices, plans, techniques, and information developed and used by the university to seek private gift support from private donors. The document reflected the university's intellectual property with respect to its development activities. By releasing the document, the university's strategies and practices for obtaining the $300 million gift would be easily disseminated through a variety of media across the nation and lead other entities—whether public or private—to use this information to their advantage and to the detriment of the university and current and future initiatives.

After the announcement of the $300 million gift, the university received many requests for copies of the successful proposal from other institutions and individuals. Because of the competitive environment, the university declined to release the proposal or any other information reflecting the business practices and methodology used by the university to secure the Walton gift.

Following a six-hour hearing in *Arkansas Times* vs. *the University of Arkansas*, the court ruled in favor of the university. The judge noted that the Freedom of Information Act should be construed in the public interest and that a common-sense approach must be taken in dealing with the act and balancing the interests involved. Gift proposals shared by the development staff are so sensitive and have such a proprietary interest in their development and creation that their public disclosure would place the university at a competitive disadvantage with other institutions in seeking charitable funds. Likewise, the judge ruled that drafts of the gift agreement, *which had not yet been finalized,* were similarly protected from disclosure.

HIPAA

In 1996, Congress adopted the Health Insurance Portability and Accountability Act (HIPAA). The law has an impact on healthcare fund raising because it requires that health organizations refrain from mailing or contacting former patients without their expressed written consent. In the past, "grateful patients" were prime prospects for healthcare philanthropy and development officials would regularly and routinely watch hospital admittance lists to see if there were viable prospects using the hospital services.

Even though the act was adopted in 1996, institutions did not need to begin complying with the privacy standards until 2003.

Most hospital's development programs have initiated procedures that protect the rights of patients' privacy but also provides appropriate access in compliance with the act. The Association of Healthcare Philanthropy has been extremely active in providing analysis and information on HIPAA. Practitioners unfamiliar with the current law are encouraged to contact the association for information and materials.

So, what should be subject to public scrutiny and what should be kept private? Certainly, there must be a balancing and a display of common sense when answering this question.

I do not believe it is in the best interest of society to be required to reveal information about a private citizen's contribution to an institution—public or independent. Revealing information considered sensitive regarding private donors will have a chilling effect on private donations and thereby lead to reduced support for the organization in the future. Once current or prospective donors perceive confidentiality as compromised, they will be far more reluctant to trust the organization with sensitive, personal, and financial information. Furthermore, some donors will refuse altogether to consider making donations to an organization that cannot provide strict confidentiality. Funds from those donors will indeed go to other organizations that can keep their records private.

But then again, what does the public have a right to know? How does the public know the $300 million gift that was given to the university did not compromise the integrity of the institution? How does the public know that the university did not make an agreement with the Walton Foundation that compromised its academic freedom? How can the public be assured that the donor will not wield undue influence over the mission and programs of the institution?

These are important questions, and I believe that there are checks and balances that must be put in place so that the public is assured that gifts are aboveboard and without serious restrictions.

It is certainly possible to argue that any gift agreement that is consummated with a donor should be made public, particularly at public institutions. Gift agreements typically lay out how a gift can be used in the future. They can be written to protect both the donor and the public so that gift amounts are not released, if nondisclosure is specified by the donor. The real rub presents itself when the media requests a gift agreement or other document related to a gift that has not been made public and in fact the donor asks for absolute confidentiality. Certainly, governing boards have a duty and obligation to scrutinize any and all gifts that come to an organization to ensure that a particular gift is not compromising the integrity of the organization.

Freedom of information laws and how they affect the nonprofit sector will continue to be discussed for many years into the future. But what must be understood is that taking the "right to know" too far can have a damaging effect on private philanthropy. Just as reporters and editors sometimes defy court orders and go to jail rather than reveal their confidential sources to a judge, nonprofit agencies believe that they must do everything within their power to protect the confidentiality of donor records.

As sacred as confidentiality of sources is to journalists, so is confidentiality of donor records to nonprofit agencies for exactly the same reason. Once donors see confidentiality breached, they will be reluctant ever after to trust the organization or to enter into a relationship with it.

A number of donors wish to remain anonymous and to have their giving records remain private and confidential. Although colleges and universities and other nonprofit organizations many times strive to make public such gifts because they inspire other potential benefactors to make gifts as well, the organization first and foremost abides by the wishes of the benefactor in regard to any public information about his or her private dollars.

Notes for Chapter 1

1. *Giving USA 2004: The Annual Report on Philanthropy for the Year 2003*, (The Center on Philanthropy at Indiana University, The American Association of Fund Raising Council, 2004).

2. *New Nonprofit Almanac and Desk Reference*, (San Francisco: Jossey-Bass, 2002).

3. Tamala M. Edwards, "The Power of the Purse," *Time*, May 17, 1999.

4. James L. Fisher, "The Growth of Heartlessness: The Need for Studies on Philanthropy," *The Education Record* (Winter 1986).

5. John Van Til, et al., *Critical Issues in American Philanthropy: Strengthening Theory and Practice* (San Francisco: Jossey-Bass Inc., 1990), 4.

6. Michael J. Worth, ed., *Educational Fund Raising, Principles and Practice*, (Phoenix, Arizona: American Council on Education, Oryx Press, 1993), 18.

7. Waldemar A. Nielsen, *The Golden Donors, A New Anatomy of the Great Foundations* (New York: Truman Talley Books, E. P. Dutton, 1985).

8. Frank H. Oliver, "Fellow Beggars: The History of Fund Raising Campaigning in U. S. Higher Education" (dissertation, Columbia University, 1999).

9. Dwight F. Burlingame, *Philanthropy in America: A Comprehensive Historical Encyclopedia* (Santa Barbara, California: ABC-CLIO Inc., 2004).

10. Jessica Kronstadt, *Charity, Philanthropy, and Civility in American History*, eds. Lawrence J. Friedman and Mark D. McGarvie (New York: Cambridge University Press, 2004).

11. Andrea Kihlstedt, *Capital Campaigns: Strategies that Work*, 2nd Edition (Gaithersburg, Maryland: Aspen Publishers, Inc., 2002), 1.

12. William P. McGoldrick, "Campaigning in the Nineties," in *Educational Fund Raising: Principles and Practice*, ed. Michael J. Worth, 144 (Phoenix, Arizona: Council for Advancement and Support of Education, Oryx Press, 1993).

13. Kent E. Dove, *Conducting a Successful Capital Campaign: A Comprehensive Guide for Nonprofit Organizations*, (San Francisco: Jossey-Bass Inc., 1988), 5.

14. Association of Fundraising Professionals, "Stressed But Coping: Nonprofit Organizations and the Current Fiscal Crisis," (January 19, 2004).

15. "Capital Campaign/Venture Philanthropy," *Professional Fundraising Magazine*. (November 2002).

16. Ian Wilhelm, "Corporate Giving Takes a Dip, Economic Slump Forces Businesses to Be More Selective," *The Chronicle of Philanthropy* (July 24, 2003).

17. "Highlights of the Foundation Center's 2004 Study International Grantmaking III: an update on U.S. Foundation Trends. The Foundation Center 2004.

18. Ibid.

19. Ibid.

20. Deborah Bongiorno, "Globe-Trotting, the Functions of Advancement Go Global," *CASE Currents* (July/August 2003).

21. Holt Ruffin, "The Globalization of American Philanthropy," Duke University, October 31, 2003.

22. Ibid., 3

23. Ibid, 7

24. Cassie J. Moore, "Nonprofit Organizations Are Hiring Workers at a Faster Pace than Government, Businesses," *The Chronicle of Philanthropy* (June 10, 2004).

25. Heather Joslyn, "Young People Fuel Demand for Nonprofit Study," *The Chronicle of Philanthropy* (January 8, 2004).

26. Ibid.

27. Jeffrey Klineman and Elizabeth Schwinn, "Charities' Fast-Track Jobs," *The Chronicle of Philanthropy* (March 18, 2004).

28. Donna Harrington-Lueker, "The Lay of the Land; What Factors Affect Giving Today?" *CASE Currents* (September 2004).

29. Lester M. Salamon, "Nonprofit World Faces Many Dangers," *The Chronicle of Philanthropy* (January 8, 2004).

30. Epsilon and Barna Research Group, Limited, "The 21st Century Donor: Emerging Trends in a Changing Market," September 2002.

31. Harrington-Lueker, "The Lay of the Land."

32. Association of Fundraising Professionals, "Confidence in U.S. Charitable Organizations Remains Unimproved," September 27, 2004.

33. Ibid.

34. Ibid.

35. Independent Sector. 2001. Giving and Volunteering in the United States. [Published survey]. http://www.independentsector.org.

36. Lilya Wagner, "Women in Philanthropy," *On Philanthropy*, 2004.

37. Ibid.

38. Colleen Nielsen, "Leaving Their Mark," *CASE Currents* (July/August 2003).

39. Michele N-K Collison, "Collision: Where the Color Line Yields to the Bottom Line," *Black Issues in Higher Education* (May 25, 2000).

40. Roger L. Williams, "Special Cases: A Close-Up Look at Four Group's Progress and Pay," *CASE Currents* (February 1996), 20–22.

41. John A. White, State of the University Address, University of Arkansas, September 24, 2004.

42. Rebecca Gardyn, "Faith in Diversity: Religious Groups See Benefits of Hiring People from Other Faiths," *The Chronicle of Philanthropy* (July 24, 2003).

43. Paula Carabelli, "Managers Portfolio: What Great CAOs Are Made Of," *CASE Currents* (September 2000).

44. Hispanics in Philanthropy, http://www.hiponline.org.

45. Native Americans in Philanthropy, http://www.nativephilanthrophy.org.

46. Thomas Blanton, "The World's Right to Know," *Foreign Policy* (July/August 2002), 50.

47. Rick Cohen, "Donations to Public-University Foundations Ought to Be Matters of Public Record," *The Chronicle of Higher Education* (April 23, 2004).

48. David Bass, "Protecting Donors Privacy Is a Matter of Good Ethics and Good Business," *The Chronicle of Higher Education* 50, no. 3 (April 23, 2004): B15.

t w o

Readiness to Preparedness

By failing to prepare, you are preparing to fail.
Benjamin Franklin

Institutional Readiness for a Major Campaign

You may be a development officer, trustee of your organization, member of the board of directors, alumnus, president or CEO, chancellor, or simply an interested third party, but you believe your institution needs to start thinking about a capital campaign. Perhaps your endowment is lower than that of your benchmark organizations. Perhaps you have a number of buildings that need renovation or your organization is in need of new facilities. Perhaps you need to change program thrusts and raise funds for programmatic needs. Maybe you simply have a feeling that you are behind the curve, behind the times, not keeping up with the Joneses, or frustrated because other similar organizations are raising more funds. Whatever the reason may be, you have a sense your organization needs to explore moving toward a capital campaign that will garner resources for your nonprofit organization.

Many connected with nonprofit organizations may have a sense that their institution needs to move forward with a capital campaign, but they have no idea how to do it or, for that matter, what they are getting themselves into. Bill McGoldrick, former vice president for institute relations at Rensselaer Polytechnic Institute and now a fund-raising consultant, commented about campaigns in general in *Educational Fund Raising Principles and Practice*:

> ...Pressure is what campaigns are about. They are not easy to plan. They are not easy to carry out. They are highly visible. And their progress is judged differently by various constituencies.
>
> Like military campaigns, they involve leadership, planning, logistics, volunteers, execution, and persistence. The planning often takes months, even years, to complete. There are considerable risks associated with campaigning, and your institution must make the decision to move forward very carefully.[1]

McGoldrick is putting it mildly! Capital campaigns are extraordinarily complex undertakings that involve the entire institution declaring fund raising as an absolute priority. Planning a campaign, inaugurating a campaign, and orchestrating it to conclusion are extraordinarily time-consuming major undertakings for any nonprofit agency, and if one is going to "do them right," understanding this complexity is critical.

There are several right ways to do capital campaigns, and many experts in the field, particularly consultants, will give different advice on different phases of the effort. But keep in mind, there are several wrong ways to do capital campaigns as well. Unless the leaders of the organization interested in moving ahead with a campaign understand the complexities and appreciate the time involved in the campaign, they are dooming their organization to failure before they get out of the starting blocks.

Organizations considering the launching of a capital campaign must remember the following quick caveats:

- You will need an extraordinary institutional commitment.

- You will need a supportive leadership team at all levels of the organization.

- You will be using volunteers more heavily than ever before.

- You will need to sharpen your mission and your strategic plan and match your mission and plan to the objectives of the campaign.

- You will need well-understood, explainable strategic objectives in the campaign that volunteers and donors believe are high priorities.

- You will need to be cognizant of the overall general economy and know if the timing is right to move forward with the campaign.

- You will need a campaign plan and organizational structure.

- You will most likely need to augment your staff, because campaigns are extraordinarily time consuming and require a commitment of personnel over and above your normal ongoing development program.

- You will need donors and prospects you can turn into donors within a reasonable period of time. If you have no donor constituency, you have no campaign. Have your donors been educated to giving major multiyear commitments?

- You may need campaign counsel if your organization does not have seasoned professionals who have been through capital campaigns before. Even with an experienced staff, you may still want to consider hiring campaign counsel.

- You will need to create a gift table that is closely associated with your current donors and prospects. Does your organization, in fact, have major gift prospect potential? Can you secure six- and seven-figure gifts within a reasonable period of time?

- You will need to surround yourself initially with a small group of volunteers and benefactors who take ownership of the campaign and will work alongside you in establishing campaign priorities and structure.

- You will need the staff to take ownership of the campaign, to sign on for the life of the effort, and to make a commitment that they will, in fact, remain in their positions during the life of the campaign.

- You will need to establish a campaign budget early on, and senior officers of the organization will need to be aware that the campaign will require additional resources and funding to be successful.

- At some point, you will need campaign communications pieces, brochures, case statements, and other materials that will require the hiring of persons with writing ability and publication know-how. You may need to contract this work if staffing levels are not sufficient.

As you can see from the above very cursory assessment, there is much to do when planning a capital campaign. You are indeed getting ready to "go to war." It is, in fact, a major institutional commitment that should not be taken lightly. If you're going to launch a capital campaign, then do it the right way, with an appropriate institutional commitment, resources, budget, staffing, and campaign know-how.

Critical Questions

Although all of the above questions and observations are important and will be dealt with individually later in the book, there are several questions that need to be answered before making a final decision to launch a capital campaign. These specific questions actually go to the heart of the issue of capital campaign timing. Unless each of them can be answered appropriately, your organization may, in fact, not be prepared to move ahead. These are questions that must be asked of every organization preparing for a campaign. Boards of trustees and CEOs would be wise to spend considerable time reviewing and answering the questions as honestly and succinctly as possible.

When considering a major capital campaign, the following questions *absolutely must be addressed*:

Chief Executive Officer

- **Is the chief executive officer of the organization committed to a capital campaign?** Are you certain that your chief executive officer fully supports launching a capital campaign? This commitment must be more than a simple nod of the head or a complacent pat on the back, sending his or her development personnel off to fight the war without him or her. Without a doubt, the person who is crucial to the success of a capital campaign is the president and CEO of the organization. If the president/CEO does not take ownership of the campaign early in the planning phase, then success will be in jeopardy. G. T. Smith states in "The Chief Executive Advancement" that "Success in institutional advancement depends ultimately on the chief executive and that officer's willingness and capacity for leadership in the advancement effort."[2]

    There are many CEOs who certainly agree with planning for a major campaign. There are many CEOs who nod enthusiastically and offer support to the development office "as necessary."

    There are many CEOs who know how the game is played and pay lip service to their constituencies. Not only must the CEO wholeheartedly accept and welcome a capital campaign, but he or she must also be prepared to be the principal spokesperson, the driving force, the individual who takes total ownership of the effort and is engaged in planning and ultimately executing the campaign. The CEO must be willing to proclaim the campaign an absolute top priority of the organization and to spend a predominate amount of time over the coming years to see the campaign through to closure.

    In addition, the CEO must appreciate what it takes to run a capital campaign. New resources, new staff, and an overall commitment by the entire organization will be required for success. The CEO must be at the forefront, pushing, prodding, and diligent in the quest for financial support. Without the CEO's leadership, the capital campaign will wither. It will never become an institutional priority and will never be as successful as it could be.

Capital campaigning is tough business. There can be endless rounds of meetings, cultivation of prospects, heavy travel, speaking engagements, stewardship events, and many, many activities that don't always have much to do with the day-to-day management of the organization. Many CEOs find the task anathema to their current responsibilities. They believe that fund raising is something the development director should do and may not want to be bothered with tasks that don't deliver an immediate payoff.

Fortunately, early in my career, I was exposed to a CEO who understood the issues of ownership and of taking hold of the campaign and making it his own.

Dr. Roy B. Shilling Jr., president of Hendrix College in Conway, Arkansas, and later Southwestern University in Georgetown, Texas, knew he must adopt the campaign as his own and work alongside his staff to make it successful. Both Hendrix College and Southwestern University were dramatically transformed through private gift support as a result of his leadership.

Dr. John A. White, chancellor of the University of Arkansas, also understood the importance of the CEO in the campaign process. Early on, he adopted the capital campaign as one of his institutional goals and spent enormous amounts of time engaging volunteers and soliciting prospects. His time commitment was critical to the success of the campaign.

During the campaign, he saw the endowment increase from $119 million to $700 million six years later. Over the seven-year timeframe of the campaign, he never lost interest, and he never stopped pushing, prodding, and insisting on campaign success.

Although all of those in the development office worked very hard to achieve the goal of the campaign, no one was more dedicated than Chancellor White in ensuring campaign success. The volunteers, the donors, the alumni, and friends knew very well that he had taken ownership early on and was not about to let the campaign fail.

At Penn State University, during its first capital campaign in the 1980s, Dr. Bryce Jordan was also an important leader who declared private gift support as one of his main presidential goals. Dr. Jordan's enthusiasm and commanding presence contributed hugely to the success of that campaign.

Suffice it to say that institutional leadership at the top is an absolute requirement for a successful campaign. Staff members, volunteers, donors, and all others involved with the campaign should never have to apologize to the CEO for expending their time or engaging their services in the campaign.

Governing Board

- **Has the governing board taken ownership of the campaign?** The governing board of the organization must acknowledge that the capital campaign will be the most important event at the organization in the coming years. Nothing else can take precedence. The governing board must unmistakably signal that the campaign has top institutional priority and must back the president and development staff fully in pursuing the goal.[3]

Too often governing boards are not engaged in the campaign early on and are not seen as endorsing the campaign until the CEO or development staff brings it to their attention.

Staff members would be wise to engage the governing board early on in the campaign and let them take individual and group ownership of the project. In fact, the most successful capital campaigns are those where the governing board is applying a degree of pressure to the staff to consider a capital campaign. Governing board members should serve on appropriate campaign committees, certainly in the initial phase of the planning, and the governing board should be kept fully informed of each step in the campaign process.

Members of the governing board also must commit their own resources, time, and talent to the campaign. This may be a challenge for those governing boards that are made up of political appointees, particularly for public institutions. Admittedly, many public university governing board members do not have the financial ability to make major commitments to a capital campaign. Yet all of them, regardless of financial resources, do have the ability to participate at some level. Their participation will be crucial to the success of the campaign.

As Kent E. Dove states: "Without the board's visible and unanimous commitment, it would be difficult, if not impossible, to motivate others to participate and it is the governing board members, independent of others, who must eventually commit themselves to seeing that a stated goal is reached because they themselves are unanimously determined that it will be."[4]

CEOs and staff members would be well advised not to get too out in front of their governing boards when it comes to the endorsement of a capital campaign. The governing board will most assuredly be asked to participate in the effort, financially and otherwise. CEOs must be certain that their governing board supports placing additional resources in the development program in anticipation of a campaign, and the board must be educated about the nature of campaigns and their purposes, organizational structure, and institutional commitment.

There is nothing more damaging to a campaign than when a CEO and a chief development officer suddenly realize that the members of their governing board have not taken ownership of the campaign and are standing aside, watching the effort from afar.

For those public universities that have relatively small boards composed of political appointees, it may be necessary to build excitement and enthusiasm around a development board or committee. Even in this instance, however, CEOs would be advised to keep the governing board totally informed and engaged in campaign matters.

Staff

- **Do you have a professional staff in place to execute the campaign?** You are not ready to launch a capital campaign if you do not have a professional staff in place that can organize and execute the effort. Although it is mind-boggling to consider, many organizations approach capital campaigns without really giving much consideration to the staffing requirements involved. In many instances, the current staff heading the development program does not have capital campaign experience or expertise. Staff members are expected to organize a campaign from start to finish without any formal or informal training or, much less, experience in campaigns. CEOs and boards can see the campaign as simply an add-on responsibility to development staff and may not understand that they are entering into a new ball game that will require a commitment of resources.

It is also important that the principal staff members guiding and leading the campaign are willing to see the campaign through to completion. In other words, they should sign on for the life of the campaign and commit fully to their organization that they will stay put until the campaign has been concluded or at least until resources have been identified to bring the campaign to closure.

Many organizations lose the chief development officer two or three years into a six or seven year capital campaign. The chief development officer is lured away by another institution with the promise of an increased salary and perquisites. Stabilizing staffing is most important in a campaign, and institutions should do all that is possible to ensure staff stability through appropriate compensation, contractual arrangement, and other perquisites.

Staff members below the senior development officer level should also remain in place during the campaign. Continuity in the development office is vital, and those signing on to a capital campaign should give assurances to their supervisor that they will see the campaign through to its conclusion. Changes in key staff positions can have a debilitating effect on the campaign, and staff stability should be an important priority when organizing and implementing the program.

Senior Officers

- **Have other senior staff members in the organization taken ownership of the campaign?** It is not enough that the CEO is totally committed to a capital campaign, even though that is the most important element in judging the internal readiness of an organization to start campaign planning. Other senior officers must be equally as committed and supportive before planning can begin.

  A key player in this respect is the chief financial officer. In most organizations, this individual controls resources, staff, personnel, and institutional operations. Although many chief financial officers are astute about capital campaigns, do not assume that the chief financial officer understands how capital campaigns work and certainly do not assume that he or she supports the effort. One chief financial officer was overheard to tell a major donor to the organization that private gift support wasn't really all that important. He told this individual who had given well over $15 million in an endowment to the organization that his endowment gift did not produce enough income at the institution spending rate to make much of a difference in the bottom line. The chief development officer's jaw dropped, and the benefactor exclaimed, "Then if it's not that important to you, why don't you just give my $15 million back!"

Of course, the real answer to the question about impact is that the careful targeting of resources can have an enormous effect on an organization and can be transformational when spent wisely. The $300 million gift from the Walton Family Charitable Support Foundation to the University of Arkansas will generate approximately $15 million a year in spendable income, with a spending rate of 5 percent. Some may say that $15 million is a small portion of the overall university budget. However, the targeting of $15 million year in and year out on programs of excellence will most assuredly transform the institution.

The chief development officer has the duty and responsibility to educate and inform his or her colleagues. Chief financial officers who do not believe in the worth of private giving, much less a capital campaign, can make the life of the chief development officer miserable and derail the campaign. It is simply not possible to run a campaign smoothly without the cooperation of other officers of the organization. Activities such as timely acknowledgement of gifts, valuation of securities, appropriate investment of gifts to assure a maximum return, advance funds for campaign planning, and sign off on strategic objectives all can be under the control of other officers of the organization and are crucial considerations in campaign planning.

It would be wise to involve senior officers of the organization in integral campaign planning and to develop a partnership between the development personnel and other institutional officers.

Not to be naïve, this is sometimes difficult to accomplish. Admittedly, other chief officers have their own responsibilities and do not always want to be drawn into fund-raising efforts.

The implementation of a capital campaign is outside of their normal operations. Drawing chief officers into discussion about the campaign can require extra effort. However, these officers can open doors that no one else—including the CEO—can open as quickly and as efficiently. A good working relationship with these officers and the campaign office will make life much easier in the initial stages of the effort. Other institutional officers must also be owners of the campaign, and this can only be accomplished by involving those persons from the outset of the effort. Prudent institutional officers will realize the importance of the campaign and will appreciate being approached in the early stages.

In a college or university setting, the chief academic officer is also vital to the appropriate functioning of a campaign, particularly in the formation of the strategic priorities.

The chief development officer and the chief executive officer will be spending a great deal of time together on campaign implementation, particularly when the cultivation process begins for volunteers as well as major gifts. These two persons will be doing a great deal of traveling together and spending time discussing prospect strategies. Development officers should keep in mind that this can become somewhat frustrating for other officers of the organization who also need time from the CEO. Jealousies can develop quickly, but much of this can be avoided by early involvement of other senior staff members.

One thing is for certain. No campaign can move forward efficiently unless all senior team members of an organization are committed and involved. Development officers are encouraged to spend real quality time communicating with their colleagues.

Constituency

- **Is there an organizational constituency ready and willing to make major gifts?** A small regional museum in a southern state had been supported for years by one principal family in the area. It had solid works of art, sculpture, paintings, and mosaics as well as many historic artifacts from the surrounding area. The museum was well attended by school children and curiosity seekers and operated on a small budget paid for almost exclusively by funds from the primary benefactor. There was no friends organization, no dues. The board of directors consisted of four people. A consulting firm was asked to advise the organization on whether it could raise a $50 million endowment to ensure its future.

How do you raise those kinds of funds if you do not have a constituency? Whom do you go to for major gifts when you have done nothing to build a volunteer or donor structure through your many years of operation? Nothing is going to happen in raising big gifts if you don't have prospects and a supportive constituency. Fund raising is not about finding a magic bullet or hiring a magician. To raise major gifts, it will be necessary to have a primary constituency that will be generally supportive of the need for a campaign and willing to place their own resources in the effort early on. The issue here is direct support in a major, important way as well as personal involvement of a group of volunteer leaders who spark interest and support from others. A capital campaign is not the sole province of the development staff. The development staff, even though intimately involved in every detail of the campaign, should be considered facilitators and implementers. Without a solid constituency, the campaign will not be successful.

Institutional Readiness

If the CEO of the institution is solidly behind the concept of a campaign, and not just in name only, but is vigorously promoting and supporting the concept, then the organization is one essential step closer to planning for a campaign.

If the governing board has shown support and enthusiasm for the concept and has taken ownership and made it their campaign, then the organization is a second step closer to planning for a campaign.

If the institution has a cohesive development office with vigorous and visible leadership that plans to remain a part of the organization for the foreseeable future and is willing to learn more about capital campaigns or engage the services of experts who have knowledge, then the institution is another step closer to planning for a campaign.

If the development officer involves other senior officials of the organization in supporting fully the campaign and these officers are willing to devote their time and the organization's resources to planning and promoting the campaign, then the organization is another step closer to planning for the campaign.

If the institution has supportive and consistent major gift prospects as well as campaign volunteers ready and willing to assist the organization in taking on leadership roles, then the institution is another step closer to planning for a campaign.

Kent Dove, in the second edition of his *Conducting A Successful Capital Campaign*, proffers a nifty tool he called the Dove Preparedness Index (DPI). Essentially, the DPI considers 10 important prerequisites to campaign readiness. Dove assigns a score to each of the prerequisites, and if the overall score meets a predetermined figure, then the institution is well positioned to move forward with its capital campaign.[5]

Note the emphasis is still on planning. By no means should the institution precipitously launch an effort. All that has been determined is that there is a favorable climate internally to planning for the campaign. Whether the institution is ultimately in a position to launch the effort requires further study.

All of the elements listed above are critically important to the planning effort. All of them are requirements for early success.

Beginning the Planning Process

At many institutions, planning for a capital campaign never ceases. Before a campaign has ceased operation and the final date of campaign counting has arrived, development officials are already planning for the next, inevitable major fund-raising effort.

It is likely that a one-year planning cycle is not enough in which to get ready for such an undertaking. Not all institutions have the luxury of extended planning time, but those institutions that have some breathing room before a campaign is mandated by the president or governing board would be well advised to spend considerable time in a planning mode, most likely anywhere from 18 to 24 months. Some capital campaigns are in a planning mode for two or three years—and beyond.

Some institutions are even planning the campaign at the same time they are executing the effort. This gives development staff the feeling they are inventing the product and selling it at the same time. In many campaigns, the start date of the effort is actually the start of the planning toward the campaign. Organizations begin counting gifts while in the planning phase and don't generally launch the effort publicly until a percentage of the goal is in hand. This aspect of capital campaigns will be discussed later, but at this point it is most important to communicate the absolute necessity of planning the effort appropriately. Planning will help relieve problems down the road, and there is simply no substitute for a solid working plan in place as the capital campaign begins.

Historical Perspective

One of the very first items to accomplish in the planning process is to develop a historical perspective of the development program and how it has benefited your organization. Development staff should create a written document that outlines the fund-raising program in detail from an historical perspective. An organization that wants to launch a capital campaign and attract major gifts cannot possibly look to the future without knowing its past. Knowledge of an organization's ability to raise major gifts is essential in the planning process. Is there a history of strong major gift fund raising at the organization? Has it been successful in garnering financial support for capital projects in the past? Is there a significant annual fund program that can provide a feeder for donors at more significant levels?

Development officers planning for a capital campaign should review total gift support to their institution for the past 10 years, examining their ability to progress incrementally from year to year in their development program. Many times, organizations want to push aggressively for a capital campaign but cannot show any historical progress in the involvement of volunteers or major gift support. In fact, some organizations are unable to show a history of annual support to their institutions. It would be unwise to push aggressively for a capital campaign with absolutely no historical base of support from which to draw. Many development officers, and particularly CEOs, will proclaim that their organization has the ability to raise big gifts, and they intuitively believe that they can launch a major capital campaign when they have no base of support from the past.

As Kent Dove states in his book, *Conducting a Successful Capital Campaign*, "Realism is necessary in determining capital campaign goals or, indeed, whether an institution is even ready to enter into a capital campaign. . . . Past performance as well as current trends in giving must be analyzed. An institution annually raising $500,000 is not likely to be prepared to mount a successful campaign for $30 million."[6]

The creation of a historical perspective need not be a difficult undertaking. It should contain a three-to-five-page document which lays out the size of the contributions that have come into the organization in the past, the level of planned gifts the organization has received, the level of annual gifts, and the overall philanthropic support received by the organization. Determining where the development program has been historically will be an important indicator of what is possible for the future. Creating the historical perspective will be much more valuable in the planning process than simply declaring that the institution fulfills an important mission and therefore deserves major gift support. That statement can most likely be made by 90 percent of the philanthropic organizations in this country.

Strategic Planning, the Case Statement, and Strategic Objectives in the Campaign

At the outset, when discussing case statements, it should be noted that there are actually three distinct documents. Many nonpractitioners, and even many practitioners, confuse these three basic elements in the planning process of a campaign. Let's try to clear up some of the confusion.

Every donor, volunteer, development officer, CEO, beneficiary, and anyone, for that matter, associated with the campaign wants to know, "What are we raising funds for?" It really all boils down to a definitive list of verifiable objectives that, when funded, will have a dramatic effect on the organization. Questions such as, "Why is this campaign necessary?" and, "What are we raising funds for?" and, "How are you going to use the money we raise?" all have to do with the strategic objective of the campaign.

Years ago, development professionals called this listing the "needs list" or "wish list" of a campaign. Certainly, a much more sophisticated label is "strategic objectives."

But how do we get to a listing of strategic objectives unless the organization has built a strong case for support as an outcome of a strategic planning process?

The words "strategic planning" were the buzz words of the 1970s and 1980s. Everyone wanted to have a strategic plan. If you weren't in a strategic planning process, you weren't on the "cutting edge," and something must be wrong with your organization and its leadership.

To this day, one wonders if organizations really understood what a strategic planning process was supposed to accomplish. There are numerous stories of organizations creating strategic plans that took two, three, and four years to accomplish and involved everyone in the organization at every level. Some academic institutions created multiple committees across the university and took months, if not years, to produce a document that was labeled the strategic plan. At one well-known major public university in the East, the process lumbered along for three years, involving hundreds of faculty and staff members, creating numerous reports, observations, and white papers and producing a "strategic plan" that was both controversial and uninspiring.

Having said this, strategic plans do have their place and are certainly important to the formation of a campaign case statement. In a June 2003 article in *Advancing Philanthropy*, Jacklyn P. Boice makes the very important point that strategic planning goes to the heart of why an organization exists.[7]

Development officers must know what they are expected to raise funds for, and although they can certainly advise a governing board and the CEO as to strategic objectives, it really is not the responsibility of the development staff to determine the projects for which philanthropic gifts will be secured. Some form of planning process that involves the principal figures of the organization—both internal and external—should take place before the launching of a capital campaign. The case statement of the campaign and the strategic objectives should be created through, or certainly should be an outgrowth of, that process. Conversely, the development staff should certainly be involved in the planning process to advise the organization on strategic priorities that will have a better chance of being funded in a capital campaign mode.

After an organization has participated in strategic planning or some sort of planning effort, the next step is to develop a case statement for the capital campaign. Alongside the case statement, and many times part of it, is the development of a strategic objectives' list, which specifically outlines those projects and programs that will be funded, or at least attempted to be funded, during the campaign.

John H. Hanson, in his article in the *Journal of Nonprofit & Public Sector Marketing*, actually believes the creation of a case statement can serve as an intervention to get organizations to focus on change.[8]

Boice also believes that a successful strategic planning process actually enhances an organization's philanthropic efforts. Based on a series of interviews with nonprofit executives, Boice lays out a number of "lessons learned" about the strategic planning process. In her article in *Advancing Philanthropy*, Boice makes the following observations:

> Do not simply bring together a well-respected and well-intended group to decide off the tops of their heads what the organization should do. This is an "opinion-rich and information-poor" plan, with everyone working very efficiently and with total commitment on all the wrong things. Create an inclusive, honest and open process.
>
> • The CEO should meet personally with people in all departments to get the complete message, rather than relying on trickle-down information.
>
> • Volunteer leaders and the board need to exude confidence and passion. Otherwise, the effects are extremely detrimental.
>
> • Don't "overdo" strategic planning. Good direction can hold your organization for three to five years with just an annual review. You do not have to start from scratch every year.

- Don't delay. Create the strategic plan, test it with internal and external constituencies, and follow through with implementation.

- Even a small group can make a difference and affect change in a community.

- The strategic planning process needs to involve all constituents, not just senior management who then hands the plan to the board.

- The plan must be truly mission driven.

- The process can be really exciting if you make it that way, resulting in greater teambuilding and motivation.

- You have to have strong leadership at both the board and staff levels.

- Know how you will make your strategic plan operational. That is an entire dance in itself.

- Never forget the basics.

- Reach high and don't limit your vision.

Therefore, after an organization's planning process has taken place, the next step is to turn to the creation of a case statement that is an outgrowth of that planning process. Gerold Panas, a long-time fund-raising consultant and author, has recently written a book about the creation of case statements. Panas, the founder and chairman of the Institute for Charitable Giving in Chicago, says that an effective case statement "grabs a person and never lets go." In his book, *Making the Case: The No Nonsense Guide to Writing the Perfect Case Statement*, he gives advice on how to create a case statement for a nonprofit organization.[10]

So what exactly is the case statement?

Definition of a Case Statement

The case statement is an internal document outlining the history of the institution, its mission, its long- and short-range plans. It presents a basic rationale for the campaign and details the reasons why an institution should move forward with the effort. The following may be a helpful guide to what is intended to be accomplished by the organization's campaign case statement.

Elements of the Case Statement

- A case statement can be considered the "preamble" of a campaign. The creation of the case statement early on in campaign planning is important to the overall effort. It is an insider's document that presents a basic rationale for the campaign and details the reasons why the organization should move forward with the effort at this time.

- The case statement works best when it is an outgrowth of a planning process that has involved the entire organization. The case statement articulates the theme of the campaign; it describes the organization's strengths, historic and current performance, and vision for the future; it conveys the primary objectives of the campaign; and it states the rationale for private support. The case becomes the organization's endorsed rationale for the importance of increased private gift support and serves as an important tool in educating, recruiting, and motivating volunteer leadership for the campaign.

- The case statement should be a statement of the goals and mission of the organization as realized through a strategic planning process.

- The case statement links the goals and mission with the need to provide resources that will enable the goals and mission to be achieved.

- Generally, the case statement describes the major areas that have been identified as critically important priorities for funding. In other words, what are the areas in which the campaign will seek funds? These areas generally include endowment, annual support, bricks and mortar, program support, and other areas for funding that have been identified as an outgrowth of the strategic planning process.

- The case statement is primarily an internal document, not necessarily used for a wide audience beyond major volunteers. It can be used in a feasibility study process and briefing sessions for volunteers and potential benefactors. It is generally addressed to the lead constituency of the organization and describes the thinking of the organization with regard to the capital campaign and the basic elements for funding.

- It is not necessary to describe every element of the campaign in the case statement. The organization's strategic needs statement in general form can be made a part of the case statement, but it is not necessary to describe every strategic need in the case statement. Instead, the case statement outlines the campaign needs in general terms. The needs statement becomes a more definitive guide for prioritizing activities in the campaign, but the case statement should list some specific projects to be funded and should be fairly definitive on exactly what categories, programs, and projections will be funded during the campaign.

- The case statement is generally a multipage document that lays out in detail the rationale for the basic components of the campaign. However, a case statement of 5 to 10 pages should suffice. Volunteers, interviewees of a feasibility study, and other potential major donors will not want to read a document of much greater length.

While the case statement is generally used in the early stages or advanced gift stages of the campaign, much of the information contained in the case statement can be used in the creation of a campaign brochure (to be discussed later).

Mark J. Drozdowski succinctly captures the difference between the case statement and the lead brochure:

A case statement presents a rationale for the campaign; a brochure presents an emotional appeal. The case statement is text-driven and always appears in draft form so readers can recommend changes. The brochure is a glossy, full-color, high-end piece dominated by photos of the campus and faces. A case hinges on logic and data; a brochure hinges on testimonials.

We share the case statement with a small group of influential donors before the campaign even begins. The brochure appears as we approach the public phase and try to involve as many people as possible. While the content of the case will inform the brochure, the two are fundamentally different in appearance, tone, and use.[11]

Mr. Drozdowski makes an important point about keeping case statements in draft form. Case statements are designed to illicit comment and create dialogue among major benefactors and volunteers. Stamping the document as a "draft" and "for internal use only" gives those persons reading the case a sense that you are looking for their input and advice and that the case is a fluid document subject to change and revision, if necessary.

Although hundreds of campaign case statements have been created for hundreds of campaigns, two case statements are presented in the "Campaign Tools" CD. The first is a case statement from Westminster College, a small liberal arts college located in Central Missouri. The second case statement from the University of Arkansas was created in 1998 and supported the $900 million capital campaign that ended up raising over $1 billion.

Creating the Strategic Objectives

In large complex organizations, it may be difficult to bring together all of the various internal and external constituencies to arrive at a document that lists the strategic objectives of the campaign. This can be particularly true when dealing with complex colleges and universities with academic units and multiple campuses. While the case statement may articulate the general needs of the institution, the needs statement is a more specific document that characterizes the funding components.

Development personnel are charged with the responsibility of gathering financial resources to meet the needs most critical to their organization. Development officers do not and should not determine the strategic priorities in a capital campaign. The strategic objectives in a capital campaign should be determined, after careful strategic planning, by the senior leadership of the organization. Development staff members should certainly be involved in the process and should assess the likelihood of success in meeting the strategic objectives, but leaving the creation of the needs statement to the development staff is wholly inappropriate. The senior officers, and particularly the chief executive officer, should participate in every aspect of determining the strategic objectives of the campaign. In large, multicampus research universities or other complex organizations, the creation of the strategic objectives can take many months of work with input from literally scores of staff members.

The strategic objectives should reflect the most important and critical priorities of the organization and must be designed to bring the institution to new heights of achievement. When a campaign has been completed and the predominant needs items addressed through philanthropic support, there should be a clear sense internally and externally that the organization has improved across the board. The strategic priorities of the campaign must be the priorities of the organization, and therefore there must be input from the organization's personnel.

The typical call for a listing of strategic objectives across an organization will generally produce a list far and above what is practical to fund in a capital campaign. Again, it is the organizational leadership, the president, CEO, and other senior officers that must finally determine what will be targeted for fund-raising objectives.

Also, it is important to note that in a major capital campaign, generally only *60 to 70 percent of the needs statement or strategic objectives are ever actually funded*. This is not to say that the dollar goal of the campaign will not be met, but the strategic objectives goal is rarely achieved in its entirety. Often donors want to give to projects that have not been listed as a priority, and if the campaign is a comprehensive campaign that counts all private resources during a specified time period, then it is entirely possible that the dollar goal will be met but the strategic objectives goal will not.

Strategic objectives in a campaign should also be considered fluid through the life of the campaign. Changing campaign objectives should not be taken lightly, but since campaigns sometimes extend five to seven years, it is possible that strategic objectives could change as well. Changes should only be made if there have been major program changes at the organization that would make a needs statement or strategic objective item obsolete.

While the case statement is general in nature, the strategic objectives should be more specific and should outline in some detail the specific objectives of the campaign. This would include the desired number of endowments to be created as well as the bricks-and-mortar projects, special program items, and other efforts to be funded with campaign proceeds.

The strategic objectives become the guide for prioritizing activities by the development staff. Development staff members should not deviate from the statement when attempting to seek support from benefactors. Development personnel should focus on the major campaign objectives contained in the listing of priorities.

It is also important to monitor the listing of strategic objectives to be certain that the campaign is actually raising funds for the highest priorities of the organization. Institutions should not simply be raising funds and "running up numbers" but actually funding the highest priorities of the organization as determined by the strategic objectives.

A number of nonprofits in recent years have launched massive campaigns with multimillion-dollar and even billion-dollar-plus goals. This rush to set big goals has created races among competing institutions to have the biggest, largest, and most comprehensive campaign. Somewhere along the way, institutions have lost sight of the fact that campaigns are supposed to be designed to improve institutions and organizations and serve as a "change agent" in building quality programs.

Campaigns are not about running up totals and trying to be the organization with the biggest goal. Later, we will discuss campaign counting. It should be noted that raising funds for the strategic priorities of the organization and meeting those priorities, or at least 60 to 70 percent of them, in a campaign environment is just as important as the dollar amount that is raised. In fact, it is much more important than the dollar amount raised, and accepting gifts in kind and property that skew the figures can damage an organization's credibility. Development officers should keep in mind that the campaign is about making progress and meeting funding goals, not trying to raise more than your counterpart institutions so that you have bragging rights.

This is not to say that institutions should back away from communicating dollar goals to its external constituents. Institutions should certainly be proud of the dollar goals that are reached, assuming those dollar goals are a reasonable expression of what the institution can raise in a prescribed period of time. The public will be interested in tracking the progress toward the dollar goal, and institutions have an obligation to report it.

But it is also wise to communicate progress toward the specific need and priority of the organization. Campaigns are not ends in themselves, but means to an end—to strengthen the organization for more effective service to its constituencies by supporting programs, facilities, equipment, and endowments. Development officers need to go beyond generalities and discuss these specifics of their campaigns and their targeted objectives. Alongside a report of the progress on the dollar goal should be a report on the progress of reaching strategic priorities, keeping careful track of an organization's progress on raising funds for specific priorities, such as scholarships, endowed positions, facilities and equipment, programs, and specifically, which administrative units within the organization are meeting or exceeding their strategic priorities and which are not.

It is vitally important for an organization's constituency that the general public knows that the organization is raising funds for specific, targeted needs. Progress must be reported in terms of the organizational needs and priorities as well as the overall dollar goal. Excesses will put institutions at risk not only with external constituencies but with persons within the organization. When constituency organizations announce that they have raised millions of dollars in a capital campaign yet only a small percentage of the funds are actually available to the organization, it can create skepticism and mistrust.

Setting the Preliminary Goal of the Campaign

Determining the actual monetary target of the campaign can be a most difficult process. Too often, development staff members, and certainly volunteers, have no idea how to go about setting the goal. They arrive at a dollar figure that has been determined haphazardly with no sense as to what is logistically possible for their organization.

The following are three wrong ways for an organization to set its campaign goal:

1. Goal Determined by Competing Organizations

A goal is set at a particular level because an organization of similar scope and size is currently operating with that goal. In other words, nonprofit A is in direct competition with nonprofit B and believes its goal for the capital campaign must be at least as high as that of nonprofit B to avoid public criticism and embarrassment. One would be amazed at the number of organizations in this country, particularly colleges and universities, that set their goal with this very thought in mind. A prestigious Big 10 university does not want to be embarrassed when it launches a campaign with a goal smaller than a competing Big 10 university, even though they may not have the historical gift support the other institution has enjoyed through the years. That institution still wants to be seen as a competitor and in the same ballgame and moves forward with a goal that may be unrealistic and impractical.

There is a certain "keeping up with the Joneses" philosophy to this goal-setting process. This philosophy has no basis in data but simply chooses a figure that might be totally wrong for the organization.

When Penn State launched its $1 billion campaign in the 1990s, there was a rush by other competing institutions to follow suit. In fact, one major institution launched a billion-dollar campaign soon after Penn State's announcement, indicating that it would take 10 years to complete the campaign. One wonders what the motivation behind their thinking was. Was the institution more concerned about "keeping up with Penn State?" This scenario happens more often than one would think and is certainly a dangerous way to set a goal for any organization.

2. Goal Determined by Strategic Priorities

Under this scenario, an organization sends out the clarion call for needs and strategic priorities and arrives at the goal based on the total aggregate of these needs. This is neither a practical nor a politically wise approach and can lead to setting a goal much higher than can realistically be obtained. Rarely can any organization launch a campaign that will solve all of its problems and meet all of its needs. It is completely unrealistic to think that private gift support can solve all of the organization's problems and that the campaign is the magic bullet that will put the organization on a firm footing for the rest of time.

The strategic priorities of the organization should be dealt with separately when using them to determine the final dollar goal of a campaign. There is never any correlation between the needs of an institution and the ability to fund those needs.

After the deans and program officers were asked to submit a listing of their strategic objectives in the Campaign for the Twenty-First Century at the University of Arkansas, those needs totaled more than $2 billion. Yes, that's right, more than $2 billion, and senior leadership knew that it was totally unrealistic to think that amount could be raised in a campaign. We knew we had a major job ahead of us to pare down the goal and to seek a more realistic number. The final campaign goal was preliminarily set at $500 million and then raised to $900 million later in the campaign after success had been achieved.

In many capital campaigns, development officers are encouraged to keep what might be called a shadow list or secondary list of priorities. These are important priorities for the organization, but they have not been declared as a first priority on the strategic priorities list. They are best described as "hip pocket" needs that are most important to the organization but were deemed as a secondary priority when seeking private gift support. The so-called shadow list of a campaign can often help to smooth ruffled feathers for program officers who don't have their projects make the first priority list. The original campaign for Penn State had a goal of $300 million but a shadow list of another $300 million.

3. Setting the Goal for Public Relations Purposes

A number of institutions set their goal because it has a particular ring to it from a public relations standpoint. This has been especially true for a number of major institutions over the past 10 years that have rushed to set $1 billion goals because the figure sounds awesome and impressive to the public at large. One well-known public university a few years ago decided to set its campaign goal at $180,750,000. The goal was set with no scientific data whatsoever, but since the institution was founded in 1875, adding a few zeros to the founding date seemed to be a nifty thing to do.

There are a plethora of institutions nationwide that have set their goal at $100 million on the anniversary of their 100 year founding—a rather unscientific 100 for 100 approach. This practice certainly ignores the basic premise that a goal should be directly related to the number of major gift prospects available.

A More Scientific Approach to Goal Setting

Keep in mind that it really isn't necessary to set a final goal in a campaign until the public announcement that generally is some months or years down the road. An organization will know much better about its ability to attract philanthropy after it has been in a solicitation advanced gift phase for a year or two. Although a preliminary working goal can be set, institutions are advised not to set the final goal until the public announcement. One to two years of solicitation can make a huge difference in the life of the campaign and can cause an organization to increase or decrease the goal based on the advanced phase.

How does one go about setting the goal for a campaign that is based on logic and realism and that has some scientific basis?

The following are some specific thoughts on goal setting that should assist an organization at arriving at its working goal as well as its final goal:

- **Program Momentum.** An organization should look to the momentum of its fund-raising program in the years prior to the campaign. What has your organization been raising philanthropically the last 5 to 10 years? Review cash commitments and the size and frequency of major pledges. Look at the annual fund growth. Has it been steady and reliable? Review the size of bequests, charitable remainder trusts, gift annuities, and other planned giving instruments. Has your organization been able to track corporate and foundation support the last five years? What other major gift focus campaigns have been launched previously by your organization and what is their success ratio?

- **Leadership Prospects.** What is the gift potential from your leadership prospect pool? These would be your largest donors to past programs. What is the size of their commitments and has your organization been able to garner major gift support from those closest to you? Do you have a climate for philanthropy and have your benefactors been taught about the importance of major gifts, not just annual gifts below $1,000? Do you have individuals of wealth and influence among your constituents who can lead the way in a campaign, realizing that 95 percent of your contributions will come from fewer than 5 percent of the donors to the campaign? Do you have a sufficient volume of major-gift donors you can rely on for support to reach your goals?

- **Depth of Prospect Pool.** What is the depth of your rated prospect pool for the campaign? How many prospects do you have at the six- and seven-figure level? Have you put together a gift chart that shows the number of rated prospects at certain levels in the campaign? Do you have any history of these rated prospects contributing to your organization or even other organizations in the community?

- **Volunteer Structures.** What is the breadth and strength of your current volunteer structures? Do you have a strong board of governors? Have they tended to promote the organization with their own philanthropic support? Are there other volunteer structures that can be called on to provide leadership and gift support to the campaign? Can you point to three to five volunteers and/or board members who will help lead the campaign and occupy important volunteer positions, giving of their time and leadership as well as their financial resources?

- **Investment in Staff and Program Resources.** What kind of an investment does your organization put into development staff and resources to raise funds? What size professional staff is in place? Does the organization plan to add staff members as it plans for a major campaign? Will the organization provide funding not only for new fund-raising positions but also for infrastructure and programs?

- **Benchmarking.** Has your organization benchmarked with other similar organizations? This might give you a sense of the level of support those organizations have attracted as well as the size of their staff and program budget. While this may be a slippery slope, it is always a good idea to compare resources with competing institutions of similar scope and size. Realizing that all organizations are different and unique in some ways, benchmarking is an important exercise when discussing campaign goals.

- **Counting Policies and Timeframes.** Do you have counting policies in place for the campaign? What will you count? Cash gifts, planned gifts, bequests? This will certainly affect the bottom line. Does your organization plan to use national guidelines that have been promulgated for counting gifts?

  What is the timeframe of your campaign? Do you plan to accept gifts in a three-, five-, or seven-year timeframe?

- **Advanced Gift Phase.** What has your success been in the advanced gift phase or quiet or prepublic phase of the campaign? Have your constituents responded generously? Have your volunteers taken ownership of the campaign? Are you out there all alone?

- **Involvement of Key Officer.** Can you count on the involvement of the CEO of the organization to spend the appropriate time and personal commitment to the effort? Is this campaign larger than the development staff? Is it supported by senior officers of the organization, and have they taken appropriate ownership? Is the governing board behind the program and has it taken appropriate ownership? Is there stability among senior officers of the organization, and is it likely that the CEO and the development staff will be in place for the life of the campaign?

- **Feasibility Planning Study.** In the final analysis, one of the most practical and accurate ways to determine the goal of a capital campaign is to conduct a feasibility planning study. A properly conducted study should give a reasonably good indication of the likelihood of major gift support from an institution's top-level benefactors. Feasibility planning studies can be expensive, difficult to administer, and time consuming, but I believe they are still an accurate and appropriate tool when determining the size of any capital campaign goal.

Prospects, Prospects, Prospects

No doubt, everyone who has purchased a piece of property, particularly a home, has heard the words time and time and again that real estate has everything to do with location, location, location!

Capital campaigns have everything to do with prospects, prospects, prospects!

As noted above in the discussion of setting a campaign goal, so much of goal setting has to do with the number of available prospects and the level of their rating. It probably is not overstating the case to advise that the most important aspect of a major capital campaign is prospect management and the evaluation and rating of major gift prospects. As previously noted, most campaigns today still validate the tried and tested formula that 95 percent of the gifts come from fewer than 5 percent of the donors. No campaign of any size will be successful unless it can secure major commitments from its constituency. While many of these major commitments should be secured early in the campaign, it will be important that major gift prospects continue to flow steadily throughout the entire life of the effort. Your campaign can be doomed to failure if you are unable to produce early major commitments and are unable to show a steady stream of prospects for future support.

Implementation of a Prospect Management Program

Too often, organizations in capital campaigns track prospects in a haphazard, nonsystematic fashion. There is little or no device for appropriate follow up, and campaign solicitation breaks down into a hit or miss mess. To be sure, the fund-raising business has a lot of speculative components.

The creation of a structure, a systematic program that requires daily follow up, patience, determination, and refusal to give up, is a requirement for anyone who wants to be a major success in the fund-raising business. Therefore, building a system that serves the needs of your organization, as well as your needs personally, and that tracks and moves forward prospects at an appropriate pace is a critical priority.

Most sophisticated development programs today have a prospect management effort in place. They may be in varying degrees of sophistication, but their purpose is to assist development officers in moving a prospect to a point of solicitation for a major gift. Campaigns that do not have such a structure in place will be greatly hampered and perhaps even doomed to failure. Prospects are the lifeblood of a campaign. Nothing can be more important than spending quality time, resources, and energy on developing an appropriate system for your organization.

A successful major gifts effort must include the implementation of a prospect management program. The basic purpose of the program is to guide and direct activity with major gift prospects, using volunteer involvement, senior officers of the organization, and development personnel. Organizations of any size should implement a prospect management system early on in campaign planning or fine-tune their existing system so that it will serve not only their ongoing development program but also the capital campaign.

When fully implemented, the prospect management program will regulate all major gift activity for the organization and will be standard operating procedure for major gift fund raising.

Basic Elements

Some of the basic elements of a prospect management program are as follows:
- All major gift prospects being pursued for eventual solicitation at a level that has been predetermined by the organization should be assigned to an appropriate prospect manager. This manager

should be in charge of the prospect from start to finish and should be given the authority to move the prospect forward with appropriate cultivation toward the eventual solicitation through the campaign. The principal manager continues an appropriate level of stewardship once a pledge or commitment has been made.

- Regular prospect management meetings must be held to discuss the cultivation process as well as additions and deletions to the prospect management list.

- The staff member assigned to a prospect will be identified as the "principal" for that prospect. The principal is responsible for the gift solicitation of that prospect. The principal, in consultation with volunteers and other organization officials, makes the decisions regarding solicitation, size of the gift request, and the particular appropriate proposal that will be forthcoming to a prospect. The principal is held responsible for moving the solicitation process forward at the appropriate time.

- Many times volunteers are assigned to a prospect, but I recommend that a staff member continue to be maintained as the principal assigned. This may be difficult to do in development shops that have few development staff members. Organizations should be careful in assigning total responsibility of a prospect to a volunteer unless that volunteer has proven to be diligent in his or her effort in following up and cultivating a prospect.

- A senior development staff member should be given the overall responsibility for managing the prospect management program, and this person should be the only one authorized to change prospect assignments.

- Requests for assignments and/or deletions of prospects in the prospect management program should be handled routinely at prospect management meetings.

- The development office should maintain a permanent record of prospects, and this record should be available for review by appropriate development personnel.

- Every active prospect appearing on the prospect management system should be assigned a principal. This will ensure bottom-line responsibility for the cultivation and solicitation process of all substantiated prospects.

- Sometimes, in large organizations, many staff members will have identifiable relationships with a prospect. Sometimes the chief fiscal officer is well acquainted with a prospect and may have an identifiable interest in that prospect. A prospect management program should allow for these competing interests by designating a "secondary assignment," confirming an additional link with the prospect. This second position affirms another interest in the prospect and keeps that interest active and in front of development staff.

- Every prospect should have a detailed "next step" in the cultivation and solicitation process. Activity with prospects should be monitored centrally so that next steps are in fact implemented appropriately. Prospects that have little or no activity by their principal managers should be moved to other principal managers or removed from the prospect system.

- Generally speaking, prospects should be visited regularly by the staff principals. Some professionals will argue that a prospect should be visited or have some contact at least every six months. If a prospect is not important enough to be contacted within this period of time, then that prospect may not have a bona fide gift potential or the principal manager may not be doing his or her job.

- In consultation with senior development officials, the principal assigned to a prospect should be responsible for defining the status and rating of that prospect. The principal should make the final decision on the appropriate size of the gift request.

- Prospects should not be visited or solicited without the permission and advanced notice of the principal assigned to the prospect. This will assist in the elimination of duplicate solicitations and multiple visits of prospects by competing organization personnel.

Evaluation and Rating of Prospects

One of the most difficult questions to answer for development professionals is, "What should the size of the ask be for a particular prospect in the campaign?"

Obviously, all development personnel want to ask for the maximum gift possible, one that would require a prospect to "stretch" his or her giving. Stretch gifts are what make capital campaigns successful, and determining which prospects are capable and inclined to make such gifts is a critical factor in campaign planning.

Asking a prospect for a gift below their capacity is the proverbial "train wreck" for campaigns. It is also important not to "overshoot" a prospect's capacity and run the risk of embarrassing the prospect to the point where he or she decides not to participate. Development professionals used to hold to the theory that "you can never ask for too much" and that potential benefactors are complimented when a gift ask is much larger than their capacity. Experience, however, has shown that it is indeed possible to shoot too high. When an individual is solicited at a level that is totally inappropriate for their financial circumstances, it can do more damage than good in the cultivation process.

While it is certainly true that benefactors generally never give away their last penny, and it is a development officer's challenge to encourage a benefactor to stretch his or her giving, it is equally as true that the gift ask should be appropriate and affordable for the prospect. While challenging the prospect to new heights of philanthropy, the ask should not be so high that it is unrealistic and unachievable for the donor.

Recently, a member of the development staff at the University of Arkansas was asked for a major commitment to a local nonprofit organization. Even though the staff member makes a very good salary and is financially comfortable, the gift ask was for $100,000. The nonprofit development team way overshot the potential of the prospect and created embarrassment not only for the prospect but also for themselves. Any degree of investigation and research would have revealed that a gift of that magnitude was not realistic. That kind of solicitation is sloppy, uninformed, and simply unnecessary for any professional organization trying to raise private funds.

There are some tried and tested ways that a campaign can work to determine the evaluation and rating of prospects. The more sophisticated organizations with larger staffs will participate in all of the following methods:

- **Professional Prospect Research Personnel.** A number of organizations with relatively sophisticated development programs employ research staff to evaluate prospects. Even in a small shop, organizations would be well served to consider employing research personnel, if only part time, and particularly during the capital campaign years. As Bobby S. Strand says, "The goal of prospect research is to support the evaluation of individuals or organizations as perspective donors and to aid in the development of cultivation and solicitation strategies."[12]

  Researching prospective donors involves gathering, organizing, and synthesizing information that is then analyzed, screened, and presented in a clear and concise format. Researchers may use proxy statements, Dun & Bradstreet reports, financial data, and other information to determine the wealth of particular prospects.

In addition, identification of new prospects is a continuing responsibility of the researcher, who will use a number of resources and techniques to accomplish a steady flow of prospects. Much information about prospective donors may be gathered from development officers who are engaged in the cultivation process. Development personnel are encouraged to complete reports of contact and include relevant information that might be of assistance during the process of cultivation and solicitation. After every visit to a potential benefactor, a development officer should write a briefing giving firsthand observations, information, and other data that might not be available elsewhere. The Association of Professional Researchers for Advancement (APRA) has developed a code of ethics and fundamental principles.

- **Electronic Screening.** Electronic screening of prospects has been around for well over 15 years. It is primarily based on geodemographic data available publicly and supplemented with other wealth indicators. Electronic screening is used regularly by a number of organizations to help in the identification of constituents who may have significant assets. These screening services use a number of different data sources. These sources can identify key demographic characteristics and wealth indicators such as estimated income and real estate value. A plethora of different sources exists, some provided by federal government data banks and others provided by database companies such as Acxiom, headquartered in Little Rock, Arkansas, as well as Dun & Bradstreet. Most of these databases can be accessed electronically and will provide a host of information that can be useful to nonprofits. Dun & Bradstreet, as an example, identifies business ownership and biographical information on more than nine million individuals and six million companies. It also makes it possible to access information regarding more than 2.8 million contributors to federal election campaigns. There are also databases that give information on nonprofit boards of directors, self-employed individuals, and insider trading of securities, to name a few.

Mary Lawrence, director of research at the Loomis Chaffee School, gives a very good description of electronic screening in *NEDRA News*:

Electronic screening is used often during capital campaigns to identify constituents with significant assets (e.g., high value real estate, multiple properties, securities holdings, private company ownership). It also can be used to identify planned giving prospects, target annual fund upgrades, and identify the constituents who are most likely to support you.

Using a company for electronic screening is not inexpensive. For this reason alone, many nonprofits choose to refrain or even ignore electronic screening as being too costly.

Many offices are hesitant to contract with an outside vendor because of the high cost associated with electronic screening. While electronic screenings are a major expense (on average, $30,000 for 100,000 records), it's important to look at the big picture before negating their efficacy. According to David Lawrence, president of P!N, the average turnaround time for screening results is four to eight weeks at a cost of approximately $6 per major gift prospect. If the same research was done in-house by one researcher who could qualify an average of one major prospect per day, at six to eight hours of research each, this would cost an average of $269 per prospect, or 16+ years at a cost of over $600,000![13]

Any organization that decides to contract with an outside agency to do electronic screening should have a definitive plan in place when the data arrives at the development office. Screening done electronically requires a significant financial investment, as well as a major investment of time. To balance the inevitable barrage of well-meaning suggestions and enthusiastic inquiries, spend ample time before the data comes back to put together a clearly articulated and agreed implementation plan.

Andrea G. Dickens writes in a 2003 *Connections* article that "Creating a detailed implementation plan before your data are returned will save you time and frustration and provide the entire fund-raising staff a clear understanding of what to expect."[14]

Amy Minton, director of development research at Bowdoin College in Brunswick, Maine, makes the following statement on electronic screening:

> Choosing a vendor for a wealth assessment of your donor database is an overwhelming process. The decisions don't end with a signed contract! One of the challenges you will face is determining how to most effectively share the returned

data with the people who really need it—your front-line colleagues. . . . The plan should allow the research staff to prioritize the work inherent in verifying and analyzing data and ensure that front-line fund raisers begin receiving data as soon as possible."[15]

Two other references are worth reviewing for those interested in pursuing electronic screening. Cecilia Hogan, the development researcher for the University of Puget Sound in Tacoma, Washington, has published a book on prospect research. She says:

Screenings—researcher designed, peer centered, or commercial versions—don't just cut a path to efficiency. They bulldoze a runway to it. The best and even the not-so-best screenings drive the names of capacity-rich constituents to the top of the heap. Do they elevate every capacity-rich name? Of course they don't. They are, after all, designed by humans, so they have flaws. Do they deliver enough capacity-rich names to keep a fund-raising team productively raising money? Of course they do, if that team has executed a thoughtful plan to deal with the screening results.[16]

A counterpoint to that view is expressed by Susan Cronin Ruderman, who is a former development researcher at MIT and Harvard and is currently a consultant. She makes an interesting case for bucking the trend of mandatory screenings and believes putting funds into the hiring of prospect researchers is a better investment.[17]

- **Volunteer, Peer, and Group Screening.** One of the best and most reliable ways to determine if an individual is a prospect is to gather information from informed volunteers. Often the volunteer can provide sensitive information about a particular prospect and the ability of that prospect to make a major commitment to your organization.

  One way to ensure the free flow of information from volunteers is to conduct group and peer screening reviews. Group and peer screening is a traditional prospect evaluation and a rating system that is used by a number of nonprofits. This screening involves several volunteers reviewing lists that are provided in advance by the development staff. Generally, the list has been refined by the development staff. The staff is attempting to gather information about an individual's asset base and likelihood of being a major gift prospect.

These group screenings can be open discussions or silent screenings, depending on the sensitivity of the volunteers. Based on the number of prospects to be reviewed and the anticipated giving levels, various methodologies can be used. For example, when reviewing a relatively small group of high-potential prospects, an initial silent screening by the group, followed by an open discussion, can be most useful.

Many institutions have become much more formal in group ratings and have created carefully orchestrated programs to conduct group sessions around the country. Several years ago, Penn State University launched its leadership evaluation and assessment program (LEAP) in an attempt to identify a new wave of major gift prospects in anticipation of its second major capital campaign. LEAP meetings were conducted in over 25 cities with large concentrations of Penn State alumni. During these sessions, specially selected alumni were asked to screen lists of potential major-gift benefactors and rate what their giving capacity might be in another campaign. These lists were then put into a database and manipulated along with data from other screening sessions. The result was a source of information based on personal knowledge of alumni who work and reside in the same geographic area as the new prospects who have been rated. Additional information on the leadership, evaluation, and assessment program is contained on the "Campaign Tools" CD.

For Virginia Commonwealth University, conducting peer screenings proved to be most valuable. Patricia Ambler, director of prospect research at Virginia Commonwealth, suggests this:

> The screening and qualification process revealed what our current and most influential contributors thought others could give to the organization. We also discovered some valuable connections between our board members and other philanthropists and organizations in the community. I also found it helped to have buy-in from both the board and development committee chairs. In some cases, the rating assigned was less useful than the information obtained during the qualification phase. . . . In addition, the peer screen-

ing activity proved to be a productive method of engaging former board members in the fund-raising process. It also helped them see themselves as contributing and valued members of the organization in a way outside of financial contributions."[18]

Peer screening definitely assists campaign volunteers in taking ownership of the effort early on. In a campaign mode, it is important to fully involve your board members and top prospects. Many are very sophisticated about fund raising and glad to help out with screening research.[19]

Electronic Fund Raising

Fifteen years ago electronic communication was something the geek professor was doing with friends and associates at other universities. Today, of course, it is mainstream America. It is estimated that within the next five years, one-half of the American population will use electronic communication in one form or another. In 2003 it was estimated that more than 50 million Americans were using the Internet on a weekly basis.

In "Using E-mail and the Web to Acquire and Cultivate Donors," Nick Allen writes:

While even the organizations most successful at raising money online still raise 30 times more offline than online, a wide range of groups are beginning to use e-mail and the World Wide Web to find new donors and cultivate the ones they have.

With more than 50 million Americans using the Internet every week—and many of them using their credit cards, too—the audience is there. Computer use is growing across class and race lines, and more and more people have access to computers through public libraries and schools, if not in their homes.[20]

With increased frequency, organizations are using electronic communication to inform their constituents on a regular—if not daily—basis. Many national organizations send daily e-mails to their constituents, keeping them abreast of the latest issues affecting their membership.

Fund raising over the Internet has worked best by using a direct approach to an organization's constituency. The organization's Web site will give a simple, quick way to make a donation to a philanthropic organization. There are also a number of appeals through electronic communication that are being made by nonprofits. These direct e-mail fund-raising appeals have met with success.

Allen goes on to say:

> Direct fundraising has been the most successful way to raise funds online and will probably continue to be. Direct fundraising online includes getting people to join your organization through your Web site or asking for money through e-mail.
>
> Most successful organizations put attractive membership offers on their Web home pages and throughout their Web site and include a "Donate" link on every page.[21]

The Baby Boomer generation's children use the Internet for their very existence. If you cannot buy it, do it, or research it on the Internet, then to this generation it must not be worthwhile.

Anyone who has to communicate with others had better be able to do it online. Many people have already made the Internet and e-mail their preferred method for connecting with the world. For many in the new generation, if you're not on the Internet, you don't exist.

But what does that have to do with fund raising? AT&T said it best with this comment:

> It isn't about technology; it's a new dial tone. Watch an 11-year old on the Internet, and you'll see that young people are as comfortable online as their elders are on the phone. The kids have been raised in an electronic, connected world. The Internet is how they communicate. If you aren't there, you are not part of their world. They are your future donors, volunteers, and stakeholders.[22]

Stories from chief development officers about closing major gifts on the Internet are rampant. At the University of Arkansas, major benefactors regularly communicate through e-mail about major gifts and use electronic transfer technology almost on a daily basis. Recently, over the holidays, a major benefactor transferred $5 million worth of stock electronically to the university. The entire communication about the transfer, as well as the transfer itself, was performed electronically. The university was closed between Christmas and New Year's. It was the preferred mode of communication for the donor and saved time and effort on both ends.

Sherri Begin recalled in *Crain's Detroit Business:*

> In the fall of 2000, Lawrence Technological University used the Internet to land a $500,000 donation from an alumnus on the West Coast. The gift wasn't made on Lawrence Tech's Web site but after an initial, face-to-face meeting, most communication with the donor took place through e-mail over a couple of months. . . . In the end, the gift of stock was made through an electronic transfer.[23]

Nathan Shaver with Changing Our World, Incorporated, a fund-raising and philanthropy consulting firm, has a number of interesting observations about "ePhilanthropy:"

> While the tools and methodologies of "ePhilanthropy" were once the unique responsibility of the IT department, nonprofit professionals have increasingly become more comfortable with the technology involved in raising money and connecting to constituents online. With the improved accessibility and lower costs inherent in a field that constantly improves upon its last breakthrough, one can assume that ePhilanthropy will one day be a full-integrated component of the development office—a component that all nonprofit professionals will use with ease.
>
> What is perhaps most important to remember as we budget and plan for the new year, is that fund raising will never be a completely digital enterprise. ePhilanthropy can help us become more efficient, but it will not radically change the type of work we do. The Web, e-mail, and other technological tools will instead become fundamental to how we do that work. Face time is and will always be crucial, and while some parts of our endeavors can never be converted to zeros and ones, some important aspects of it can be with great effect. From the more accurate targeting of prospects to the less expensive and more personal cultivation of donors, technology has come of age and our nonprofit universe and will benefit every one of us.[24]

While using the Internet and electronic communication for major gift fund raising is still in the infant stages, there are examples of electronic communication being used with increasing frequency to raise big gifts. Most fund raising through the Internet, to date, has been built around annual fund raising and ongoing support. There are a number of companies that have moved into the electronic communication fund-raising business and tout it as an extraordinarily inexpensive and effective way to raise considerable resources for nonprofits.

The unprecedented growth of ePhilanthropy in just the last 5 to 10 years is causing all nonprofit professionals to reevaluate their skill sets and be certain that they are in tune with this ever-changing and evolving future direction of fund raising.

In an article in the *International Journal of Nonprofit and Voluntary Sector Marketing Success* entitled "ePhilanthropy: Using the Internet to Build Support," Theodore R. Hart writes:

> The growth of ePhilanthropy has required even the most seasoned nonprofit professionals to learn new skills and to re-evaluate how

they approach nearly every aspect of fund raising. These tools add a new dimension of efficiency and require higher levels of integration for nearly every offline approach to attracting philanthropic support.

Success will come not from an emphasis on the technology, but from cultivating and enhancing relationships. The Internet provides countless highly efficient opportunities to enhance relationships, improve donor satisfaction and, therefore, to raise more money. Those who give online, however, are those who are invited to give online. Therefore, strategies must be devised and deployed to identify, cultivate, solicit and steward philanthropic support. [25]

Nonprofits would be well advised to spend considerable time reviewing their electronic communication and how it can assist them in the future. One thing is for certain, ePhilanthropy is like a freight train coming at us at full speed. We either get out of the way, get on board, or get left behind!

Ongoing Fund Raising During the Capital Campaign

A nonprofit's development organization is in the business of garnering resources on an ongoing basis. A question that is frequently asked is, "How does the ongoing development program, particularly annual fund, continue forward within the aegis of a capital campaign?"

Some development professionals have argued through the years that capital campaigns are no more than a revved up major-gift program that has been happening at the institution on an ongoing basis. They argue that the organization of a capital campaign is unnecessary, because such campaigns are simply an ongoing statement of institutional needs and priorities and that organizations should continue to vigorously raise funds with or without the framework of a capital campaign.

Of course, the main purpose of a capital campaign is to sustain an intensified, systematic program of major gift fund raising with a defined target, goal, and giving opportunities, using the assistance of a volunteer network. Without the context of a campaign, there is little opportunity to "rally the troops." There is no question that a five-to-seven-year capital campaign instills a fund-raising process that will continue to benefit the institution many years into the future.

But it is important to note that a capital campaign does not mean that day-to-day development activities should be suspended during the life of the campaign. What it does mean is that the major components of a development operation should be keyed into campaign activities. Annual fund, planned giving, corporate and foundation giving, and the offices that provide development services should all become a part of the overall campaign.

Many former clients used to talk about the need to hire campaign staff under the context that "those people would be running the campaign." Many clients thought that campaign activity was separate and apart from ongoing fund raising and that the organization would simply "hire somebody to do the capital campaign."

The reality is, however, that in a major comprehensive capital campaign, the entire development structure must become part of the effort supporting and nurturing the campaign through to fruition. You want your total development organization to take ownership of the campaign and not believe that it resides in another office down the hall or in another building, on another floor.

This is one reason why some development professionals resist the title of director of the campaign. They do not want other development personnel to feel as though the campaign is somehow broken away from the mainline development function and is being handled by a director who is not really in the mainline, ongoing fund-raising program.

There is no question that a five-to-seven-year capital campaign instills a fund-raising process that will continue to benefit the institution in years ahead. While the day-to-day development activities should by no means be suspended during a capital campaign, all components of a development operation should be keyed into the campaign activities. Development activities should not exist in a vacuum and should work in tandem with campaign activities.

Annual Giving During the Capital Campaign

Many nonprofit organizations have rather large constituencies. They may be friends of the organization, dues-paying members, annual fund donors, or volunteers. At a college or university, the largest constituency is, of course, the alumni base.

Regardless of the size of the organization, the vast majority of its constituents will not be given the benefit of a personal call by a volunteer or staff member on behalf of the campaign. It is simply not feasible or practical for large numbers of constituents to be contacted personally and asked for a gift during a campaign. Remember that 95 percent of the gifts that flow to the campaign and make a difference in campaign totals will come from fewer than 5 percent of the donors. Concentration on the bigger gifts is vital to the success of any campaign, and, as one development professional put it, "ringing doorbells with proposals" will not make for campaign success.

Nevertheless, an annual fund program of an organization must continue to raise funds for vital programs but should do so with regard for the larger campaign effort.

Some organizations have left the annual giving program undisturbed during the capital campaign and have focused their efforts on major gifts from the 5 percent of its constituents as mentioned previously. Under the scenario, the annual fund is allowed to send the same type of mailings and perform the same kind of telephone solicitations that it has always done. Communications with constituents proceed as if the capital campaign was an add-on.

Many professionals will signal that this is a mistake. Certainly, the annual fund of an organization should continue to seek gifts during the capital campaign but should recognize the campaign in promotional literature. The preferred mode of operation is to have annual fund literature carry a description of the campaign so that an organization's constituents are made to feel that their annual gifts are helping, even in a small way, to satisfy campaign needs.

Extreme care should be taken, however, so that constituents do not believe that their annual gift is necessarily their only gift to the capital campaign. Most annual gifts are below $1,000, and many of the constituents might have the wherewithal to make gifts at a much higher level. Every discussion of capital campaign operations will include the issue of "preemptive gifts." A preemptive gift is one that comes to an organization either through the annual fund or without formal solicitation. This type of gift can make it most difficult to go back to the individual for a larger, more appropriate gift. Preemptive gifts can hurt a campaign, and organizations would be wise to implement policies that will help to avoid preemptive gifts.

The following are some potential ways of avoiding a preemptive gift to a capital campaign:

- Delete from annual phone or mail gift solicitation those major-gift prospects who will be asked personally to contribute to the campaign with a multiple-year pledge. Even though this mechanism solves the problem of receiving a preemptive gift through the mail, it is not recommended under all circumstances. Unless the capital campaign has a large staff that is capable of reaching constituents quickly, it could mean that certain donors will go unsolicited for several months if not even years. Excluding a constituent from an annual fund mailing solicitation in an attempt to reserve him or her for a capital campaign "ask" may simply have the effect of "losing the annual gift." Extreme caution should be taken when making any decision to eliminate major-gift prospects from annual fund-raising appeals.

- Seeing the prospect within a reasonable period of time is most important. The double ask will require the education of an organization's constituents, and donors must be aware that they are making separate and distinct commitments, both of which count in the comprehensive campaign.

- Another option is simply to continue annual giving appeals full throttle and make them a part of the overall campaign by using the campaign logo and campaign information in all annual fund literature. Constituents are educated regarding the importance of continuing their annual giving to help support and sustain the organization and in making a capital gift that might be paid over a defined period of time. Most religious organizations do, in fact, ask for an ongoing annual gift for church or synagogue operations even when they request a capital gift for a particular project that has been identified as a priority.

With proper education, constituents will, in time, recognize the difference between an annual gift and a capital gift, and the organization will be much healthier in the long run.

Tax-Exempt Bonds and Capital Campaigns

Federal and state laws allow for debt financing for capital projects on a tax-exempt basis. This can be extremely advantageous for nonprofit organizations, because it allows for a financing method that costs less than borrowing funds from financial institutions on a conventional long-term basis. Individuals who buy tax-exempt bonds do not pay federal income tax on interest they receive; they accept a lower interest rate.

A number of jurisdictions also exempt state income tax from the bonds, thereby giving an added benefit to bond purchasers. The largest user of tax-exempt bonds has historically been governmental entities such as schools, municipalities, and other government-owned functions that need to improve construction, infrastructure, and other projects requiring a large infusion of resources.

A number of private organizations, however, may also receive benefits of tax-exempt financing, particularly those organizations that are exempt from federal income tax under section 501(c)(3). Because of this "inexpensive" way to finance capital projects, a number of nonprofits are turning to the use of bonds for bricks and mortar rather than conventional methods of borrowing. This has the added benefit of preserving endowment funds or institutional reserves and allows for an institution to finance new bricks-and-mortar projects on a long-term basis at a low interest rate.

Federal tax regulations govern the investment and expenditure of tax-exempt bonds and are quite detailed and complex. It is important, however, to exercise caution in this tax labyrinth to avoid the characterization of bonds as "arbitrage bonds."

The relationship between bonds and carrying out fund raising for certain capital projects have a number of legal restrictions that require special note. Arbitrage bonds are bond proceeds that are invested, or used to "replace" funds that are invested at a higher interest rate than the interest rates on the bonds. This has the result of losing the tax exemption on the bonds. As Rachel H. Pollack indicates in her 2000 *CASE Currents* article, "Development officers unfamiliar with bonds might think, 'This sounds great! My campus will use bonds to pay for a new residence hall, raise money for it at the same time, then use that money to pay off the bonds.' There is only one problem. It is illegal."[26]

Fortunately, there are other ways to achieve the same results. Fund raising and bond financing can be accomplished in a manner that does not lead to arbitrage. The 501(c)(3) organization should make sure that any solicitation for the building project is open ended and does not specify a particular capital project purpose for the pledge. Any gift agreements, acknowledgment letters, or other formal pledge agreements should not specify the particular bricks-and-mortar project. It may also be a simple matter of structuring a gift agreement to state that the organization's board of governors will have the authority to specify how the gift is to be used rather than having to specify it is for the capital project.

Suffice it to say, development officers, boards of governors, CEOs, and others at nonprofit organizations should be made aware of this bond-financing issue when linked to fund raising. It is a little understood part of the tax law that can have unfortunate consequences if it is not dealt with adequately and appropriately.

Pay Incentives

Recently, a CEO of a nonprofit suggested that, "Let's just hire a hot-shot fund raiser and give them 10 percent of the proceeds that they raise as a motivator and see how fast they get the job done!" While pay incentives, bonuses, and sales percentage incentives have long been used to motivate employees in the for-profit sector, nonprofit organizations have been slow to realize the benefits of such compensation packages. Only in the last 10 years or so have these incentives been used more aggressively in the nonprofit sector. In recent years, a number of higher education institutions have adopted incentive pay-plans, including the California State University System, Duke and Michigan State Universities, the University of California at San Diego, and the University of Minnesota. [27]

Martin Grenzebach, chairman of Grenzebach Glier & Associates, in Chicago, has long advocated the use of incentive plans for nonprofits. "They should operate on principles that have succeeded in business," he says. "This is one of them."[28]

Others in the business, however, are more skeptical. Since fund raising requires teamwork and total institutional commitment, it is not always certain who is actually the "closer" of the gift and which person in the organization ultimately caused the gift to happen. Most major gifts have multiple fingerprints on the gift. Awarding a bonus or pay incentive to an individual when several persons have been involved in meeting a goal or in particular project funding can be more damaging to an organization than not providing the incentive.

Through the years, practitioners with some longevity in the business have maintained that bonuses or incentives destroy the concept of building a climate for philanthropy and cause development personnel to think of their own financial bottom line rather than what's best for the organization and the donor. Sometimes, recommending that a donor make a certain gift in a certain way may not be in the best interest of the donor, and if a development officer receives a benefit directly by virtue of the gift, a huge conflict of interest can arise.

Amy Smith, director of development for the University of California at Riverside, believes that, "Performance pay tarnishes a sacred calling. Raising money for higher education is about relationship and trust. People who are incentivized by bonuses should go sell cars."[29]

The one area that has seen an explosion of incentive-based programs in the nonprofit sector is the health-care industry, with hospitals and medical institutions. CASE has long been opposed to a straight bonus plan for fund raisers and has maintained that position for more than 10 years. In recent years, CASE has been less definitive of the issue of incentive-based plans, and this has caused some movement in the area among nonprofits.[30]

Bonuses have not always included a cash outlay, and other incentives are being offered to fund raisers that meet their goals. Some of those compensation incentives include the following:

- Low-interest loans given to development officers for meeting certain performance levels
- Automobile privileges

- Professional conference travel to a warm climate as determined by the development officer
- Car allowances, housing allowances, entertainment allowances for certain development officers that historically meet goals and funding objectives
- Country club memberships and golf privileges for the most productive personnel[31]
- Flexible benefits
- Day care
- Time off
- Retirement plan contributions[32]

What is certain, however, is that incentive-based pay plans are becoming more and more prevalent in the nonprofit sector as organizations compete for the best talent.

In response to the United Way scandal, Congress implemented a number of new penalties for nonprofits that pay their officers excessive salaries or offer excessive bonus plans. It is more important than ever that nonprofits be careful with the bonus plans they are offering employees, so that they do not appear out of line or excessive for the work being performed.

AFP has commented more extensively than CASE on incentive compensation plans. The AFP president and CEO, Paulette V. Maehara, explains it like this:

> The AFP Code of Ethical Principles and Standards of Professional Practice permit incentive compensation when structured properly—that is without basing the incentive amount on a percentage of dollars raised. Incentive compensation is a growing trend. In the *AFP Compensation and Benefits Survey* completed last year, 19 percent of U.S. members surveyed and 15 percent of Canadian members surveyed received some type of incentive compensation.
>
> Tom Watson makes the case in his 2004 article in *OnPhilanthropy* that, "There are several reasons for the growth of this type of compensation. The shortage of senior development professionals is challenging organizations to be more creative in their compensation packages. Many organizations use this type of compensation in order to retain fund-raising professionals and as a way to reward their performance. In addition, organizations use incentives as a way to motivate and reward staff to achieve large goals, such as a billion-dollar campaign for example.

There are incentive compensation strategies that are not dependent on a percentage of dollars raised. I encourage the use of non-financial variables such as number of volunteers involved, number of new annual fund donors, major gifts and bequests."[33]

While pay-incentive plans have made serious inroads into the workplace and the nonprofit sector, in the July/August 1999 *CASE Currents*, author James W. Asp II notes there are some cautions and guidelines that should be considered:

- Tying extra compensation to specific gifts can be problematic.

- Tying extra compensation totally to fund-raising totals is not always a fair assessment of an organization's fund-raising progress and can end up compensating the wrong development officer.

- Work to find the real qualifiers for success such as the number of new donors, the number of major benefactors at the level of $10,000 and above, the number of deferred gift expectancies, the number of charitable remainder trusts, gift annuities, and other indices that show work in progress.

- Be certain that incentive-pay programs benefit the entire organization and not just the top management. Sometimes the actual fund raising is being carried out by middle-level managers whose credit is never realized.

- Don't forget to incentivize the team player and the person who works for the total organization's welfare, not one particular department or program.

- Be certain that the pay incentive program is definitive and well structured so that everyone knows the parameters of the program.

- Always be fair and appropriate in dealing with employees and their compensation, and be certain that they completely understand how it is possible to obtain a bonus or incentive.[34]

Salary Gap

Finally, in the area of compensation, it is important to remind nonprofits that female executives are paid less than their male counterparts. CASE's *2002 Salary Survey*, conducted by Carnegie Communications, shows a wide disparity between women's and men's salaries (see Figure 1).

FIGURE 1. HOW PAY FOR MEN AND WOMEN DIFFERS AT NONPROFIT ORGANIZATIONS

Median Pay for Fund Raisers

	Men	Women
Chief executive officers	$68,333	$49,167
Chief development officers	$73,000	$50,000
Deputy development officers	$65,250	$48,000

Source: Association of Fundraising Professionals' 2000–2001 Compensation and Benefits Study. In the survey of 1,200 association members, 67 percent of respondents identified themselves as female.

College Fund Raisers' Pay Ranges

	Men	Women
Percentage who earn $20,000 to $40,000	11.9%	27.4%
Percentage who earn $40,001 to $60,000	27.8%	38.1%
Percentage who earn $60,001 to $100,000	41.1%	28.5%
Percentage who earn $100,001 or more	19.3%	5.5%
Percentage who earn $100,000 or more in their first year	15.0%	4.0%

Source: The Council for Advancement and Support of Education's 2002 salary survey, conducted by Carnegie Communications. In the survey of more than 10,000 council members, 65 percent of respondents identified themselves as female.

Median Pay for Executive Directors

25 percent of groups with annual budgets of $5-million or more are headed by women.

Size of budget	Men	Women
More than $50-million	$271,032	$186,088
$25-million to $50 million	$175,913	$143,188
$10-million to $25-million	$135,885	$111,545
$5-million to $10-million	$105,699	$91,179

Source: 2002 GuideStar Nonprofit Compensation Report

As Heather Joslyn states in her 2003 article in *The Chronicle of Philanthropy*, "Survey after survey shows that female executives and fund raisers make less than males in similar jobs at comparable organizations and that women, while heading the majority of all charities, are far less likely to lead the largest ones."[35]

The nonprofit sector should be a beacon for women's salaries and on the leading edge. Tolerating such a huge disparity in male and female salaries in the nonprofit sector is a travesty of justice and a black mark on philanthropic organizations. Organizations must work diligently in the months and years ahead to bring the salary levels in line and at acceptable levels. To do anything less would be to compromise the integrity of the nonprofit sector and call into question the entire fund-raising profession.[36]

Forthcoming Wealth Transfer

Much has been written in recent years about the coming wealth transfer. In the next 30 years, there will be a tremendous amount of wealth being transferred from one generation of savers to the Baby Boomer generation. Those persons born in the 1920s and 1930s, or what Tom Brokaw referred to as the Greatest Generation, are a generation of savers and conservators. As they die and leave their fortunes to the next generation, two things are likely to happen. First of all, the wealth transfer will precipitate a number of major gifts as persons implement estate planning devices to lessen the tax bite. Secondly, a new generation with new thinking, new giving patterns, and perhaps a less-conservative approach to philanthropy will emerge. Individuals in their late 40s, 50s, and early 60s will inherent significant wealth and will be positioned to take up the mantle of philanthropy as a new generation of givers. Paul G. Schervish and John J. Havens of the Social Welfare Research Institute believe the wealth transfer will be larger than first thought:

> On the basis of a recently developed Wealth Transfer Microsimula-tion Model, we estimate that the forthcoming transfer of wealth will be many times higher than the almost universally cited 55-year figure of $10 trillion. Our low-range best estimate is that over the 55-year period from 1998 to 2052 the wealth transfer will be $41 trillion, and may well reach double or triple that amount. Depending upon the assumptions we introduce into the model, we estimate the wealth transfer will range from a lower level figure of $41 trillion, to a middle level figure of $71 trillion, to an upper level figure of $136 trillion. These estimates are not back-of-the-envelope projections. They derive from what to our knowledge is a first-of-its-kind microsimulation model of wealth accumulation and transfer.[37]

This wealth transfer most assuredly will spawn a new generation of phi-lanthropists and bode well for future capital campaigning. Those institutions that are favorably positioned to take advantage of the wealth transfer will thrive in the philanthropic marketplace. Organizations that have built a solid program base, have used volunteers, and have professional staff in place will receive extraordinary benefits from the wealth transfer. Likewise, institutions that are not well positioned and have not created a climate for philanthropy will no doubt miss this future wave of giving much like a number of institutions missed the giving spree of the early-to-mid 1990s.

Selecting a Campaign Name or Theme

Institutions can spend a wasteful amount of time trying to determine a campaign name or even campaign theme. Not to denigrate the naming of a campaign, but it will not have a material impact on the success of the effort. Some of the campaign names that have been experienced through the years are:

- Budget Equilibrium Program
- Continuity and Renewal
- The Campaign for Academic Excellence
- The Futures Campaign
- The Becoming One Campaign

One donor once commented that the title of the campaign "Budget Equilibrium" reminded her of an inner-ear infection.

Preliminary Word on Campaign Phases

Before this book goes much farther, perhaps a brief discussion on campaign phases would help set the stage for later discussion. There are seven major phases in a capital campaign. Our discussion to date has centered on the first phase which we can call Precampaign Planning. The other phases are:

- The Quiet Planning Phase
- Advanced Gift Phase
- Public Phase
- Plateau Phase
- Final Phase
- Post-Campaign Phase

Each of these phases will be discussed at length elsewhere in this book, but perhaps listing them in this chapter will give the reader a better sense of direction as to where we are in the campaign process. It is certainly helpful to look at a capital campaign as a series of phases. These phases often overlap, and sometimes it is difficult to determine when one phase has been completed and another one has begun. The phases are interconnecting and interwoven, and each one has a specific purpose in the preparation of a capital campaign. Throughout this book we will touch on each of the phases, and a later chapter features a much more specific discussion about how the phases interact. For now, suffice it to say, we are still in the precampaign planning phase.

The Feasibility/Planning Study—Essential Tool or Relic of the Past?

Ten to 15 years ago the feasibility study to determine the goal and probability of success of an organization in a capital campaign was simply conventional wisdom. Most fund-raising consultants across the United States recommended feasibility studies to determine goals, and there was even a stigma attached to those organizations that publicly launched campaigns without going through the time-consuming process of a feasibility study. Feasibility studies were as necessary as goal statements and case statements to a capital campaign, and it was practically considered to be "a given" that an organization would conduct a feasibility study if it was, in particular, discussing a multimillion-dollar goal.

What Is a Feasibility Planning Study?

The feasibility planning study is a systematic process undertaken to determine the readiness of an organization to launch a capital campaign. Generally, it uses face-to-face interviews with the organization's most important benefactors. It includes a questionnaire that attempts to determine if an individual prospect is ready and willing to be solicited for a major commitment to the institution. Robert Hoak, a consultant and former development vice president, suggests the feasibility study is a market survey that tells you how close your key volunteers and prospects are to full commitment. Unless they are fully informed, fully involved, and fully committed, they will not make their best effort for the upcoming capital campaign.[38]

How else could an organization really know what it was capable of raising unless it interviewed its top constituents? How else could an organization set a fund-raising goal if it did not know the level of support that might be forthcoming from the organization's major benefactors? How can the organization successfully set a "stretch goal" unless it knows where the funds will be coming from and if its major benefactors will step forward and take ownership of the campaign?

However, once considered an essential element of a capital campaign, the feasibility study has increasingly fallen into disfavor and disuse. The last 10 to 15 years have seen a number of major campaigns planned, launched, and successfully completed without ever having conducted a feasibility planning study.

Robert Hoak also believes that feasibility studies are an important component of any campaign:

Having worked for 15 years in development, I have seen a number of organizations struggle with the concept and added expense of conducting a feasibility study before launching a major campaign. The feasibility study is an objective evaluation of an organization's perceived strengths and weaknesses, effectiveness, financial capabilities, leadership, accountability, board strength, staff professionalism, and ability. It also establishes a starting point for the director, the campaign counsels, and the volunteer leadership to initiate a campaign, and it is an important cultivation step to introduce the project's basic objective and the elements essential to the campaign's success. More importantly, it gives an organization a strong indication of the potential donor's financial capability, philanthropic interest, leadership potential, dedication to the organization and project, and finally, a sense of their potential financial commitment to the campaign.[39]

Hoak goes on to suggest that individual interviewees will open up and reveal themselves as well as their opinions during the interview process. His experience has been that donors and persons close to an organization want to vent their frustrations and inner feelings during a confidential interview. The person conducting the interview can gather important information that can be used to determine an organization's next steps in a campaign. Hoak states:

Once completed, the study findings should be a blueprint for your success. By evaluating the potential owner's reactions, the consultant can assess an organization's true financial potential and campaign leadership capabilities. Feedback from the study will allow the organization to craft a case statement around the donor's priorities and help create a priority list of initial solicitations to set an example of generosity that will inspire other potential supporters to consider a challenge gift."[40]

To be sure, however, a number of practitioners believe the feasibility study is a relic of the past. William J. Moran concludes in his article, "An Alternative to the Campaign Feasibility Study," that "The conventional feasibility study is a flawed vehicle for conducting a pre-campaign fund-raising evaluation. Even though these flaws increasingly hamper fund-raising campaigns, the conventional studies are still being conducted for lack of a better approach. It is time for the fund-raising community to adopt viable alternatives to the conventional feasibility study."[41]

Campaign feasibility studies are typically conducted by fund-raising consultants or persons external to the fund-raising organization of a given nonprofit. Most fund-raising consultants do not like to interview fewer than 40 or 50 persons and prefer an interview number of 60 to 75 persons. Moran believes that the process is flawed from the very beginning and that consulting companies are more concerned about getting "their foot in the door" for a long-term consulting contract than giving really good, solid advice about the potential of a campaign. He cites the fact that most feasibility studies are positive, and very few give a negative report on an organization's ability to raise funds.

Moran also states that since the client wasn't participating in the collection of the data, little valuable information is actually given to the client, resulting in a "divergence of perspectives."[42]

Moran's alternative to the common feasibility study is to have the staff conduct informal interviews with key supporters. While still generally in favor of the concept of feasibility studies, Toni K. Goodale also analyzes some of the pitfalls:

> Conducting a study, however, is an expensive, time-consuming process that places significant demands upon an organization's often over-stretched budget and staff. In some cases, it is possible to establish a campaign goal and identify potential leadership without incurring the cost of a formal study. For these reasons, you might find yourself balancing the benefit of a feasibility study against the extensive resources that it requires.[43]

Goodale goes on to point out that many nonprofits are quite sophisticated in their fund-raising programs, and they already know a good deal about their major gift prospects and have already identified leadership for the campaign. A feasibility study would provide very little additional information.

One thing is for certain. Many feasibility study interviewees are approached by competing organizations, and they are growing quite weary of being approached again and again. One fund-raising consultant recently conducted an interview with an organization's major prospect only to be told that it was the fourth interview in six months that the individual had participated in, and he was always asked the same questions by different organizations.

Goodale concludes her article with the following caveat: "If your organization, however, has an experienced development office, a clear sense of its constituency and, most importantly, a flexible goal, then you should consider the possible advantages of foregoing a feasibility study. Doing so may enable you to preserve your organization's most precious resources: time, money, and finally, the enthusiasm and interest of your biggest donors."[44]

Two somewhat dated articles on feasibility studies are worth mentioning. The first is by Arthur C. Frantzreb, titled the "Pros and Cons of Feasibility Studies." Frantzreb presents the view that "feasibility studies reflect only momentary attitudes and impressions that can change very quickly." He further states that most of these feasibility studies are simply "guesstimates" and not real scientific surveys of available support.[45]

The second article is from *Fund Raising Management* by Christopher Walton. It is an interesting statement of some of the pros and cons of feasibility studies.[46]

One fund-raising consulting firm that continues to believe quite strongly in the importance of campaign strategic planning studies is the Grenzebach Glier firm (GG&A) of Chicago. GG&A is one of the largest consulting firms in the nation and has conducted hundreds of campaign feasibility studies for colleges and universities, health organizations, museums, and a host of other philanthropic organizations. GG&A believes strongly that a properly conducted strategic planning study will lead to consensus building for an organization and will assess the potential to reach the fund-raising goals. However, GG&A does not conduct feasibility studies without specific leadership briefings designed to inform the constituents of the organization's plans.

A major goal of this consulting firm in conducting a feasibility study is to gather data on not only philanthropic interest, but on volunteer interest as well. GG&A believes that personal donor attitudes about an organization will influence dramatically their willingness to step forward with time and resources.

Through a series of confidential, individual interviews, GG&A explores an organization's image, campaign goals, and funding objectives. The information gathered from these interviews form the basis of key findings represented to the nonprofit organization.

GG&A notes, however, that an important secondary purpose of the feasibility planning study is to educate key constituents about the coming campaign. Interviewees receive an initial letter as well as the case statement describing the coming effort. This letter generally arrives at the interviewees' home or office a week before the interviews take place. It is hoped that the interviewee will read the case statement and be prepared to answer a series of questions as laid out by a representative of the GG&A firm.

It is also important to note that this consulting firm has begun requiring an evaluation of staff and resources as part of the overall feasibility program. This firm wants to be certain that the resources are available internally to run an effective campaign and, therefore, proposes a review of internal resources as well as external resources. GG&A focuses on six fundamental criteria when conducting the external feasibility study:

1. Is there a positive institutional image on key constituent groups?
2. Is there strong and engaged internal leadership?
3. Is there a clear and compelling case for support?
4. Are ample funds available to meet the goals?
5. Is there respected and committed volunteer leadership among the constituent group?
6. Do the favorable timing and competitive positioning necessary to be successful in a major campaign exist?

At the conclusion of the study, this consulting firm gives lengthy reports that analyze all of the data and presents findings to the organization.

Other consulting firms have similar approaches to the feasibility planning study. Although feasibility studies have fallen in respect in some quarters, they still appear to be a valid and effective way to gauge the overall ability of an organization to be successful in its campaign. Even with its bumps and bruises and discounting the last 10 years or so, feasibility studies continue to be the most effective way for an organization to determine its goal. The problem simply is that no other viable alternative has been presented that does as good a job as the feasibility planning study in gathering appropriate data and assisting an organization in goal analysis. As will be seen later, it is important, however, that no organization rely exclusively on the feasibility study to determine its capacity for a capital campaign. Numerous other important indicators are discussed in upcoming chapters.

Alternatives to the Standard Feasibility Planning Study

Some institutions have begun using large group meetings, where potential benefactors, volunteers, and interested friends are questioned in a group setting about their interest in and support for a major campaign. This method can yield valuable information about institutional readiness and potential for campaign support. It does not gather specific information about potential major benefactors to the campaign and their interest in contributing, but it can be an alternative approach in gathering data and gauging the readiness of external constituents.

FIGURE 2. KEY COMPONENTS OF A FEASIBILITY PLANNING STUDY

- External consultant conducting the study
- A case prospectus to be read by interviewees
- Potential of leadership briefings of interviewees and other constituents
- A minimum of 50 to 75 interviewees are major potential benefactors in the campaign
- An interview request letter signed by the organization's CEO or board chair
- Competent staff to arrange the interviews and follow up appropriately
- Interview questionnaire designed to elicit information about the case statement and campaign goal
- Biographical information for interviewer on potential interviewees
- Testing of potential volunteers in the campaign
- Thank-you letter for persons interviewed
- Final letter to interviewees with synopsis of study results

Telephone Study

A few institutions have used telephone surveys to gather information from constituents about the feasibility of launching a campaign. In fact, some firms conduct telephone interviews of a larger, wider audience in addition to conducting individual interviews of a small sample of major gift benefactors. The advantage of the telephone survey is obvious. A much larger sampling of potential benefactors can be contacted and more data can be accumulated and processed. However, the reliability of the data can be suspect and only general information about campaign goals and objectives is forthcoming over the telephone.

Mail Study

A few institutions have sent questionnaires to constituents in an attempt to gather information about their likely support of a proposed capital campaign. This approach does not allow for the careful analysis of a professional that might come about in a personal one-on-one interview with a prospect. Often, benefactors are reluctant to put answers in writing, and the reliability of the data can be questionable.

Internal Staff and Volunteers Conducting the Study

The use of staff members and volunteers to actually conduct the feasibility study is another method that is being used more widely. Volunteers and staff members are assigned to make individual calls on potential benefactors and to determine the level of support that might be forthcoming from the interviewee. It is, in many cases, a peer-to-peer study when volunteers question other volunteers, and can result in important data. It's debatable, however, whether potential benefactors will be forthcoming with information to volunteers and staff members with whom they may be well acquainted. The advantage of outside counsel is that they can more readily protect the confidentiality and anonymity of the interviewee, which may be important in sharing confidential data.

Information Systems

When gearing up for a capital campaign or any major gift effort, an organization must be certain it has an adequate information system that is fully functional. A successful fund-raising operation cannot operate without a user-friendly, flexible, and reliable management information system.

With that in mind, three critical aspects of a good system should be reviewed:

1. Application Software
2. Data Management
3. Resources

Many information systems are literally homegrown and built over a period of years. As more sophisticated systems become available, this landscape is changing dramatically. Today's market offers a variety of sophisticated information systems that meets the needs of all types of philanthropic institutions.

Application software programs typically address multiple areas of information: biographical data, gifts and pledges, prospect management, membership information, and fund-management tracking.

Biographical information has become much more than name and address. Today's fund raisers need to be aware of family relationships, interests, business information, volunteer activities, preferred mailing address, preferred mailing name, nicknames, and on and on. The system needs to be capable of generating personalized mail with preferred salutations in an efficient manner. Donors have grown accustomed to receiving specially tailored mailings with personal addresses and personalized data.

Likewise, gift and pledge information can be complex, and a system must handle this data with ease. Gifts that are split between husband and wife, matching gifts, pledge payments, pledge reminders, gift receipts—all have to be integrated into a system and provide the users with flexibility to meet the individual needs of the institution.

Although the mark of a good information system is its capacity to store information in a variety of ways, the true test is its capability to provide that information in a useable format. Today's advancement professional requires more information in more ways in less time. The combination of high-speed networks, sophisticated software programs, and advanced technology has reduced turnaround times by significant amounts. Accurate, timely reports provide critical information and play an important role in the decision-making process for campaign asks.

Duff Batchelder writes in *Fund Raising Management* (October 2002):

Fund-raising database software has gone from being a luxury to an everyday necessity for most development programs. However, unlike most other software genres, instead of facing few choices, purchasers are confronted with a multitude of options—at every price level—from comprehensive proprietary packages with sophisticated add-on modules to introductory-level shareware or freeware programs available on the Internet. As a result, one of the most common computer-related questions voiced by development officers is, "How do we evaluate and choose a fund-raising database program that best meets our needs?"

We know we need a database for recording, tracking, reporting, managing, and implementing our development program, but where do we begin? Begin your search with a thorough analysis of your current development program. Map out all of the following on paper before you begin to look at different software packages:

- Initiatives: What are the specific elements for individual and/or institutional giving in your annual fund-raising program plan? (e.g., direct mail, corporate and foundation grants, special events, planned giving, major gift program.)

- Computer equipment: How many computers are in your office, and with what chip, speed, RAM, and storage capacity? If you have a network, how many are on it and what is your network software? Do you plan to expand in the near future?

- Budget: How much can you spend?

- Staffing: What is your departmental structure? If you have fund-raising software, who inputs data? How many currently use your database software and at what level of proficiency? Will additional users be added in the future?" [47]

The explosion of technology in the nonprofit sector over the past 10 years has been phenomenal. An extraordinary number of companies now offer software packages catering to the needs of the nonprofit sector.

Nicole Wallace, in a 2004 article in *The Chronicle of Philanthropy*, states:

A growing number of investors are putting their energy—and their money—into building software for fund raisers. Several large corporations have bought companies that produce fund-raising software, and two companies that focus entirely on producing software for nonprofit organizations have gone public in the past year—Kintera in December [2003] and Blackbaud in July [2004].

She goes on to quote Chuck Longfield, chief executive of Target software, a Cambridge, Massachusetts company he founded in 1992, as saying, "The fund-raising software industry has been discovered." Wallace continues:

The entrance of large public companies and investment capital into the nonprofit-software field started in the late 1990s, and the phenomena has been gaining steadily ever since.

- In 1999, SunGard, a Wayne, Pennsylvania company with $3 billion in annual revenue, bought BSR, a company whose fund-raising system is widely used by colleges and universities.

- Since its founding in 1999, Convio, an Austin, Texas, company that offers Web-based software to help charities raise money online, has raised $37 million in venture capital.

- Intuit, a Mountain View, California company, acquired American Fundware, a company that made accounting software designed for charities and government agencies, in 2002.

- Before it went public in December 2003, Kintera, a San Diego company that provides Web-based fund-raising software to nonprofit organizations, raised more than $32 million in venture capital. Its initial public offering netted $36.1 million, and a July sale of stock brought an additional $18.8 million.

In 2001 Best Software, in Irvine, California, bought Micro Information Products, a company that produced accounting software for nonprofit organizations. A year later, it purchased the company that made the Millennium and Paradigm donor databases, and then in 2003, the company that produced the fund-raising software packages GT Pro and Rainbow Software.[48]

Thus, database management systems in the nonprofit sector are seeing extraordinary change in evolution and the change that has taken place in the last 10 years has been particularly phenomenal. Divine Tabios, associate director at Changing Our World, Inc., states:

As the adage goes, change is constant and inevitable. As technology increases exponentially, operating systems and database platforms themselves must evolve. Most products now have estimated life cycles. As those life cycles come to their end, companies often discontinue support for the product. This is a major problem; it will become harder as time goes by to find people to do the day to day management of the program.[49]

John Covaleski says that the biggest concern for nonprofits when purchasing database systems is being certain that they are buying the right technology. "Wrong decisions can be particularly infuriating when today's rapid technology development could mean finding the right solution might be a matter of just looking further or waiting longer."[50]

While the nonprofit sector has been viewed as lagging behind in providing appropriate software technology, there has been a trend over the last year or two toward upgrading some major databases at prominent organizations. Reports Craig Causer in *The Nonprofit Times*:

Nonprofits are often viewed as being behind the proverbial eight ball when it comes to technology. But in fiscal 2003, a number of prominent organizations allocated funds toward new and enhanced technology services. Spending ran the gamut from information technology design to software and technology consulting and Web site construction.[51]

To list all of the companies that provide information technology support to nonprofits would fill this entire book. The industry is constantly changing, and as soon as the list was printed, it would be grossly out of date!

Notes for Chapter 2

1. William P. McGoldrick, "Campaigning in the Nineties," in *Educational Fund Raising, Principles and Practice*, American Council on Education, Michael J. Worth (Phoenix, Arizona: Oryx Press), 145.

2. G. T. Smith, "The Chief Executive in Advancement," in *Handbook of Institutional Advancement: A Modern Guide to Executive Management, Institutional Relations, Fundraising, Alumni Administration, Government Relations, Publications, Periodicals, and Enrollment Management*, ed. A. Westley Rowland, 697 (San Francisco: Jossey-Bass, Inc., 1986).

3. Robert L. Krit, *The Fund-Raising Handbook*. Scott Foresman Professional Books, 1991), 54.

4. Kent E. Dove, *Conducting a Successful Capital Campaign: A Comprehensive Guide for Nonprofit Organizations*. (San Francisco: Jossey-Bass Inc., 1998), 32.

5. Kent E. Dove, *Conducting A Successful Capital Campaign: The New, Revised, and Expanded Edition of the Leading Guide to Planning and Implementing a Capital Campaign*, 2nd ed. (San Francisco: Jossey-Bass, Inc., 1999).

6. Dove, *Conducting a Successful Capital Campaign*, 7.

7. Jacklyn P. Boice, "Achieving Dreams Through Strategic Goals," *Advancing Philanthropy* (May/June 2003): 14–18.

8. John H. Hanson, "Dead Man Walking: Case Statements as Organizational Change Narratives," *Journal of Nonprofit & Public Sector Marketing* 10, no. 2 (2002): 83.

9. Boice, "Achieving Dreams Through Strategic Goals," 16.

10. Jerold Panas, *Making the Case: No Nonsense Guide to Writing the Perfect Case Statement* (Chicago: Institutions Press, 2004).

11. Mark J. Drozdowski, "Not Making the Case," *Chronicle of Higher Education Chronicle Careers* (August 9, 2004).

12. Bobby J. Strand, "Building a Donor Information Base," in *Handbook of Institutional Advancement: A Modern Guide to Effective Management, Institutional Relations, Fundraising, Alumni Administration, Government Relations, Publications, Periodicals, and Enrollment Management*, ed. A. W. Roland, 337 (San Francisco: Jossey-Bass, Inc., 1986).

13. Mary Lawrence, "Lights . . . Camera . . . Action! Screening Prospects for a Capital Campaign," *NEDRA News* (Summer 2003).

14. Andrea G. Dickens, "Getting Ready for the Data: Preparing an Implementation Plan," *Connections* (Summer 2003).

15. Amy Minton, "What Now? Working with Wealth Screening Results: Lessons I Learned," *Connections* (Summer 2003): 8.

16. Cecilia Hogan, "Viewpoint: To Screen or Not to Screen?," *Connections* (Summer 2003): 14.

17. Susan Cronin Ruderman, "Viewpoint: Go Ahead—Skip the Screening," *Connections* (Summer 2003): 15.

18. Patricia Ambler, "Getting to Know Them," *Connections* (Summer 2003).

19. Lawrence, "Lights . . . Camera . . . Action!"

20. Nick Allen, "Using E-Mail and the Web to Acquire and Cultivate Donors," *Nonprofit World* (January/February 2003): 27.

21. Ibid.

22. Steve Epner, "Surviving Fundraising on the Internet," *Nonprofit World* (March/April 2004): 17.

23. Sherri Begin, "Support System: Online Fund Raising Grows, but Nonprofits Say It's Still a Long Way from Being the Main Avenue," *Crain's Detroit Business* 20, no. 46 (November 15, 2004): 11.

24. Nathan Shaver, "Technology in 2005: The Rise of ePhilanthropy," *OnPhilanthropy* (December 17, 2004).

25. Theodore R. Hart, "ePhilanthropy: Using the Internet to Build Support," *International Journal of Nonprofit and Voluntary Sector Marketing* 7, no. 4 (November 2002): 353.

26. Rachel H. Pollack, "Bond Issues," *CASE Currents* (January 2000).

27. John L. Pulley, "Embracing Performance Pay," *The Chronicle of Higher Education* 49, no. 36 (May 16, 2003): A28.

28. Ibid.

29. Ibid.

30. Ibid.

31. Jeremiah Hall, "When Your Donations Fund Insider Perks," *Christian Science Monitor* (June 21, 2004): 13.

32. "Create an Incentive Program that Is Effective, Not Excessive," Kern-DeWenter-Viere (KDV).

33. Tom Watson, "Philanthropic Landscape: A Fundraiser's View," *OnPhilanthropy* (February 20, 2004).

34. James W. Asp II, "Pay for Performance," *CASE Currents* (July/August 1999).

35. Heather Joslyn, "Charity's Glass Ceiling: Salary Gap Persists for Women in Nonprofit Organizations," *The Chronicle of Philanthropy—Managing* (March 20, 2003).

36. Ibid.

37. Paul G. Schervish and John J. Havens, "Recent Trends and Projections in Wealth and Philanthropy," Social Welfare Research Institution, Boston College, November 1, 2000.

38. Robert Hoak, "The Value of the Feasibility Study Best Practices," *OnPhilanthropy* (August 8, 2003).

39. Ibid.

40. Ibid.

41. William J. Moran, "An Alternative to the Campaign Feasibility Study," *Fundraising Management* (April 2000): 28.

42. Ibid., 29.

43. Toni K. Goodale, "Is It Feasible?" *Fund Raising Management* (November 2001): 40.

44. Ibid., 41.

45. Arthur C. Frantzreb, "The Pros and Cons of Feasibility Studies," National Society of Fundraising Executives, *Advancing Philanthropy* (Winter 1997–98).

46. R. Christopher Walton, "Rethinking Feasibility Studies," *Fundraising Management* (September 1997): 14.

47. Duff Batchelder, "Evaluating and Choosing a Fund-Raising Database Program," *Fund-Raising Management* (October 2002): 4.

48. Nicole Wallace, "Building Better Technology," *The Chronicle of Philanthropy* (September 16, 2004).

49. Divine Tabios, "The Why and How of Database Change," *OnPhilanthropy* (October 22, 2004).

50. John Covaleski, "Getting Value from Application Resellers," *NonProfit Times* (October 15, 2003).

51. Craig Causer, "Special Report: Technology Spending Is Picking Up," *NonProfit Times* (November 1, 2004).

three

Organizing for a Campaign

He who gives when he is asked has waited too long.

Seneca

Let us assume that your organization has now made a decision to move ahead expeditiously with the launching of a major capital campaign. The chief executive officer of the institution has given his or her unqualified support and is ready to work vigorously on behalf of the campaign and to appropriate the time commitment that will be required. Your governing board has given its endorsement and approval, and you are confident that a number of your board members will support the campaign generously with their time and resources. Other volunteer leadership groups, particularly those associated with public institutions, have also indicated support, philanthropically and through volunteerism. You feel confident you will be able to tap volunteer leadership for the campaign and have individuals closely associated with your organization who will take the necessary ownership and work alongside staff members to make the campaign a reality.

You have conducted an appropriate feasibility study, which indicates that resources are available among your constituents and that you have the "philanthropic muscle" to raise the resources necessary to meet your needs. The senior leadership of the institution has prioritized the campaign as the most important happening the organization will experience over the next several years. You have prioritized your needs, and they have been appropriately juried by senior leadership as well as by the academic leadership in institutions of higher education. You believe you have professional staff members in place appropriate to the task at hand, and they have committed to remain at the organization during the campaign years, dedicating themselves to building a successful campaign organizational structure. Everything seems to be pointing in the direction of a capital campaign, and the basic elements discussed in chapters 1 and 2 appear to be in place. It is now time to create a campaign organizational structure that will, in fact, ensure campaign success and get the job done.

Creating a campaign organization for any size institution is no small task. Without a campaign organization in place, it is highly likely the campaign will not be successful, volunteers will become frustrated, and there will be a general appearance of little or no activity toward campaign objectives. Capital campaigns need an organizational structure in place. This includes a staffing model, a volunteer model, and an organization that ensures that the various elements of a capital campaign are functioning smoothly.

Of course, the creation of a campaign organization cannot and should not wait until all of the elements mentioned in chapters 1 and 2 are firmly in place. Instead, the steps in the process must move forward somewhat simultaneously. The campaign organizational structure must be in place, or at least the process toward forming a structure must be substantially in place, early on in the campaign.

The Importance of Institutional Integration of Advancement

Most nonprofit organizations have staff members who perform various external affairs functions. Sometimes they are vested in one person in a small shop and other times multiple staff members perform the various duties and responsibilities associated with what has become known in the college and university genre as "advancement." The integration of advancement under one chief officer of an institution has long been a point of discussion among development, public relations, and alumni personnel. While the issue of integration may be more aggrandized at colleges and universities, it also is an important consideration for any nonprofit organization, particularly when preparing for a capital campaign. Basically, the institutional advancement model places the major communications-oriented units that work in external affairs under one senior officer of the organization. At colleges and universities, the university advancement model has been the model recommended by the trade organization, the Council for Advancement in Support of Education, for a number of years. The notion of combining fund raising with other traditional external relations positions under the authority of a single officer was first proposed at what has become known as the Greenbriar Conference in 1959, where a number of education public relations personnel met to discuss institutional advancement.[1]

Since the Greenbriar Conference, many institutions have adopted the institutional advancement model. Under this model, typically the development, or fund-raising branch, the public relations branch, and the alumni branch all report to a central vice president. The model has been endorsed by a number of professionals and research scholars, but not all believe this is the appropriate model. Since the predominate number of advancement vice presidents come out of the fund-raising arena, justifiably a strain has been placed on the relationship of development with the other mainline functional areas of advancement (public relations and alumni relations).

A recent article in the *The Chronicle of Higher Education* by Mark J. Drozdowski, the director of corporate, foundation, and government relations at Franklin Pierce College, discussed the differences between marketing and development in higher education. He makes a number of interesting points about the issue of advancement integration:

> Few advancement vice presidents (and presidents, for that matter) would deny the primacy of fund raising. After all, most of them rose through the development ranks and still maintain a portfolio of top donors and prospects.
>
> On the other hand, communications professionals could persuasively argue that fund raising is a subset of marketing, and that we development officers are marketers with a narrowly defined purpose. . . . What matters is that understanding among all advancement professionals that they need to function as a team, mutually reinforcing one another. A gulf between marketing and development serves no one. Each side has to appreciate that these aren't discrete functions. Fund raisers are indeed public relations ambassadors, and marketers are, in the broadest sense, fund raisers. . . . And, to presidents on campuses where marketing and development report separately to you, I say reconsider your structure. Think about establishing an advancement office under a vice president or director.[2]

Since the Greenbriar Conference, literally hundreds and hundreds of articles, books, manuscripts, and professional presentations have been written and made about the issue of integration and centralization versus noncentralization of development functions. In 1995 John L. Dietz addressed the issue of "University Fund Raising: Is There an Ideal Management Model for the Development Operation of the Large, Public Research Institution?" This master's thesis explored in detail fund-raising organizations at large public research universities and the various management models used by these institutions when engaged in major gift fund raising.[3]

The advancement model for large university systems was discussed recently in a September 2004 article in *CASE Currents* written by Susan Brenna. Her article examines system advancement models at the University of Texas, the State University of New York, the University of Nebraska, and the University System of Maryland.[4]

Another article, written by Mary Ellen Collins in *CASE Currents*, April 2001, reviewed the University of Virginia's efforts to complete a unified campaign at a highly decentralized institution.[5]

An excellent article in the same publication by Margarete Rooney Hall explores the inherent strengths of both centralized and decentralized advancement structures. Her discussion of key operational issues and which model is better in the long run provides an excellent overview of the various issues on centralization and decentralization.[6]

Peg Hall also participated in a study that compared characteristics of successful academic unit fund-raising programs with their counterpart advancement office in public relations and their successful programs. Using interviews and surveys it explores whether academic unit fundraisers value the roles and responsibilities that align with identified strategic-managerial and historical-technical characteristics in public relations, whether demographic differences affect the role perception of the fund raisers, and whether the universities provide support for programme excellence. Hall concluded:

> Fundraising programmes exhibit most of the characteristics of successful public relations programmes and that the academic units in which these fund raisers work provide support for them to do excellent fundraising. Both fundraising and public relations seek to build mutually beneficial relationships between organizations and their key stakeholders, albeit with a more narrowly defined set of stakeholders in the case of fundraising. The two fields might be able to learn from each other and adapt each other's best models and practices.[7]

The issue of integration, centralization, and decentralization has also been discussed within specific areas in units of fund-raising organizations. Susan K. Martin of the Georgetown University library touches on organization and process for library fund raising, particularly as related to the development function of a major institution.[8]

Robert M. Beagle reviews the issue of athletic fund raising as part of a central development program and the importance of integrating athletics development into the overall fund-raising effort of a college or university.[9]

Another article that discusses the advantages of a centralized advancement research office can be found in *Connections,* Fall 2002.[10]

While discussions of integration of advancement personnel, centralization, and decentralization are important concepts for the academic researcher, they are also of great importance when recommending which model is preferred while preparing for a major capital campaign. Should the various advancement functions be integrated under one senior officer of the organization? Or, in the alternative, should the various advancement functions all report directly to a CEO? The integration of advancement personnel has been a constant issue during my years of professional consulting. From 1995 to 1998, I consulted with more than 20 colleges, universities, health agencies, philanthropic organizations, and nonprofit agencies. Over 60 percent of them had issues dealing with the integration of advancement personnel, and most of those also had issues regarding centralization and decentralization of development functions. In 2005 I am dealing with two major organizations that have integration issues. The first, a major think tank in Washington, D.C., has distributed its advancement functions among several staff members reporting to various officers of the organization. The fund-raising function is also spread among numerous staff members reporting to various parts of the organization. A more centralized integrated model has been recommended.

The second organization is a major health center hospital, and, again, the major functional advancement areas all report to the CEO. Needless to say, coordination of duties and responsibilities in preparation of a major capital campaign has been difficult and has caused angst even in the early stages of planning.

I have long believed that the best model of organizational structure for a development program entering a capital campaign is the advancement model of an integrated system. Having all of the people who deal with the public on a regular basis, particularly in the public relations arena, development, and constituent/alumni/membership arena reporting to one senior officer of the organization makes it much easier to plan a capital campaign. All of these units will be called on to support the campaign in some form or fashion. It is simply not possible to organize an effort without the involvement of these mainline advancement units.

In 1989 a major study was undertaken that surveyed 10 institutions nationwide that then were engaged in a capital campaign. Five of the organizations used integrated structures in planning and initiating their campaigns. The other five organizations used nonintegrated structures. The study concluded that the institutions that had integrated organizational structures were much better able to prepare for their campaigns, achieving cost savings and better use of existing staff resources. Unhealthy competition among advancement units was reduced considerably. The organizations with integrated programs operated more efficiently and effectively and moved their campaigns forward with much greater ease than their nonintegrated counterparts.

I recommend that nonprofit organizations give serious consideration to the integration of their organization's advancement units before a campaign is initiated. The preparation of the case statement, the creation and continued monitoring of public relations plans, the production of campaign videos and publications, the impaneling of volunteers, and the coordination of solicitation of major gift prospects can all be enhanced through the integrated model.

A capital campaign is an intense, time-consuming project of formidable complexity. Nonprofit organizations do not need to be spending time in turf battles among staff members, all to be refereed by a very busy and occupied CEO.[11]

If an organization decides that the advancement model is worth pursuing, the first step in creating such a model is to inaugurate a vice president-level position that has authority over all institutional advancement. This vice president would also coordinate the capital campaign and would have direct-line authority over all external-relations officers who can affect the success of the campaign.

Generally speaking, the person occupying this senior role should have a fund-raising background and solid development expertise. Again, this can create competitive discord among others in the advancement areas, but it is simply a recognition of the fact that the institutional advancement component of a nonprofit must move in unison during a capital campaign. All units of advancement must come together to support, enhance, and promote campaign objectives. Without this cooperation, the campaign will not move forward as rapidly or as efficiently as necessary. Capital campaigns require teamwork, and this teamwork can only be accomplished by integrating and centralizing the advancement function.

The Engagement of Campaign Counsel

The decision as to whether a nonprofit organization planning for a capital campaign should hire professional counsel is an extraordinarily important one. The use of campaign counsel has always depended a great deal on the state of the economy and the philanthropic marketplace. Fund-raising consultants can be extraordinarily busy one year only to find their consulting contracts cut back the next. This ebb and flow has made it difficult for some of the smaller firms to remain in business, particularly after the terrorist attacks of 9/11, when consulting relationships took a dip. Some consultants indicated that their consulting relationships dropped as much as 30 percent in 2001 and 2002.[12]

Many nonprofit organizations reduced their budgets and number of staff members because of the major downturn in the economy. As the economy has begun improving in 2003 and 2004, nonprofits have once again engaged the services of consultants.[13]

Preliminary results of a national survey conducted in February 2004 by the Alliance for Nonprofit Management in Washington, D.C., show that consultants across the country are seeing increased demand for nearly all their services. Demand is heaviest for consultants who specialize in helping nonprofit organizations manage their resources and raise funds.[14]

It is important to note, however, that consultants are not only being hired by nonprofits for fund-raising expertise in major gift efforts but also to provide consultation for technology, database management, electronic screening, phone solicitation program, electronic fund raising, planned giving expertise, interim management duties and responsibilities, and organizational structure. Providing expertise in the area of technology is in high demand, and consulting companies that offer this expertise are finding their plates very full. The number of consultants who conduct executive searches for nonprofit organizations seeking fund raisers has tripled over the last 5 to 10 years.

A number of publications regularly publish a listing of higher education consultants that include fund-raising executive search firms and fund-raising consultants in general. The publication *University Business* annually publishes a directory of the 250 higher education consultants. It is a fairly comprehensive survey that includes most of the larger fund-raising consultant companies.

The Chronicle of Philanthropy publishes an annual consultants' guide for capital campaigns.

The Association of Fundraising Professionals publishes its AFP Who's Who directory of consultants and resource partners. It is an annual paid listing of consultants. *CASE Currents* regularly lists fund-raising consultants in almost all of its issues. While it would be inappropriate to recommend one consulting firm over another, the Consultants Appendix in this book lists the larger, more comprehensive firms that provide capital campaign fund-raising counsel to a number of nonprofit organizations.

Engagement of Counsel

If your nonprofit organization decides that campaign counsel is a necessity, consider employing such counsel early in the planning stages rather than asking counsel to join the team after key decisions have been made, which would be a disservice to both the organization and the consultant.

The ultimate decision to employ campaign counsel is always a difficult one. Depending on the assigned consultant, campaign counsel can be difficult, stubborn, definitely expensive, time consuming, and argumentative. Some development officers believe that hiring campaign counsel is a "necessary evil."

The employment of campaign counsel is an expensive proposition. Currently, most of the larger, more established firms charge a minimum of $2,000 a day plus expenses. A few consultants are even charging $3,000 to $5,000 per day and billing portal to portal. Fees can be negotiable and should depend greatly on the level of expertise and experience of the person assigned to the organization.

Determining if Campaign Counsel Is Necessary

Many nonprofit organizations are reluctant to spend the kind of funds necessary to hire campaign counsel. The decision to move forward with the employment of a firm can be an arduous task for many a chief executive officer and chief development officer. The following circumstances might benefit from campaign counsel:

- The current development staff has limited experience in major gift fund raising and little or no experience in conducting a capital campaign.

- The institution has made a decision to employ a chief development officer without heavy campaign experience for one of several reasons: limited resources, inability to attract a top-level professional to the organization, longevity of present personnel, and so forth. Campaign counsel can bring to the table the necessary knowledge base to organize the campaign more quickly.

- Some members of the organization's "leadership team" do not appear to be supporting the campaign with the necessary vigor discussed earlier. Campaign counsel often can help shape the president's opinion about the need for additional resources for the campaign and can provide "political muscle" to convince organizational leadership of the need for new resources, additional staff, and commitment of CEO time.

- Development staff members need assistance to verify their management and organizational decisions. The employment of campaign counsel brings a new and different perspective that can augment the opinions of internal development staff. The right counsel professional will have experience conducting other campaigns in a diverse range of circumstances.

- Campaign counsel brings knowledge of cutting-edge development initiatives from other institutions and organizations. Although it is rare that campaign counsel will share confidential information (and certainly inappropriate to do so) about other institutions' capital campaigns, general knowledge about new initiatives can be most helpful in campaign planning.

- Campaign counsel can provide the motivation to volunteers and a certain comfort level that the campaign is progressing appropriately and on target and that it is organized in the best professional manner. Campaign counsel verifies to the major volunteers that the campaign is progressing on schedule.

- Campaign counsel can provide specific expertise in conducting a planning study, staffing, or feasibility study; helping to publish the lead brochure; producing a video for the campaign; or providing technical planned giving expertise. Having campaign counsel advise on these tasks can save valuable time for development personnel who are concentrating on the cultivation and solicitation of major gift prospects.

- Campaign counsel can serve to broker information to CEOs and other senior staff about issues and problems that need to be solved in order to move the campaign forward. The carrying of bad news or even difficult news is sometimes better handled by external campaign consultants.

- Development personnel often need a sounding board for confidential campaign problems, particularly in the area of personnel decisions. Campaign counsel can serve as a confidant who is connected to the campaign and is in the inner circle of campaign planning but is not a direct member of the development staff.

Guidelines for Selecting Campaign Counsel

When choosing a firm as campaign counsel, be certain that you interview and are most familiar with the individual who will be assigned to the account. Do not hire just the firm, but also the individual who will be assigned to you. All well-established, highly recommended firms have members of their consulting team who are much better than others. Particularly, in good economic times, firms tend to scramble to hire campaign consultants just to keep up with the level of business they are experiencing. Sometimes they get sloppy and hire people who have no business being in the consulting arena.

Choosing counsel should be more about the individual fit assigned to the project rather than the reputation of the firm. It is not always necessary to choose the largest, most well-established firm. With increasing frequency, institutions are even choosing senior development officers at major institutions to serve as campaign counsel. This can present a conflict of interest unless handled with extraordinary professionalism. I advise that campaign counsel from other organizations that perform consulting as an add-on to their current responsibilities limit their consulting to particular geographic areas. They certainly should not be consulting with an organization that is in competition with their own institution. A vice president or senior development officer of a nonprofit organization providing counsel to another organization with which they compete is a definite conflict of interest and should be avoided. Development officers of a nonprofit organization who do private consulting on the side should decidedly limit their consulting to a geographic region that presents no possibility or little possibility for conflict of interest. If a conflict of interest arises, they should immediately inform both organizations of the conflict. I have been approached numerous times by other organizations that aren't as interested in receiving consulting services as they are in wanting information about certain major donors of the University of Arkansas or Penn State University. It is a dangerous, slippery slope and should be avoided at all costs.

Selecting the best firm is a time-consuming process, but development staff and senior administrators must devote adequate time and resources to finding the proper fit. When selecting campaign counsel, consider the following guidelines:

- Conduct personal interviews with several firms when choosing campaign counsel. Both the chief executive officer and the development professional assigned campaign responsibility should be in the interview process. Likewise, they should insist that the chief executive officer of the consulting firm as well as the person who will be assigned to the account present themselves to the organization in an interview process. Campaign staff should seek wide concurrence among internal and external groups before engaging the resources of campaign counsel.

- Be certain to interview several firms before making a final decision on campaign counsel. Firms will offer different perspectives and levels of expertise. Be sure that you know the individual who is going to be providing most of the services and that you have confidence in his or her background and expertise.

- Confidential discussions with other institutions that have employed counsel you are considering is most important. It is a good way to gain a perspective on a firm and its ability to provide the necessary expertise to your organization. Check out the firm thoroughly and know what you are going to be getting for your resources.

- Ask the firm to provide a listing of the expertise it can provide you. How is the firm going to help you to achieve your goals and objectives and ultimate success in the campaign?

- Ask the consulting firm to list successful campaigns for which it has provided counsel and to include specific names of development personnel with whom members of the firm have worked. Be certain to contact references that they provide and don't hesitate to interview others who were not listed as references. Employing campaign counsel is an important decision. Investigate thoroughly the individual who will be assigned to you. If you get an individual who does not have the appropriate expertise and gives you bad advice, it could be months before you can get the campaign back on track.

- While some firms continue to place full-time senior members of the firm on site to provide day-to-day, full-service advice and assistance to campaign staff, this scenario is becoming less and less attractive to organizations. Not only can this be extraordinarily expensive to an organization, but it also may mean delegating management issues and decisions to campaign counsel that should be reserved for permanent development personnel. In today's environment, full-time counsel is assigned in only extraordinary cases where very little or no campaign experience exists among development staff. While this mode of operation existed 10 or 20 years ago, it has fallen into disuse in recent years.

- Generally, spending two to four days per month with campaign counsel will be a sufficient time allocation. Perhaps in the early days of the campaign, more time will be necessary, but two to four days a month should adequately cover all of the issues. Sessions with campaign counsel should be highly structured with definitive agendas distributed in advance of the consultant's visit. Verifiable objectives should be determined in advance so that the consultant is aware of what needs to be accomplished during that visit. Development personnel will find it difficult to spend quality time with a consultant if it becomes more than two to four days a month.

- In some cases, project specific work—drafting documents, assisting with campaign organizational structure, writing of case statements, and so forth—can be carried out offsite by the consultant and can save an organization expensive travel reimbursement.

- Campaign counsel should be required to execute a contract with the employing organization. Any firm with a good track record will insist on such a document, and the organization, likewise, should insist on formalizing the relationship through a contractual agreement. The contract should establish the terms of the relationship and the number of days per month the firm will expend for the institution. Billing procedures, expectation of payment, and ability to cancel the contract should be spelled out for both parties.

- Be certain to ask for a clause in the contract requiring the consulting firm to seek prior approval of any other relationship with an institution in the same geographic region or that might be considered a definite conflict of interest. Providing counsel to two organizations that are in direct competition or considered rival organizations could be a conflict of interest and should be avoided.

- A few firms have taken to employing the chief development officer of the institution where they are, in fact, providing counsel and sending that individual to other consulting arrangements. This is a practice that should be reviewed very closely for potential conflicts of interest. It frankly smacks of collusion and is best avoided. An organization's CEO should be fully informed and cognizant of the establishment of any relationship of this type.

- Often, campaign counsel will want to establish a close working relationship with an institution's chief executive officer as well as with the chief development officer. It should be made clear from the outset for whom campaign counsel works and to whom they are primarily responsible. Many times campaign counsel is hired for the expressed purpose of determining if campaign staff has the necessary expertise to carry off the campaign. This can place campaign counsel in a very difficult position. Some firms in the business have gotten the reputation of being "doctors of death" and being hired for the sole purpose of firing existing development personnel.

- Campaign counsel sometimes will attempt to manage and direct staff members even if they are only visiting the organization two or three days a month. There may be a natural tendency for counsel to want to provide hands-on management of the day-to-day operations of the development program. Orders and directions to organization personnel should be reserved for the development professionals at the organization, and this responsibility should not be abdicated to a consultant.

- Development personnel should be cognizant that campaign counsel have lives too! Having served as a campaign consultant full time for three-and-a-half years, I know only too well that some institutions are bent on squeezing every minute into the consultant's time onsite. They will schedule a breakfast at 7:00 A.M. and a dinner that concludes at 11:00 P.M. The consultant needs to have a break during the day to return phone calls or handle urgent messages. Be conscious of the fact that consultants have only so much stamina.

Nonprofits may want to give consideration to engaging a consulting firm that is a member of the American Association of Fund-Raising Counsel (AAFRC). The AAFRC was founded more than 60 years ago to advance the philanthropic cause and the ethical approach to fund raising.

In 1935 a group of early practitioners and consultants were aware that American philanthropy was burgeoning at a quickening pace, and they wanted to be certain that fund-raising consulting firms adopted fair practices and worked by a professional code of conduct.

The AAFRC publishes two booklets that are recognized as important sources of philanthropic information. The first is *Giving USA* and the second *Giving USA Update.* AAFRC headquarters are in New York City; the current telephone number is 847/375-4709, or toll free 800/462-2372; fax: 866/263-2491.

Campaign counsel can provide extraordinary levels of expertise. However, it is not wise to turn a campaign over to a consultant for its exclusive management. Counsel is there to serve as a partner in the relationship. They are there to help you prioritize campaign initiatives and to guide and steer you toward the right way to conduct a campaign. The ultimate responsibility of the campaign must continue to reside with the organization and its own personnel.

A First Step in Moving Ahead: The Internal Planning Group

As has been stated previously, capital campaigns are enormous undertakings that require considerable staff time, planning, and diligence. I recommend that one of the first steps in organizing a campaign is to establish what might be called an *internal planning group*, consisting of those internal individual staff members who will provide the ongoing support to the campaign. Establishing this group early on in campaign planning will help in the monitoring of every aspect of the campaign. This group should be chaired by the chief advancement officer or director of the campaign. The purpose of the campaign planning group is to lay out the basic components and the timetable of the campaign and to track the effort from start to finish. Initially, I recommend that the planning group meet almost on a weekly basis and continue to meet throughout the campaign, phasing to monthly meetings and then perhaps quarterly meetings.

All major decision making should flow through this internal committee. Recommendations to the chief executive officer, to the campaign volunteer chair, and to other volunteer leaders should evolve out of this campaign planning group. This internal planning group should provide the agenda for volunteer committee meetings, as well as campaign materials and supporting audio visual materials. The committee might even be used to monitor the lead campaign solicitations, although other committees will most likely be inaugurated to move the solicitation process forward. The internal campaign planning group would decide which decisions and recommendations will need to go before the CEO and/or the governing board or perhaps the lead volunteers. The planning group is the nerve center of the entire campaign that guides, directs, and supports all campaign initiatives from a staff perspective.

In addition to the chief development or advancement officer, members of this internal committee might include the following:

- **Development Officer in Charge of Moving Prospect Management Forward.** An individual who is charged with the responsibility of tracking major gift solicitation should be a member of the internal planning group. In small organizations, this individual might very well wear several hats. Whoever is working primarily with the major gift prospects should be a member of this internal group.

- **Development Officer in Charge of Major Fund-Raising Staff.** The individual in charge of the major development staff should certainly be a member of the internal planning group.

- **Donor Relations or Constituent Relations Officer.** The person in charge of donor relations or constituent relations of the organization should also be a member of the planning group. The planning of events, the providing of donor premiums, and the fulfillment of donor expectations and stewardship will become a very important part of the campaign in its early stages.

- **Communications Officer.** The campaign will face a number of initiatives involving communications, including press releases, video presentations, brochures, and press conferences, and they will all require the expertise of a communications professional. Integrating this important function into the campaign is vital in the early stages of the effort. In the integrated organizational system discussed previously, this official may indeed report to a vice president for advancement. In a nonintegrated system, provisions should be made to involve an individual with communication skills in the internal planning group.

- **Other Personnel.** There may indeed be other personnel who should, in fact, be in the internal planning group, and this will depend on the organization and structure of the nonprofit involved. It is important to remember, however, that the internal planning group should be composed of any person in a leadership position who can help to move the campaign forward.

The Six Phases of a Capital Campaign

Almost all capital campaigns are composed of a series of phases. These phases often overlap, and sometimes it is difficult to determine when one phase has been completed and another phase has begun. Practically all capital campaigns exhibit at least six phases that can be defined as follows:

Phase One: Quiet Planning Phase

Depending on the breadth and scope of a campaign as well as on its sophistication and complexity, this phase typically lasts anywhere from one to three years. Some institutions begin planning a capital campaign two, three, or even four years before ever soliciting the first gift. One thing is certain; nonprofit organizations generally do not dedicate enough time to planning and find themselves "inventing the product and selling it at the same time" because of lack of planning.

The quiet planning phase is just that—a nonpublic time when staff members and a few select volunteers are performing precampaign functions but not in a solicitation mode. Generally, this phase is internal, involving primarily staff members. It should be a confidential preparation time in which the various campaign elements are outlined and the staff starts moving in the direction of a campaign. For some organizations, the quiet planning phase may literally begin weeks or months after just having completed a previous major capital campaign.

Phase Two: Advance Gift Phase

This phase may last one, two, or perhaps even three years and is still considered a nonpublic phase of the campaign. During this time period, the campaign establishes an organizational structure and the campaign becomes public to a small group of benefactors and volunteers. The major campaign committees are recruited and lead gifts are, in fact, solicited and closed. This phase is generally characterized by major gift activity with the organization's most important and generous benefactors. The success of the advanced phase often determines the overall success of the campaign.

Phase Three: The Public Phase

This phase is generally characterized by a public announcement that may include a major gala event involving lead benefactors, volunteers, and constituents of the organization. The campaign is publicly announced to the media, and there is a final determination and announcement of the goal. The public phase of the campaign can stretch anywhere from two to four years depending on the overall length of the capital campaign. Major gift activity continues throughout this phase, and the garnering of gifts at all levels, particularly at the range of $100,000 and above, will be particularly important during this phase.

During the public phase, media attention may focus on the campaign. As will be discussed in the communications chapter, media attention during the public phase can be most helpful in spreading the news of campaign success and gaining additional support from people who may have been reluctant to make major commitments.

Phase Four: The Plateau Phase

At some point during the campaign, generally in the middle of the public phase, the campaign will likely enter into what might be called the plateau phase—a time when volunteers and benefactors tire of the campaign and are ready for its completion. Volunteers become fatigued and ready to get the campaign behind them. They are tired of the solicitation process and attending multiple meetings, and they just want the campaign to reach its goal. These are truly the "dog days" of the campaign.

It is important to note that not every campaign experiences a plateau phase, but if it does occur, the organization should find ways to reinvigorate those involved in the effort. Many times, organizations will use the plateau phase to declare a new goal or a raised goal and some even have a mid-campaign event to excite and involve volunteers and benefactors. It is important to find ways to breathe new life in to the campaign should the plateau phase be experienced.

Phase Five: The Final Phase

The final phase of the campaign is built around the achievement of the goal and pushing toward successful completion. Goal attainment in itself energizes the committee, and many benefactors who have not already made commitments will come forward in an effort to help put the campaign over the top. At this time, previous benefactors will often increase their commitments in hopes of achieving the goal. Second and even third campaign commitments will often happen during this phase.

During the final phase, donor recognition events should take place to honor major benefactors for their philanthropy. An organization may also hold a final campaign event that brings together the various constituencies of the campaign honoring them and their achievements in declaring campaign success. The final phase is an important time for the organization to assess what the campaign has meant in terms of additional resources and volunteer engagement.

Phase Six: Post-Campaign Phase

Upon the conclusion of the campaign, campaign staff should evaluate the success of the campaign and create a plan to continue major gift support. Even though the campaign is concluded, major gift fund raising must remain an important and integral part of the organization's development program. It is hoped the organization will have reached a level of gift support that can be sustained, even in the off years of the capital campaign. The capital campaign should also be expected to boost the level of annual giving. It is hoped that this level of annual giving will be sustained as well.

The post-campaign phase is a time to sharpen the focus of the development program and to decide where resources can best be directed to continue to attract the highest level of gift support possible.

Campaign Planning Document and Timetable

Staff members would be well advised to create a campaign planning document early on in the campaign. The campaign planning document would have all of the various elements of the campaign and would be a general blueprint that might be used primarily for internal staff members and major lead volunteers. It can be particularly helpful as the volunteer structure of the campaign is being organized. Many campaigns actually use the campaign planning document in the recruiting phase of the volunteer network or distribute it at the first meeting of the lead campaign committee. A wise person once said, "If you can't write it, you can't do it." The campaign planning document allows an individual to read the document and gain a general understanding of how the campaign will proceed and the various elements and phases that will move the project forward.

The following are categories that might be contained in a campaign planning document:

- **The Case for Support.** Information about the case statement and the strategic objectives of the campaign is placed under this heading. The case generally lays out the reasons for launching a major capital campaign and the various strategic objectives to be funded.

- **Results of the Feasibility Planning Study.** A general discussion of the feasibility planning study falls under this category, and if the study has been completed, the results of the study can be outlined under this section.

- **Establishment of the Campaign Name.** Under this heading, the name of the campaign is mentioned for discussion and final action by the lead campaign committee.

- **Establishment of a Working Goal.** The working goal of the campaign can be examined, and volunteers should be involved in a thorough discussion of the goal that will finally be decided for the campaign.

- **Inauguration of Internal Planning Group.** This section has previously been discussed in detail, but the purposes, duties, and responsibilities of the planning group are detailed in this section.

- **Prospect Identification.** Prospect screening, demographic screening, as well as volunteer screening sessions are discussed under this heading.

- **Duties and Responsibilities of Campaign Officers.** Within this category, the duties and responsibilities of the various officers of the campaign, including the campaign chair, vice chair, campaign treasurer, and other officers are examined in detail.

- **Duties and Responsibilities of the Campaign Cochairs and/or Vice Chairs.** If the campaign engages volunteers as cochairs and/or vice chairs, their duties and responsibilities are listed in this category.

- **The Roles of Internal Staff, Including the Chief Executive Officer, Chief Development Officer, and Other Campaign Officers.** The duties and responsibilities of the various internal staff members for the campaign are listed under this category.

- **Communications Plan.** A communications plan is outlined under this heading.

- **Campaign Naming Opportunities.** No doubt there will be a number of naming opportunities in the campaign, and this area features a general discussion of those naming opportunities.

- **Campaign Management Reports.** Development personnel produce monthly campaign management reports showing progress toward the goal.

- **The Gift Range Chart.** The gift range chart and its purposes are outlined under this category.

- **Pledge Term.** A general discussion of the term of pledges that will be accepted in the campaign is set forth in this category.

- **Campaign Organizational Structure.** This section presents a general discussion of the organizational structure of the campaign and how the various committees will be staffed and organized. An organizational chart should be contained under this heading.

- **Duties and Responsibilities of Campaign Committee Members.** This section lists the duties and responsibilities of campaign steering or executive committee members who operate as the lead campaign committee. Also, the various subcommittees of the campaign are discussed in detail.

- **Campaign Phases.** A general discussion of the various campaign phases is contained in this area.

- **Broad-based Campaign and Its Relationship to the Major Gift Effort.** A general discussion of the broad-based campaign in annual giving during the capital campaign and how it will be handled in relationship to the major gift effort is addressed in this section.

- **Volunteer Training Program and Volunteer Guide.** Most campaigns have training sessions for volunteers, and a discussion of this important project within the campaign is contained within this category.

- **Campaign Accounting.** What gifts will be counted in the campaign is an important decision point for campaign leadership. This section outlines the various gifts that can be counted in the campaign effort.

Each element of the campaign planning document mentioned above is discussed at length in various chapters of this book.

Campaign Action Items

The following is an attempt to list every conceivable action that may be required in the capital campaign. This is an accumulation of several action items for major capital campaigns that may be adopted for use in a timeline.

- Receive CEO and board direction for campaign planning.
- Conduct internal audit for campaign readiness.
- Complete case prospectus.
- Conduct feasibility study external interviews to determine if campaign is feasible from external perspective.
- Deliver study results to CEO and appropriate parties.
- Establish confidential working goal for advanced gift phase.
- Formalize campaign planning document.
- Form internal campaign planning group and begin meetings.
- Establish resource and staffing plan and campaign budget.
- Establish space needs for campaign staff and office.
- Create preliminary campaign planning committee of volunteers.
- Conduct electronic screening of prospective donors.
- Conduct prospect research on principal and major gift prospects.
- Pull select data from computer or data files on cumulative donors and evaluate past giving.
- Conduct rating and screening sessions with volunteers in key areas.

- Continue cultivation plan of top 200 principal gift prospects.
- Establish a definitive list of campaign priorities based on the campaign needs statements and case statement.
- Review database system infrastructure.
- Link campaign strategic priorities to constituency unit and principal/major gift prospects.
- Finalize gift range chart.
- Establish volunteer organizational structure.
- Create job descriptions for campaign committees and officers.
- Develop campaign management reports.
- Develop preliminary campaign communications plan and campaign publications.
- Decide on final campaign name.
- Begin campaign counting period based on campaign counting guidelines.
- Formalize naming opportunities.
- Establish pledge term and pledge form.
- Recruit campaign chair and officers.
- Plan campaign publications.
- Recruit lead campaign committee.
- Begin leadership gift solicitations, including principal gifts.
- Solicit lead campaign committee.
- Solicit governing board.
- Solicit other major boards of organization.
- Continue principal gift solicitations at $250,000 and above.
- Hold first meeting of the lead campaign committee.
- Form appropriate major gift organizational structure if necessary.
- Conduct major gift solicitations below $250,000.
- Deliver campaign public announcement and hold appropriate gala event.
- Continue gift solicitations at the principal and major gift level.
- Conduct staff solicitation program.
- Consider broad-based solicitation program, using annual fund.

- Consider midcampaign event if plateau phase occurs.
- Continue announcements of major gifts to galvanize donors and prospects.
- Consider raising goal if necessary to help galvanize prospects and volunteers.
- Plan concluding gala event and announcement of campaign success.
- Conclude campaign counting period.
- Host concluding gala event after counting period concludes.
- Begin post-campaign planning and consideration of next campaign in three to five years.

A Word About Phases and Components Specific to Colleges and Universities

College and university fund raising is unique to the extent that it has both internal and external constituents that can be solicited for campaign support. It is certainly true that any good campaign at any nonprofit organization should indeed solicit its staff at some point in the campaign timeline. Some persons may argue that staff solicitation should occur early on to show external constituents that the organization's employees support the effort. Others will argue that this phase of the campaign should come later, particularly in the public or even plateau phase. In any event, staff solicitation in any campaign is an important component and should be given due consideration.

Faculty and Staff Component at Colleges and Universities

Regardless of the size of the college or university, there should be a faculty and staff solicitation component of the campaign. Although some experts will claim that faculty and staff giving to a capital campaign increases the likelihood of corporate and foundation support to the institution, there seems to be no research to support this conclusion. There are a number of foundations, however, that are interested in faculty and staff giving and require that information in application procedures. In general, faculty and staff giving does not directly affect corporate and foundation support of a capital campaign.

This is not to say that faculty and staff giving is unimportant. It can certainly serve a positive purpose to help ignite good feelings on campus among faculty and student groups. Much positive communication can surround a faculty and staff campaign to heighten awareness of the effort in general.

A number of institutions will turn over the faculty and staff component of the campaign to the annual fund program. This is particularly true if the annual fund component has been soliciting faculty and staff on a continuing basis prior to the capital campaign. Different institutions deal with faculty and staff solicitation during a capital campaign in different ways, but I have the following two specific recommendations:

- **Program-Specific Solicitation.** Many institutions choose an all-university strategic priority or objective that might appeal to a large number of faculty and staff members, such as the renovation of the main library, the creation of faculty fellowships, the creation of student scholarships, or the endowment of library holdings. Faculty and staff members are then asked to contribute to this need each year for the life of the campaign. Many times a multiyear pledge is requested, and faculty and staff members are solicited by their peers during a defined period of one to two months.

  The advantage of this mode of solicitation is that it creates a unified rallying point for all faculty and staff members as well as a specific objective to be funded during the campaign. It also may allow for increased giving if faculty and staff members continue their previous current giving to other programs and projects of their choosing.

  The disadvantage of this method is that it does not allow faculty and staff members to designate their giving toward a particular entity or discipline of their choice. In other words, a professor of history may want to contribute to the history department or to the liberal arts college. Program-specific fund raising does not encourage contributions to the area of the faculty or staff member's choice.

  It also has the disadvantage of detracting from the overall annual giving program that previously may have benefited from annual gifts from faculty and staff. A faculty or staff member may decide to simply designate their giving to the specific capital campaign project and discontinue their giving to the annual fund during the life of the campaign.

- **Annual Fund Designation.** Another method of solicitation of faculty and staff during a capital campaign, particularly at major universities with multiple campus and schools, is to allow faculty and staff members to designate their giving on an annual basis to an entity of their choice. A multiyear pledge is still possible, or the institution can simply solicit the faculty and staff annually throughout the life of the campaign. The annual fund may want to create a campaign look to their mail solicitations to give faculty and staff members a sense of belonging to the campaign.

If annual solicitation is to take place, then major gift prospects among faculty and staff members (and there may, in fact, be a number of them who are major gift prospects) should take place long before the faculty and staff campaign begins. Or, in the alternative, these faculty and staff members should be solicited with major gift asks and particular proposals to designated areas of interest.

The Student Component at Colleges and Universities

Colleges and universities should also give serious consideration to a student component of the campaign. A student component can help to galvanize volunteers and campaign leadership. Although resources garnered by such an effort may be limited, the communications value of this undertaking will be extremely important and will also increase the likelihood that students will become life-long donors to their alma mater.

The student component is probably best organized around living units, for competition between these units can be brokered. An alternative to student living units is the use of student clubs and organizations.

It is likely that students will want to rally around a particular campaign need or project, and they should be given the opportunity to choose one that will directly benefit students.

For those colleges and universities that do not have an annual fund student campaign, this may be an opportunity to integrate such a program. The annual student or senior class gift could, in fact, become the gift to the campaign and, in a sense, these gifts could be merged during the life of the campaign. Because of the matriculation of students, the student campaign might be better organized on an annual basis throughout the life of the overall capital campaign. This will help to alleviate the problems of student continuity.

The Alumni Association of Colleges and Universities

Most colleges and universities have alumni offices that may be associated with the advancement unit but are separate and distinct entities, not necessarily involved with fund raising. Multiple models exist throughout the country.

These alumni offices may take the form of separate legal entities with private governing boards. In some smaller independent institutions, the alumni office is governed entirely by the institution, and the separate alumni association board serves in an advisory capacity to the college or university. Regardless of the type of governing unit of an alumni association, there will be a need to determine how to use an alumni support group, alumni association, or alumni office during the capital campaign. It is likely that members of the alumni association governing board or the staff in the alumni office will want some sort of role or list of responsibilities and duties during the campaign. The campaign will become the most important effort undertaken by the institution during a prescribed period of time, and any healthy, active alumni association will want to be involved in a meaningful way.

Possible roles and responsibilities of the alumni association or alumni office are:

- Invite the alumni association's governing board to pass a resolution in support of the capital campaign.

- Invite the alumni association governing board to fund a particular identified project within the campaign such as a scholarship, fellowship, or even an endowed chair. Support for this project could come from the association's own assets (those with dues-paying members). Development personnel will want to be careful that the association does not solicit alumni in conflict with the ongoing annual fund effort in order to fulfill its own campaign commitment.

- If the alumni association has clubs and/or chapters in certain geographic regions, these clubs or chapters can serve as excellent vehicles for a communications program about the campaign. During the public phase of the campaign, clubs and chapters might be asked to allow campaign volunteers and staff to speak about the campaign, informing the general alumni body about the effort, its objectives, and how it is affecting the university or college.

- Alumni chapters or clubs can also sponsor individual scholarships from their particular geographic region. A number of alumni associations have chapters that are successful, functioning entities unto themselves and generate revenue on an ongoing basis. They might be invited to fund scholarships to be given to prospective students from their geographic region.

- Alumni associations could be of great assistance in conducting rating and screening sessions in particular geographic regions. Care should be taken to be certain that the appropriate persons are invited to the rating and screening sessions so that appropriate information is gathered from the most knowledgeable alumni in the region.

Keeping the alumni association or alumni office strategically involved in campaign planning is very important to the welfare of the overall campaign. Potential conflict between the association's and the capital campaign's objectives should be avoided at all costs, and the alumni association should support and endorse all campaign objectives. Open communication and coordination with alumni personnel and volunteers are highly recommended.

Athletic Fund Raising at Colleges and Universities During the Capital Campaign

Athletic fund raising, particularly at Division 1-A colleges and universities, consists to a large extent of priority seating and premium ticket options. These programs generally do not interfere with the ongoing process of development for academic programs and, in most cases, are not part of the ongoing development effort of a college or university. While change is in the wind in this regard and a few institutions have started collaborating more closely with athletic fund raising, this is still the exception rather than the norm.

Even though the major revenue for athletic programs comes chiefly from priority seating, a number of institutions have major gift fund-raising programs in athletics, and a handful have endowed coaching positions and even player positions. Pennsylvania State University has long had a major gift component of its athletic program and has refused to scale its stadium, which could dramatically increase ticket and priority seating revenue. The major sports arena on the Penn State campus was built entirely with a state appropriation and private funds.

At the University of Arkansas, athletic fund raising has been enormously successful primarily as a result of the guidance of the university's long-time coach and athletic director, Frank Broyles, and the president of the Razorback Foundation, Chuck Dicus. All of the university's major sports facilities have been built with private gift support.

In the last 10 years, athletic fund raising at colleges and universities of all sizes has become more and more sophisticated and aggressive. I recommend that college and university capital campaigns include a component of the campaign for the athletic department. This may simply include counting athletic gifts if the campaign is a comprehensive effort or identifying a specific program to be funded with campaign gifts from those interested in the welfare of athletics. Suffice it to say that a discussion should take place early on in campaign planning regarding where the athletic program fits in to the overall capital campaign.

Parent Giving in the Capital Campaign at Colleges and Universities

Many colleges and universities regularly solicit parents for contributions to the institution. Often, this is conducted through an institution's annual giving program and may include a phone or mail campaign.

During a capital campaign, an institution should not ignore the potential of *major gifts* from the parent population. Parents, and even grandparents, have the potential to contribute to annual fund gifts as well as be the prime prospects for capital gifts or major gifts at higher levels. Parents should be treated as any other constituent group, and many of them will have the potential to make major gifts during the life of the campaign.

Don't Forget the Local Community Component

All capital campaigns of any prominence should give consideration to a local community component of their effort. This is an opportunity for smaller businesses, associations, and other entities in the region surrounding the nonprofit to participate in the campaign by making a pledge commitment. A community-based campaign should not run throughout the life of the capital campaign, but rather have a defined window of solicitation that might occupy a six-month to one-year period of time. Volunteers are recruited to solicit local businesses and associations for pledge commitments to the campaign.

A local community component is not advised for every capital campaign. It is time intensive and involves a large number of volunteers. Generally, businesses and associations are targeted by dividing them among multiple solicitors in certain categories such as banking and financial institutions, professionals, doctors, lawyers, accountants, and so forth. Any solicitation effort of this type would involve training sessions for volunteers who would be given a definitive period of time in which to make their solicitations and then report back at the end of that period.

The local community component of the capital campaign is another way to galvanize support in the local area once the advance and major gift phases are fully operational. Those businesses, associations, and other entities in the region that have major gift potential should be solicited in the principal and major gift phases of the campaign and should already have been contacted and had proposals delivered to them long before a community campaign is organized and launched. This will help to ensure that preemptive gifts of a smaller size are not made to the campaign.

Notes for Chapter 3

1. M. D. Richards and G. R. Sherratt, "Institutional Advancement Strategies and Hard Times," ERIC Report No. 2 (Washington D.C.: American Association of Higher Education, 1981).

2. Mark J. Drozdowski, "A Phantom Menace," *The Chronicle of Higher Education* 50, no. 25 (February 27, 2004): C3.

3. John L. Dietz Jr., "University Fund Raising: Is There an Ideal Management Model for the Development Operation of the Large, Public Research Institution?" (master's thesis, Pennsylvania State University, Graduate School and the College of Education, April 1995).

4. Susan Brenna, "Buddy Systems?" *CASE Currents* (September 2004).

5. Mary Ellen Collins, "Campaign Strategies: Orchestrating a Harmonious Campaign," *CASE Currents* (April 2001).

6. Margarete Rooney Hall, "Two Approaches, One Goal," *CASE Currents* (April 2002).

7. Margarete Rooney Hall, "Fundraising and Public Relations: A Comparison of Programme Concepts and Characteristics," *International Journal of Nonprofit and Voluntary Sector Marketing* 6, no. 4 (November 2002): 368.

8. Susan K. Martin, "Academic Library Fund-Raising: Organization, Process, and Politics." *Library Trends* 48, no. 3 (Winter 2000).

9. Robert M. Beagle, "Competing Interests," *CASE Currents* (October 2003).

10. Nanci Olson Gundry and Peter McKinley, "Advantages of a Decentralized Advancement Research Office," *Connections* (Fall 2002).

11. G. David Gearhart and M. Bezilla, "Fund Raising Success Takes Teamwork," *Fund Raising Management* (March 1991): 42–44, 46.

12. Peter Panepento, "Clamoring for Consultants," *The Chronicle of Philanthropy* (March 18, 2004).

13. Ibid.

14. Ibid.

four

Staff Roles, Responsibilities, and Essential Services

We are not interested in the possibilities of defeat.
Queen Victoria

Staffing Requirements

The number of staff members required for a capital campaign will depend, of course, on the scope and size of the institution. Coverage of certain essential services is necessary, however, for a campaign of any magnitude undertaken by a nonprofit of any size.

In large, major philanthropic organizations that are raising multimillions of dollars on an annual basis and have capital campaign goals in the hundreds of millions of dollars, the regular staff can be in the range of hundreds of people. Major public and private universities that have been in the fund-raising business for many years often have regular, ongoing fund-raising staffs of more than 100 persons.

The following is not necessarily a listing of positions but rather those essential services that need to be covered in any capital campaign. For the smaller shop, many of the services will be conducted by the same staff member who will, naturally, be called on to wear many hats. In larger, more sophisticated organizations, the services may be spread among multiple persons with job descriptions that are specific and unique to the required service. The important point in discussion of staffing is that, regardless of the number of people employed by the organization, there are essential duties, responsibilities, and services that must be covered for any comprehensive capital campaign.

It is also important to point out that in some organizations certain services are outsourced to consultants or to for-profit organizations that will fulfill a particular need or cover a particular professional area (such as planned giving) for the nonprofit organization.

Staffing coverage essential for campaign success includes an overall campaign manager or director, prospect management and solicitation staffing, prospect research, and corporate foundation relations.

Overall Campaign Manager or Director

Someone must be designated and perhaps even anointed with overall campaign responsibility. This campaign director or manager is the senior official leading and guiding the campaign on a day-to-day basis. He or she must give the campaign total and complete attention. The individual charged with this responsibility makes the campaign his or her life! The campaign director thinks about the campaign first thing in the morning and the last thing at the end of the day. It is a job that requires complete and total attention to campaign goals and objectives and should not be undermined by less-important priorities.

Certainly, any individual who occupies the position of campaign manager or director must be at the very senior level of the development operation. After all, the CEO of the organization and the governing board have supposedly determined that the capital campaign will be the most important effort undertaken by the organization and will be deemed the highest priority over the next four to seven years. Pivotal campaign decisions will need to be made and carried out by the individual occupying this critical campaign position.

A substantial argument can be made that the person occupying the chief development officer or vice president role in the organization should, in fact, also be designated the director or manager of the campaign. If the CEO and board have, in fact, designated the campaign as a top priority, then it is axiomatic that the chief development officer or vice president for development or advancement guide and lead the campaign on a daily basis. There is no way that the chief development officer can be left out of decisions pivotal to the campaign's success. Establishing a layer below the vice president or chief development officer can create a burdensome and cumbersome bureaucratic organizational structure.

A contributing factor to the decision to hire a separate campaign director from the chief development officer will, naturally, be the size of the organization and capital campaign. Larger organizations may find it necessary to have this key position filled by someone who is not burdened with the day-to-day responsibilities that a chief development officer or vice president may have. Personnel issues, budget, and the myriad and unending lists of duties and responsibilities of a chief development officer may argue for the position of the campaign director to be separate and distinct from the chief development officer or vice president.

It should also be noted that employing a single individual to be a campaign director sometimes sends a signal to the rest of the development or advancement organization that the campaign is somehow distinct and apart from the normal development office operations. This can be harmful to any organization that does not weave the campaign into the fabric of the ongoing development efforts. The development team and the entire development operation and structure should be seen as serving the campaign on an ongoing basis. Creating a separate structure within the organization can oftentimes send the wrong message to other development officials.

The preferred model is to have the vice president or chief development officer serving also in the capacity of director of the campaign. This does not mean, however, that that individual needs to take on the title of director or manager of the campaign. Many large, highly successful campaigns do not have a staff position titled director of the campaign, preferring that this task be performed by the vice president or chief development officer in charge of advancement or development for the organization. Senior administrators, the governing board, and volunteers need to agree that the person directing the campaign on a daily basis is a high-ranking official of the organization and has the chief executive officer's ear. That sends a strong message about the critical nature of the campaign and the importance of the undertaking.[1]

Some development professionals in these senior positions may ask, "How can I do the work I am doing now and be campaign director all at the same time?" The obvious answer is that there is nothing more important than the planning and implementation of the capital campaign for the chief development officer, and other less-important duties and responsibilities may need to be shifted to other personnel or take a temporary backseat to the ongoing campaign responsibilities. If the chief development officer does, in fact, become the campaign director and manager, then he or she may need to reprogram and reevaluate duties and responsibilities that do not directly influence campaign activity.

First and foremost, the campaign director, manager, vice president, or chief development officer (whatever title is appropriate) must provide staff support to the chair of the campaign and the CEO of the organization. All prospects assigned to the chair and the CEO should be under the direction of the campaign director. The campaign director should know those prospects intimately and view them as his or hers during major gift solicitation.

Anytime a solicitation is made by the chair or CEO without the director of the campaign, the director should promptly debrief the chair and CEO. The director should provide written reports of contact even though he or she may not actually make the solicitation with the CEO or chair. In short, the campaign director and manager provides support to the CEO and campaign chair on an ongoing basis and makes certain that reports of contact, proposal letters, and acknowledgment letters are prepared in a timely and efficient manner.

Supporting the chair and CEO is a critical and important priority for the campaign director. The campaign director is also the staff liaison to the top volunteer committee. He or she must maintain weekly contact with all members of the volunteer committee. The campaign director should accompany the CEO and/or chair of the campaign on major gift solicitations when appropriate. Care should be taken that no more than three individuals be involved in a solicitation, generally speaking, at any one time.

In short, the campaign manager or director is the architect, the progenitor, and the facilitator for the entire campaign. Without a strong person guiding and leading the effort, the campaign will not be successful. The CEO and lead volunteers must have a campaign director who is hardworking, diligent, energetic, and enthusiastic, and who is always looking for the next major gift to the campaign.

The chief development officer's agenda should be focused on getting the capital campaign up and running. The following is a partial listing of the duties and responsibilities of the individual who has overall staff authority over the campaign. The director of the campaign:

- Is the staff member in charge of total operations of the campaign.
- Is the liaison with lead volunteers, particularly the officers of the campaign.
- Chairs campaign internal planning group meetings.
- Monitors staffing and budget issues for the campaign.
- Moderates decision making on principal and major gift prospects and helps to move the solicitation process forward.
- Creates a campaign organizational structure and accompanies the CEO to tap membership of the lead campaign committee.
- Creates agendas for campaign meetings and subcommittee meetings.
- Creates campaign planning document.
- Monitors timeline of the campaign and works to keep the campaign on schedule.
- Makes decisions on campaign announcements, media attention, and general campaign communications.
- Monitors campaign gift recording and campaign counting policy.
- Accompanies volunteers and chief officers on solicitations of lead campaign gifts.
- Keeps CEO and other senior organization officers informed of campaign progress.

- Monitors campaign stewardship plan and donor recognition events.

- Serves as chief officer directing the campaign and planning every aspect on a daily basis—providing analysis of plans and fund-raising potential.

- Creates campaign proposals in a timely and efficient manner and follows up with prospects after solicitations have been appropriately delivered.

- Creates appropriate call reports and campaign solicitations and builds campaign files on campaign prospects.

- Serves the president and chair of the campaign and other campaign volunteers and oversees solicitations and other responsibilities.

Prospect Management and Solicitation Staffing

Every campaign needs an individual to monitor constantly the prospect list and make certain that solicitations for the principal and major gift prospects (particularly those at the six-figure level) are moving forward with deliberate speed. The individual charged with this responsibility:

- Maintains principal and major gift prospects list for solicitation.

- Maintains proper assignments to development personnel, CEO, and volunteers for solicitation/cultivation purposes.

- Supervises electronic screening program, prospect screening sessions, and compilation of database information for accumulation of prospects.

- Monitors follow up on prospects to be certain that the solicitation is performed in a timely manner and follow up to the prospect is appropriate.

- Develops the principal and major gift solicitation list, adding and subtracting from the list throughout the campaign timeline.

Prospect Research

Many smaller organizations do not have the resources to fund a prospect research office. Unfortunately for these small shops, research seems to be the last development service funded in a capital campaign. Development research is a vital component of any capital campaign and should not be overlooked. Some smaller operations will blend the services of a prospect management director with the research responsibility. In larger organizations, the research office may employ several persons to perform that function. This individual:

- Identifies potential major gifts prospects.

- Develops profiles of individual, corporate, and foundation prospects having principal and major gift potential.

- Prepares profiles, particularly for review before cultivation and solicitation by volunteers, CEO, and development personnel.

- Uses appropriate research services to obtain maximum data on major gift prospects.

Adequate preparation of those responsible for solicitation is a key ingredient to success in major gift fund raising. Too often, development personnel and volunteers make critical mistakes that could have been avoided had they been properly briefed with research materials and adequate and timely information about the prospect.

Corporate and Foundation Relations

A person responsible for corporate and foundation relations fund raising is essential for large research-oriented organizations, but ideally a staff member should be assigned this area of responsibility within a campaign even at smaller institutions.

Generally speaking, corporations and foundations have been reluctant to make gifts to endowments or bricks-and-mortar projects without some close tie to the organization. Generally speaking, a nonprofit will need to find a link or tie to the corporate entity or even a quid pro quo for a corporate donor to make a major campaign commitment to their organization. Corporations have continued to position themselves to require some tangible benefit in return for their philanthropic support. Particularly, corporate entities that have stockholders want to be able to show a cost benefit for their philanthropy.

These cost benefits can range from recruitment of employees to sponsorship of academic research programs. At a major research university, these project-oriented proposals can be extraordinarily time consuming and require the diligence of dedicated staff members who will work with faculty members in applied research areas to develop proposals that match the interests and opportunities of a particular corporate entity. Major support from the corporate sector is more readily available to major organizations with close proximity to the company.

The individual assigned to corporations and foundations:

- Establishes and implements a comprehensive plan for developing support from corporations and foundations, with emphasis on capital campaign needs.

- Serves as spokesperson for the organization to corporations and foundations and assists in developing policies regarding corporation and foundation contact.

- Initiates and conducts research and analysis of corporations and foundations regarding potential for support to the campaign.

- Develops systems and procedures to coordinate all organization contacts with corporations and foundations.

- Develops a program to involve campaign volunteers in the effort.

- Establishes communication programs with corporations and foundations using publications and other media avenues.

- Provides guidance, counsel, and assistance to volunteers in cultivating corporate contacts.

- Provides information to update development records on corporations and foundations.

- Provides professional staffing on corporate and foundation matters to various groups—internal and external.

- Visits corporate and foundation executives to cultivate relationships and foster an understanding and appreciation of your nonprofit.

- Serves as the organization's spokesperson to corporations and foundations insofar as philanthropy is concerned.

- Develops systems and procedures to coordinate contacts with corporations and foundations that have an effect on fund-raising programs.

Another Word About Corporate and Foundation Initiatives in a Capital Campaign Setting

Corporate and foundation fund raising is dramatically different today than it was 10 years ago. In today's economy, greater emphasis is placed on reducing employee head count, implementing cost containment, and gaining competitive advantage. Organizations can no longer count on recruiting relationships as primary driving forces for corporate philanthropic decisions.

But entities are looking to organizations where they have the most to gain by creating an affiliation. Traditional factors, such as geographic location, current levels of philanthropic support, recruiting interests, highly placed alumni, and number of alumni can be factored into the process but are not always controlling issues.

With respect to foundations, it is well accepted that campaigns have little meaning to private philanthropic foundations. Exceptions to this general rule are those family foundations or trusts that are controlled by an individual who has a relationship to your organization. Major philanthropic foundations will be primarily interested in supporting a particular area of interest to the foundation, and very few of these major foundations have any interest in the fact that you are in a capital campaign.

The following are some key points regarding corporate and foundation fund raising in a capital campaign environment.

Campaign Objectives in the Corporate and Foundation Arena

A key objective is to maximize support from corporations, foundations, and associations during the campaign. This means the organization must create and nurture both formal and informal relationships with corporate representatives.

You must create visibility, awareness, and understanding of your organization and its programs, particularly those that are leading edge and national or international in scope or reputation.

You must bring together representatives from corporations, foundations, or associations and match them with your organization's counterparts to begin a process of discovery regarding how the organization and the corporate or foundation can best work together to meet *both* missions.

You must develop a vision, and from that, a working model and structure on how your organization can and should work with the private sector.

You must work internally with your organization to develop strategies that will maximize support from corporations and foundations.

Campaign Opportunities in the Corporate and Foundation Sector

In spite of corporate downsizing, your organization may be a key institution and a significant resource to the corporation.

Industrial sponsored research continues to be a great strength for health agencies, colleges, and universities. The organization's ability to conduct collaborative research and to aid in the transfer of technology will be crucial factors that will influence corporate support.

Your organization must stress and emphasize mutually beneficial relationships with corporate partners.

There appears to be a growing interest, particularly in the past five years, in building special relationships or alliances between corporations and organizations. The philosophy must be to build as many organization-wide relationships as possible in order to create advocacy and set your organization out as a willing, customer-driven, quality-oriented organization.

Campaign Challenges in the Corporate and Foundation Sector

The challenge is the leveling or, in many cases, the downsizing of support to philanthropy by the corporate sector.

For many corporations, and certainly foundations, a campaign initiative and timetable have little or no meaning. Foundations are driven by other criteria, and campaigns have no meaning at all. Most corporations, particularly in the current environment, are not as motivated to make special campaign gifts as they once were unless a very special relationship exists.

As much as recruiting has been a primary element in building relationships that lead to significant philanthropy, particularly in the college and university setting, the current trend of employee downsizing by corporations feeds into all of these other issues. Now many large corporations are cutting back on recruiting and are spending less time on college campuses. In many cases, corporations are limiting the number of institutions where they will recruit.

Corporations and foundations are looking with great interest to the success of the organization in diversity and minority efforts. This is a major concern and is a key factor or indicator in determining how much and where corporate support will go.

The performance of the stock market, particularly from 2000 to 2003, and part of 2004, has been a pivotal element with respect to corporate and foundation support. The past few years have not been good ones with respect to foundation portfolios and have had a dramatic impact on the level of gift support available. This has brought about a leveling or reduction of foundation grants.

A key challenge will be the ability of your organization to be recognized and visible in the foundation and corporate community.

Final Word About Corporate and Foundation Initiatives

- Attempt to identify, cultivate, and solicit corporations and foundations that present opportunities for gift support at the six-figure level. Otherwise, you will spend as much time at lower levels with significantly less pay off.

- Build broader, deeper, more involved multifaceted relationships that include philanthropy, research, continuing and distance education, vendor relationships, affiliation relationships, and other appropriate linkages.

- Don't try to do everything. Focus on coordinating and managing approaches to the top 50 corporations and foundations that have multiple ties with your organization. It is simply not possible to cover everything. Use a laser-targeted approach rather than a shotgun approach.

- Work with, train, and empower others in your organization to become more effective in identifying, cultivating, and soliciting corporations and foundations that have narrow, unit-specific interests and have regional geographic preferences. Be certain to coordinate their efforts and stay on top of their assignments.

- Refine and maintain a matrix of corporate information and relationship factors that include such items as giving, research expenditures, key employees and executives, vendor relationships, recruiting relationships, and research projects.

- Gather and maintain personal and business relationships that exist between your organization and the corporation or foundation. Use this information as needed to forge new relationships, open doors, and create advocacy for proposal acceptance.

- Use relationships with corporations and foundations to match the interests of potential donors with specific needs and wants of the campaign.

- Consider the creation of a semiannual newsletter for corporations, foundations, and associations. The purpose would be to increase awareness of your organization's programs of note, report current grant activity, and feature special areas of program expertise and distinction.

After all is said and done, corporate and foundation fund raising in a capital campaign environment is a tough business! Do not assume that major corporations and foundations are going to support your organization simply because you have a capital campaign. The bottom line is your organization's capital campaign may have little or absolutely no meaning to the corporate or foundation entity. Expecting that the corporate and foundation sector will swoop in with a major philanthropic support for your organization during your capital campaign is impractical and even naïve. Corporate and foundation support is possible to obtain but, as the above indicates, it is a "tough row to hoe."

Be Realistic—Staff Will Be Needed

Each of the staff positions or staff functions described above is instrumental for the successful launching and sufficient running of a capital campaign and should not be overlooked because of lack of resources. At major organizations, each of these components might be staffed by a single individual or several individuals. In a small shop, one individual might be charged with administering multiple responsibilities.

Experience has shown that a capital campaign invariably requires more staff members than assumed at the outset. CEOs and governing boards should not be surprised at the number of new personnel required to make the campaign a success. Each of these functions requires staffing:

- **Annual Giving Program.** Annual giving at your institution must continue even during the capital campaign years. There must be a staff member who sufficiently understands the relationship between the campaign and annual giving to keep the annual giving component of the organization alive and well.

  In a small shop, this person will most likely have additional responsibilities. At a large institution, the director of annual giving may have a rather large staff conducting phone, mail, and electronic solicitation. Whichever is the case, annual giving must not atrophy during the campaign years. A staff person needs to be assigned to this important responsibility.

- **Donor or Constituent Relations.** Another area of essential coverage is donor or constituent relations. This might be defined as the practice of donor stewardship and honoring benefactors appropriately for their major-gift support. Increased philanthropic support to an organization during a capital campaign presents unprecedented opportunities for the strengthening of donor and constituent relations. Benefactors who make major commitments to an organization require special care and attention. It will be important to assign a staff person to this area dealing with the care and well-being of major gift benefactors, not only during the life of the campaign, but afterwards as well. Major gift activity increases the intensity of this office dramatically. Major gift prospects and donors may want to deal with the chief officer of the development program or campaign, so it might be wise to physically situate the donor relations officer close to the chief development officer.

Donor and constituent relations will be addressed more comprehensively later in the book, but for now, realize this is an area that must receive attention during a campaign.

- **Proposal Writing.** Every campaign, regardless of size, needs someone to coordinate proposal writing. Every individual, corporation, or foundation solicited for a principal or major campaign gift should receive a formal, specifically tailored proposal. Casual solicitations that do not use a written proposal can spell disaster for a campaign. Preparing these proposals is essential to the success of any capital campaign. It is likely that at least one staff member, at the minimum, will be needed who can help produce the proposals in a timely, efficient, and effective manner. The proposal writer may have other duties and responsibilities in a small shop, but the ability to produce timely proposals in quick turnaround mode will be a key factor for campaign success.

- **Campaign Communications.** Every campaign, large or small, will produce communications with internal and external audiences. A staff member must be assigned this important responsibility and must possess excellent written and verbal skills to effectively produce campaign brochures, newsletters, press releases, and facilitate overall news media relations.

  In a large, complex organization, this individual might well be the chief public relations officer of the organization. In a small shop, this individual may have numerous responsibilities. In any event, there needs to be at least one staff member who understands this component of the capital campaign and can provide support and assistance on a regular basis in shaping campaign communications.

- **Fund-Raising Personnel Engaged in Solicitation.** An active volunteer campaign committee will require close supervision and support by the development staff. Many times, a trained, knowledgeable development officer should accompany a volunteer on fund-raising calls. Thus, it is important that there be a sufficient number of fund-raising personnel who are not burdened with heavy managerial responsibility or the day-to-day operations of the campaign to be available to make fund-raising calls with volunteers. They must be readily accessible and able to travel a good deal of the time, and they must respond quickly and efficiently to volunteers during the intense proposal delivery activity.

At large, complex organizations, there may be a multitude of development officers who are assigned this responsibility.

Although it may be difficult for the chief development officer, vice president, or campaign manager to find time for solicitation activity, it is absolutely essential that he or she be seen as the chief fund raiser (other than the CEO, that is), and this person must reserve considerable time for direct, face-to-face solicitations of the highest-level potential benefactors.

The most important point is that all campaigns must decide which personnel will be on the front line, making calls, delivering proposals, and following up with potential benefactors. The campaign will not move forward without a clear understanding of who has the responsibility for proposal delivery and solicitation as well as who is working with volunteers on prospects.

- **Responsibility for Keeping Appropriate Records.** Major gift benefactors will expect their commitments to be tracked, recorded, and acknowledged efficiently and effectively. Staff members must be available to carry out the function of gift recording and recordkeeping. Gift commitments and pledges must be recorded by an organization with extreme care and extraordinary accuracy. Failure to follow up on pledge commitments as appropriate requires the organization to "get the gift twice."

  Practically all organizations of any sophistication have records and data systems that are specifically used for the purpose of tracking and recording gifts.

- **Planned Giving.** Whether the capital campaign is being conducted at a major organization or by a small nonprofit organization, there must be a way to cover the essential component of planned giving. Planned giving is the area that will hold the greatest promise for major-gift commitments and certainly has the potential of benefiting organizations dramatically in the future.

If a small shop cannot afford a full-time planned giving director, or in the alternative, the expertise does not exist among other development personnel, then it may be necessary to hire a consulting firm to perform this function. Some law firms now specialize in planned giving and will understand the intricacies of a planned giving program. Ten to 15 years ago, few law firms understood the basic rubrics of planned giving, but this has changed substantially, and many firms, particularly the larger ones, can provide this expertise to a development office.

Whichever the case, irrevocable planned gifts may account for a substantial percentage of the goal of the capital campaign. Knowledgeable personnel, trained in the latest gift techniques, will be extremely important to the campaign.

- **Executive Assistant for Travel and Appointments.** Development officers are notorious for planning, planning, and planning and never executing, executing, executing!

Development staff can spend hours upon hours discussing a potential prospect and pulling together materials and proposals but never getting around to scheduling the appointment and following up appropriately. Campaign offices would be well served to hire and train an individual who is charged with the responsibility of setting up appointments and travel schedules for fund-raising personnel and volunteers. While this staff position may be a luxury in a small shop, it is an absolutely essential responsibility. The greatest plans, the greatest proposals, and the most fundable projects won't matter one single bit if appointments are not made and prospects visited. While many professionals may argue that development officers should make their own appointments with potential benefactors, sometimes it is not possible for extremely busy personnel at a senior level to do so. In a perfect world, all development officers would set up their own appointments, but assigning an individual responsibility to make appointments for certain appropriate development personnel who are on the road may, in fact, be more effective. You cannot raise funds sitting in the office! You must maintain a vigorous travel schedule cultivating and soliciting or gifts will simply not materialize.

Some particular pointers on travel and appointment making are:

- Keep an up-to-date travel log that lists those with whom you need to make an appointment. List them both geographically and alphabetically. This will allow you to be certain to visit all who are in a geographic location and track them with regularity.

- Make appointments at least two weeks in advance. It is easier to say no to development officers if they call only a few days before the desired appointment time. Don't give individuals a readily available excuse not to meet because the time frame is too short.

- Program your travel out two to three months so that you save travel days on your schedule and don't get pulled into meetings and other obligations that are not as important as solicitation. Protect your calendar far in advance so that you know you will be on the road soliciting and cultivating well in to the future.

- For those calls that are still in the cultivation process, go ahead and tell the prospect that you are not coming to ask them for a gift but rather to inform them about the campaign and try to establish a closer relationship with them. This will put them at ease, and you will be much more likely to obtain the cultivation appointment.

- Maintain diligence in seeking appointments and don't give up until the prospect tells you that they absolutely, positively will not meet with you. Persistence definitely pays off in major-gift fund raising.

It is simply not possible to run a major capital campaign without increased costs as well as increased personnel. Trying to do it "on the cheap" will backfire every time. If the CEO requires a development shop to administer a campaign without any increased staff and resources, he or she is dooming the effort to failure and is asking the campaign management team to accomplish the impossible. *The capital campaign will require increased personnel costs and budget in order to be successful.*

The Role of the CEO in the Campaign Environment

The CEO, president, chancellor, director, or whatever title is given to this important position, can and will have a dramatic impact on campaign success. As stated previously, the CEO must totally support the concept of a campaign and must be its strongest advocate. He or she must make the campaign an institutional priority and devote a substantial percentage of time to the project.

Consultants are often asked by CEOs just how much time will be required of them in the campaign. In the early stages of the effort, it is not out of the question for the CEO to devote as much as 60 to 70 percent of his or her time to campaign priorities. The real answer, however, is that the CEO must devote as much time as it takes to be successful. "Whatever it takes" is not a very scientific answer, but is probably the best answer.

The CEO must be willing to devote ample time to the following important campaign activities:

- **Assisting With and Endorsing the Campaign Planning Phase.** The CEO must be viewed as the campaign leader and progenitor. This cannot be left to campaign staff, the chief development officer, or even to volunteers. The CEO will ultimately bring the campaign to fruition and should be seen as the driving force out front, ever enthusiastic and supportive of campaign activities.

- **Recruitment of the Volunteer Campaign Committee.** The CEO must be willing to travel extensively in the early days of the effort to impanel the volunteer committee for the campaign. This cannot be left to the chief development officer. The CEO must personally recruit every member of the general volunteer committee. Recruitment should include personal calls at the volunteer's home or office. Securing the campaign chairperson will also be a most important initial task of the CEO.

- **Attendance at Volunteer Campaign Meetings.** The CEO must attend every meeting of the major volunteer group of the campaign to demonstrate to these volunteers (and potential benefactors) that the campaign is an important priority. Major volunteers will want to communicate directly with the CEO about campaign matters and he or she should be available accordingly. Missing key campaign meetings sends the wrong message to key volunteers who are expending their time and resources supporting the effort.

- **Act as Principal Spokesperson for the Campaign.** All major gift announcements should flow through the CEO's office and be made jointly by the CEO and the campaign chairperson. This demonstrates to benefactors that their gift commitments are considered vital, and it will also signal internal and external constituencies that the campaign is very important to the welfare of the institution.

- **Participate in Internal Staff Campaign.** The CEO should be a visible and active participant during the internal staff campaign. The CEO must be totally supportive of the effort. This visibility will serve as a multiplier, encouraging members of the staff to make commitments to the campaign.

- **Make a Commitment.** Campaign volunteers will want to see the CEO make his or her own personal campaign commitment of resources. CEOs should be asked to stretch their giving and make the largest gift possible for their financial circumstances. This shows extreme commitment on behalf of the CEO and will be well received by volunteers and benefactors not to mention campaign prospects.

- **Solicit Principal and Major Gifts.** The CEO will be called on to solicit or be a part of a campaign team to solicit the principal and major gifts of the campaign. These gifts can generally be defined as those in the six-figure level and above, and at major sophisticated organizations, the CEO should probably be reserved for gifts in the $1 million and above range. In larger, more sophisticated efforts, CEO involvement below the level of $250,000 should be evaluated closely. Only in circumstances where the CEO has a close personal relationship with this prospect or is soliciting a member of the governing board or campaign committee, should his or her involvement be considered below this $250,000 ceiling.

The level of solicitation undertaken by the CEO will depend entirely on the prospect list, the gift chart, and the sophistication of the organization. It is important, however, to reserve the CEO for the highest level solicitation possible. An organization should not expend a CEO's time on gift commitments that won't make a huge impact on the campaign. This is not to say that all commitments to the campaign are not important, it is simply reality that the CEO will have only so much time to expend and this time should be carefully orchestrated.

Notes for Chapter 4

1. Rita Bornstein, "The Capital Campaign: Benefits and Hazards," in *The President and Fund Raising,* eds. James L. Fisher and G. H. Quehl, 203–4 (New York: American Council on Education and Macmillan Publishing Company, 1989).

five

Volunteers and External Campaign Organization

Never give in . . . Never, never, never . . . in nothing, great or small, large or petty—never give in except to convictions of honor or good taste.

Winston Churchill

A solicitor must be well informed in regard to the salient facts about the enterprise for which he is soliciting. An adequate knowledge of the organization is necessary in order that the solicitor may be able to speak with conviction. It is of great help to know something about the person whom you are approaching. And, everyone always likes to know what other people are giving. That may be an irrelevant question, but it is a human question. If I am asked for a contribution, naturally and properly, I am influenced in deciding how much I should give by what others are doing. Never think you need to apologize for asking someone to give to a worthy object, any more than as though you were giving him an opportunity to participate in a high-grade investment. The duty of giving is as much his as is the duty of asking yours. Know as much as you can about the man to whom you go; give him a general idea as to the contributions being made by others in his group, and suggest in a gracious and tactful way what you would be glad to have him give, leaving it entirely to him to decide what he shall give. Be kind and considerate. Thus, you will get closest to a man's heart and his pocketbook.

John D. Rockefeller

Volunteerism is an American way of life. While experts differ on the number of Americans who perform volunteer duties, Independent Sector conducted a national study in 2002 that gave some definition to the number of persons who are making an impact on the American scene through volunteerism.

In that study, Wallace W. Conhaim states:

> Some 85 percent of nonprofit organizations and 92 percent of religious groups use volunteers, according to the Independent Sector. The average time each volunteer spends per week has been decreasing, but the number of volunteers has increased 10 percent each year since 1995.
>
> The study estimates that 89.3 million American adults who volunteer contribute the time equivalent of $239 billion a year—this is equal to 9 million full-time employees.
>
> Volunteerism is a quintessential American value. Americans' practice of banding together to meet a civic need was noted in the 19th century by Alexis de Tocqueville.[1]

Volunteers

The vast majority of America's volunteers work in the human services areas or religious-based volunteerism. Health-related and community service also contribute large numbers of volunteers to the overall volunteer network.

Probably one of the most extensive studies of American volunteerism was conducted in fall 2003 and published in February 2004 by The Urban Institute. [2]

Conducted by the Urban Institute and funded in part by the UPS Foundation, the Corporation for National and Community Service, and the USA Freedom Corps, the Institute claims this undertaking to be the first national study of volunteer management capacity. The study came about in part in response to President George Bush's 2002 State of the Union Address in which he urged all Americans to spend a minimum of 4,000 hours serving others over the course of their lives.

Before beginning an in-depth analysis of use of volunteers in a capital campaign, it would be helpful to review the executive summary and major findings of the Urban Institute study. Those major findings are as follows:

The Use of Volunteers

Many charities and congregational social service outreach programs use volunteers, and these volunteers play an important role in their operations. A large majority of organizations report that they are prepared to take on additional volunteers.

- **Four in five charities use volunteers.** Of the approximately 215,000 charities that filed Form 990 or 990EZ with the IRS in 2000 (required of those charities with over $25,000 in annual gross receipts), an estimated 174,000 organizations use volunteers. One in three congregations manage volunteers in social service outreach programs. Of an estimated 380,000 congregations in the United States, 129,000 manage volunteers in such programs.

- **Volunteers offer benefits associated with investments in management.** A large majority of charities report their volunteers are beneficial to their operations in a number of ways. Further, the study concludes that investments in volunteer management and benefits derived from volunteers feed on each other, with investments bringing benefits and benefits justifying greater investments.

- **Charities and congregations are ready to take on more volunteers.** More than 9 in 10 organizations are ready to take on more volunteers at their present capacity, with a median of 20 new volunteers. Without any capacity enhancements, charities could take on an estimated 3.4 million new volunteers, and congregational social service outreach activities could take on an estimated 2.5 million new volunteers.

Challenges to Mobilization of Volunteers

The greatest challenges that charities and congregations face is an inability to dedicate staff resources to and adopt best practices in volunteer management.

- **Devoting Substantial Staff Time Spent on Volunteer Management as a Best Practice.** The percentage of time a paid staff volunteer coordinator devotes to volunteer management is positively related to the capacity of organizations to take on additional volunteers. The best prepared and most effective volunteer programs are those with paid staff members who dedicate a substantial portion of their time to management of volunteers. This study demonstrated that, as staff time spent on volunteer management increased, adoption of volunteer management practices increased as well. Moreover, investments in volunteer management and benefits derived from volunteers feed on each other, with investments bringing benefits and these benefits justify greater investments.

- **Low Staff Time Spent in Volunteer Management.** Three out of five charities and only one out of three congregations with social service outreach activities reported having a paid staff person who worked on volunteer coordination. However, among these paid volunteer coordinators, one in three have not received any training in volunteer management, and half spend less than 30 percent of their time on volunteer coordination.

- **Not Adopting Volunteer Management Practices.** Fewer than half of charities and congregations that manage volunteers have adopted most volunteer management practices advocated by the field. For example, only about one-third of charities say they have adopted to a large degree the practice of formally recognizing the efforts of their volunteers.

- **Capacity-Building Options for the Future.** Despite the willingness of charities and congregations to take on volunteers, challenges prevent them from meeting their full potential. A number of actions might improve the ability of charities to work effectively with and take on new volunteers.

- **Increasing Volunteerism During the Workday.** The most prominent challenge to implementing volunteer programs among charities and congregations is recruiting volunteers during the work day, reported as a big problem by 25 percent of charities and 34 percent of congregational social service outreach programs. This suggests that groups interested in promoting volunteerism should explore ways to create more flexible workdays for potential volunteers who have regular jobs.

- **External Support of Full-Time Volunteer Managers.** The most popular capacity-building option among both charities and congregations with social service outreach activities is the addition of a one-year, full-time volunteer with a living stipend (like an AmeriCorps member), with responsibility for volunteer recruitment and management. AmeriCorps members could be particularly useful in charities that are challenged in recruiting enough and the right kinds of volunteers, but also in those that do not have time or money to train and supervise volunteers.

- **Supporting Intermediaries that Recruit and Match Volunteers.** Many charities and congregations struggle with finding a sufficient number of volunteers. Roughly 40 percent report that more information about potential volunteers in the community would greatly help their volunteer program, highlighting the important role that volunteer centers and other community information resources could play in linking people who want to volunteer with organizations that need them.

- **Developing Avenues to Help Train Staff.** Training staff members on how to work with volunteers could address a range of challenges, including recruiting volunteers during the workday.[3]

Cassie Moore discusses the Urban Institute study in an article in *The Chronicle of Philanthropy,* "Charities Must Learn to Better Manage Volunteers, Study Finds."[4]

Indeed, volunteerism in America has faced new challenges in the past 10 years. As technology is advancing rapidly, volunteers expect the organizations they are working for to keep up with the advancement. Frequently, nonprofit organizations are behind the eight ball in technology, and this proves to be frustrating and incapacitating for volunteers.

Volunteers are also feeling the money crunch, and because of the general economic climate of the past few years, many volunteers are precluded from heavy involvement with their nonprofit agencies. With the heavy work responsibilities of both spouses, there is little time for volunteerism.

Job changes are causing people to move their residency more frequently, which also creates an unstable factor for volunteerism, particularly for community-based organizations.

With the plethora of nonprofit organizations, the competition for the best volunteers in a community is acute. Word spreads quickly about those volunteers who are particularly hardworking, diligent, and effective. It's not long before a multitude of philanthropic organizations are asking good volunteers for their services. Although I heavily promote the concept of using volunteers in capital campaigns, there are a number of negative factors that should be stated and considered by nonprofit organizations:

- Emphasis on complicated, complex giving techniques, including tax considerations, renders most volunteers ineffective.

- Donors may be less likely to reveal confidential information to volunteers in a solicitation environment.

- When a donor's giving is more program oriented, volunteers may not have the special knowledge or technical expertise to explain, or for that matter, even comment on an organization's strategic objectives.

- Organizations have witnessed a paradigm shift and are using more paid staff rather than volunteers in high-level solicitations. The staff members are more reliable, more knowledgeable about the organization, and better trained to deal with high-end donors.

- Donors expect solicitation from high-level staff, including a vice president level or the CEO of the organization. They want to touch the proverbial cloth of the organization's president and feel as though their gift has been invited by the highest-level person in the organization.

- Staff members are much more experienced at major gift solicitation and will not be reluctant to make the ask. Most volunteers are reluctant to make the ask and find it difficult or even impossible to state a specific figure in the gift solicitation environment.

- Staff solicitation is much more efficient in a controlled environment. Volunteers are unreliable and unpredictable.

Richard J. Pokrass, in a 1986 article in *CASE Currents*, identified four types of problem volunteers:

- **The No Show.** His intentions may be good, but he always seems to have a reason for his absence from meetings or festivities.

- **The Procrastinator.** She requires constant nudging by others and is always late with projects.

- **The Rubber Band.** He enjoys volunteer work so much that he is stretched between so many organizations and projects that it is impossible for him to get everything done.

- **The Know It All.** Because she likes to share her opinion on everything, she causes the group to deviate from its agenda and turns 45 minute meetings into three-hour marathons.[5]

No doubt, most development officers find working with volunteers difficult, time consuming, and sometimes simply aggravating. But the truth of the matter is that few capital campaigns will be successful without the use of volunteers in an organizational structure.

The Ideal Volunteer Partner

Having worked with hundreds if not thousands of volunteers over three decades, I have developed a real appreciation for the ideal volunteer partner. John Glier, president and chief executive officer of the Grenzebach Glier Consulting Firm in Chicago, Illinois, and a chairman of the firm, Martin Grenzbach, have contributed greatly to the following list of qualities of the ideal volunteer partner:

- They are leadership benefactors who not only give time but also resources at a generous level. They can provide access and advocacy for the nonprofit organization.
- They are knowledgeable about the organization and its fundraising goals and agenda.
- They are articulate spokespersons for the case, the organization, the CEO, and the staff.
- They are patient, collaborative, and willing to work in strategic ways in making a commitment to the cultivation of benefactors.
- They are colleagues, allies, and partners in the long-term process.
- They have credibility and stature and lead with their own commitment first.
- They understand that a major-gift program, a capital campaign, is a process, not a single event.
- They engage in appropriate preparation as an important factor in major-gift solicitation.
- They understand that partner solicitation with staff members is always a stronger and more effective way to raise a major gift.
- They understand their job in a solicitation environment is to raise the prospects' sights and attempt to engage them in making the largest gift possible to the organization.
- They must be active, not passive. Supportive, not belligerent. Helpful, not condescending. They help take ownership of the program.
- They operate as partners, not independent contractors.
- They emphasize concrete tasks, not generic roles. They help get things done and are not window dressing.
- They are volunteers who encourage joint ownership in the project, emphasize communication, and follow through.

Volunteer Maxims

Many times, effectiveness of volunteers depends on the staff members servicing those volunteers. Development staff members must understand how to use volunteers appropriately and effectively. The following is a listing of important maxims when considering the use of volunteers:

- Do you have accurate, up-to-date volunteer job descriptions that pinpoint what you want people to accomplish? In today's environment, volunteers want to know what is expected of them and what their specific job is. Generic roles won't cut it any longer.

- Do you adequately explain to your volunteers the importance of their jobs and what, specifically, you want them to accomplish? Do you tell them their purpose and function?

- Have you trained your volunteers adequately to cope with their job responsibilities?

- Do you recognize your volunteers in a meaningful way? Do they know you appreciate their volunteer time as well as the giving of their resources?

- Have you recognized the severe time crunch of the 21st century and the difficulty volunteers are having in expending time for volunteer efforts?

- Are you using your best volunteers to help train novice volunteers?

- Are you up to speed on communication technologies so that your volunteers can communicate with you effectively and efficiently?

- Do you clarify the details of the volunteer job and the demands they will place on the volunteer?

- Do you regularly meet your volunteer in person and develop human contact rather than communicate by telephone and letter writing?

- Are you totally honest with your volunteers about the campaign, the expectations, and the difficulties in fund raising?

- Are you always courteous to your volunteers, regardless of their attitudes toward staff members?

- Do you listen to your volunteers and respect what they have to say regardless of the substance and efficacy?

- Are you continuously enthusiastic with your volunteers?

- Are you sensitive to the volunteer's perceptions and attitudes?
- Have you established an appropriate environment for the volunteers?
- Is your organization well respected and focused?
- Do you inform the volunteer of appropriate progress being made on the campaign?
- Have you informed volunteers of their reporting responsibilities?
- Are you serving your volunteers regularly, being certain that the volunteer feels engaged, involved in your organization's activity?
- Do you reinforce good performance among your volunteers by congratulating those who are especially helpful and supportive?
- Have you established a mechanism for recruiting new volunteers to your organization?
- Do you promote exercises that force self-examination of your volunteer network?
- Are you setting realistic expectations for fund raising so that volunteers don't fail in their activities?

Volunteers in a Campaign Environment

Volunteers are important to successful fund raising. It is not an understatement to claim that a capital campaign will not approach maximum success without the use of volunteers.

There will be many opportunities for volunteers to serve in a variety of official capacities such as campaign chair, vice chair, secretary, treasurer, as well as chairs of various campaign committees. Numerous committees and task forces throughout the life of the campaign require volunteer leadership. Volunteers should be engaged in issues involving organizational structure as well as approving key issues such as gift accounting principles, campaign timeline, campaign promotional materials, and other significant decision making that would allow volunteers to take premier ownership and develop accountability for the campaign. As key volunteers become more engaged in the life of the campaign, they will become better volunteers and hence better contributors at major levels.

Volunteers should play a key role in the solicitation of major gifts. Peer pressure can be an important factor in closing on a major or principal gift opportunity. Volunteers accompanying staff members, particularly the CEO or senior development officer, can form a powerful team to leverage a gift that otherwise might not be forthcoming.

Volunteers should always be encouraged to make their own gift commitment first before engaging others in conversations about gifts.

Volunteers, along with the CEO of the organization, can also serve as spokespeople with the news media as well as with the organization's constituencies. Many times, announcements by volunteers will carry more clout than announcements by staff, and volunteers can serve a key communications role for the campaign.

It is important to keep in mind that an organization should attempt to use only the most dedicated, committed, and energetic constituents to participate in volunteer roles during the capital campaign. Choose volunteers who have an interest in supporting the campaign through their own philanthropy. Be prepared to train volunteers in the solicitation process.

Regardless of the size of the organization or the capital campaign, the use of volunteers demands extensive staff time. Volunteers expect the campaign office to tend to their needs and answer their questions in a timely manner, and staff members should anticipate this expectation. Volunteers are a valuable resource, and staff members must treat them with care and respect. The "care and feeding" of volunteers during a capital campaign is an important staff assignment, and staff members should be prepared to spend many hours in this process.

Volunteer Recruitment

Every volunteer in a capital campaign, regardless of the level of assignment, will require formal recruitment. Whenever possible, volunteers should be recruited by the most senior campaign and staff official. In most cases, this will be the CEO of the institution and/or the chief development officer. If people involved in the campaign at lesser levels are sent to recruit major volunteers, the prospective volunteers are likely to dismiss the campaign as an unimportant and unnecessary expenditure of their time.

Recruitment of the senior volunteer leadership such as the campaign vice chair or other committee chairs should always involve the chief executive officer and possibly the campaign chair, reflecting a unified effort of both administration and volunteers. This places the priority of the campaign at the highest level and is an undeniable institutional demonstration of commitment through the campaign.

Many times, the senior development officer of the campaign will accompany the CEO and the campaign chair during the recruitment process. Bringing key volunteers online and engaging them with the campaign are very time-consuming, but extremely important undertakings.

At both Penn State University and the University of Arkansas, the CEO of both institutions recruited every member of the campaign steering committee. This was a huge task that took several months to accomplish, but it was absolutely the right thing to do. Through face-to-face engagement with the CEO or the chief development officer, and in some cases the campaign chair, the volunteers were galvanized and enthused from the beginning.

In larger campaigns with multiple committees and assignments, it may not be practical for the CEO of the organization or even the chair of the campaign to recruit volunteers past the major lead campaign steering committee. It may be necessary for key volunteers and other staff members to recruit volunteers at subcommittee levels. Be certain the recruiters have a full understanding of campaign priorities, volunteer duties, and responsibilities.

I recommend that any person tapped for volunteer leadership at any level receive a recruitment or acknowledgment letter from the CEO and campaign chair, which details the overall recruitment process. Those involved in a campaign must achieve leadership and ownership. Volunteers must take ownership of the campaign and make it their campaign from the very beginning. Every facet of the effort must have the support and encouragement of the volunteer structure.

A Word About Volunteer Campaign Philanthropic Commitments

As previously stated, an important first step for volunteers is to make their own commitment to the campaign, particularly as they begin soliciting others for commitments. Many experts in the field insist that volunteers be solicited even before they are asked to serve on major campaign committees. The thought is that a volunteer will only be as good as his or her commitment to the campaign. If a volunteer commits at a lower level than is appropriate for his or her gift capacity, then it is likely that his or her volunteer work will be similarly unimpressive.[6]

Under this theory, volunteers need to consider a particular-size gift even before they are asked to join the campaign committee.

The theory here seems solid and is difficult to argue against; however, from a practical standpoint, soliciting volunteers before they are heavily involved in the campaign and before they have experienced working with fellow campaign leaders may be a mistake.

Experience has shown that volunteers who have the potential to make major commitments to the institution are more apt to do so only after they are fully entrenched in the campaign and have been convinced that it is an extremely worthwhile effort.

A volunteer's complete confidence early on in the process may not be possible. A better tactic might be to inform the volunteers that they will be called on for a "major gift commitment" at an appropriate time during the campaign. Volunteers should be made to understand that a gift request will be forthcoming early in the campaign, and a gift at a significant level will be expected. Making this entirely clear to the volunteer is not only acceptable but necessary. However, soliciting for a specific dollar amount at this stage of the process is generally not a good idea. What you want are engagement and commitment of time and interest. Commitment of resources will follow.

One further note is important. Holding off on the solicitation until the lead campaign committee has been organized does open the possibility of preemptive gifts. Solicitation should not be delayed too long, because volunteers may preempt the campaign with a smaller gift. However, rushing in with a proposal at the same time the volunteer is being recruited for committee membership is premature and may result in no contribution and no commitment of volunteer time.

The Lead Campaign Volunteer Committee, Other Subcommittees, and Organizational Models

There are numerous ways to organize a volunteer structure for a capital campaign. The following presents several organizational models and volunteer committee structures.

Volunteer Planning Committee

It is recommended that the first committee of volunteers to be organized be a relatively small group of committed individuals who can form a planning committee in the very early stages of planning the campaign. This committee might meet on a monthly or quarterly basis and be composed of persons who not only have philanthropic interest in the organization but who also may occupy senior-level volunteer positions such as chairman of the board, chairman of a supporting foundation organization, or other key volunteers who have leadership positions in the organization. It is best to have people on this committee who have the wherewithal to make major commitments, because they will no doubt be asked to serve on the lead campaign volunteer committee when that committee is formed.

The volunteer planning committee or volunteer planning group should consist of approximately 7 to 12 members. Its function and objectives include:

- Assisting in confirming the organizational plan of the campaign.

- Assisting in establishing the working goal of the campaign.

- Verifying the strategic objectives for campaign funding.

- Assisting with the development of a strong case statement and delineation of campaign objectives on which to base the campaign.

- Establishing a climate of philanthropy and major gift activity with other volunteers, potential benefactors, and the organization at large.

- Helping in the engagement of campaign counsel, if appropriate.

- Confirming issues regarding the planning and feasibility studies and accepting the recommendations from the consulting firm.

- Making early decisions about campaign executive leadership.

- Confirming the need for additional resources and the staffing plan for the campaign.

- Reviewing the names of potential lead volunteer campaign committee members.

- Reviewing the initial list of principal and major gift prospects.

The volunteer planning committee or group should consist of a small number of volunteers who become insiders to the campaign and will help to confirm, lead, guide, and support the early planning stages of the campaign, moving it from planning to implementation.

The Lead Volunteer Committee

I recommend that every capital campaign needs a lead volunteer campaign committee of some type. As has been previously discussed, campaigns will not reach their maximum potential without the use of volunteers from start to finish. The lead campaign volunteer committee provides ongoing volunteer leadership to every aspect of the campaign.

This is the group of volunteers that has been recruited by the chief executive officer of the organization along with the chief development officer and possibly chair of the campaign. These individuals will help to guide and lead the overall effort from inception to conclusion. This committee is generally composed of people who are closely associated with the organization and have been major benefactors in the past. The committee may be composed of members of governing boards, boards of visitors, and affiliated development foundation boards as well as friends, alumni, benefactors, and other persons who have a strong affinity and interest in the welfare of the organization.

In larger organizations, the lead campaign committee may represent certain support groups, units, academic branches, or even campuses. Caution should be taken with this approach, and it is not necessarily recommended. An organization should be looking for the most *capable* and *financially viable* volunteers without regard to which units are represented. It is more important to have a *cohesive* volunteer committee composed of individuals who have the ability and wherewithal to be at a major gift or principal gift level and be able to feel comfortable with their fellow committee members. Committee members who do not have the financial capacity to make a major commitment to the campaign could feel embarrassed or even out of place in their committee membership. The predominant number of volunteers on the lead campaign committee should be of sufficient philanthropic ability so that their level of gift support will not be embarrassing or seem inadequate when compared with other committee members. If instituted correctly, the lead campaign committee will become something of a "club" of people who have come together to support the organization with their time, talents, and resources.

Some professionals would argue that no one should be asked to be on the lead campaign committee who does not have the ability to make a seven-figure gift to the campaign. While this may be impractical for some organizations, it is certainly something to strive for and should cause an organization to choose primarily persons of wealth and influence.

The size of the lead campaign committee will depend a great deal on the organization's constituency base and size. Larger, more complex organizations will often find it necessary to expand the number of committee members perhaps to 50 people and beyond. Some organizations, particularly smaller ones, may find it entirely adequate to hold committee membership to no more than 15 to 20 members. The committee should be small enough so that each member becomes acquainted with his or her fellow committee members. Ideally, they will feel like a team, feel ownership, and work toward a common goal. If the committee becomes too large and cumbersome, this special "club" effect loses strength. The size of the committee depends on the size of the constituency base, major gift prospects, current volunteer organization, and the number of people who do, in fact, have the ability and inclination to make major, principal gifts to the organization. The committee must be composed primarily of wealthy individuals who can make significant high-six and seven-figure gifts to the campaign.

This is not to denigrate smaller contributions or volunteers who do not have financial capacity. There are other ways to use their skills and support, but the lead campaign committee should be composed primarily of the organization's best prospects.

Naming the Lead Campaign Volunteer Committee

There are practically as many names for this lead volunteer committee as there are campaigns. Some of the more successful campaigns across the country have named their lead campaign committees as follows:

- The National Campaign Committee
- The Executive Committee of the Campaign
- The Campaign Steering Committee
- The National Campaign Steering Committee
- The Campaign Leadership Committee

The lead campaign committee should meet on a regular basis during the life of the campaign. Some campaigns call this committee together four times a year, while others bring the lead committee together twice a year. Meeting frequency will have much to do with other levels of the campaign and the engagement of volunteers at those levels.

Duties and Responsibilities

Duties and responsibilities as well as expectations of the lead campaign committee members are as follows:

- The committee consists of friends of the organization from professional, corporate, civic, and philanthropic backgrounds.
- The committee will be asked to attend regular committee meetings, with the potential of additional subcommittee meetings as needed.
- The committee develops and implements strategic planning for the campaign.
- The committee ensures the fulfillment of campaign objectives and particularly helps keep the campaign on track toward meeting the most important strategic objectives of the organization.
- The committee promotes the campaign to the public, and members serve as spokespeople to the wider community, as necessary and appropriate.
- The committee assists in identifying, cultivating, and soliciting gifts to the campaign through personal involvement in garnering resources for the organization.
- The committee reports progress on campaign objectives to the organization at large, including the governing board and other appropriate constituency groups.

- The committee assists in the identification and recruitment of key campaign volunteers at all levels of the campaign.

- The committee members will be knowledgeable about campaign objectives and strategies, the mission and case for support, and the role the campaign plays in the advancement of the organization.

- The committee provides executive leadership to the campaign and guides the effort through its multiyear term.

- Each committee member will be invited to make a significant stretch-gift commitment to the campaign, keeping in mind that gift commitments are always a personal and private decision of the committee member, his or her spouse, and family. It is hoped, however, that lead committee members will make the largest gift possible to assist the organization in advancing the goals of the campaign.

Campaign Executive Committee

Depending on the size of the lead campaign committee, it may be necessary to create a smaller working group to meet on a more regular basis. This executive committee could consist of the officers of the campaign, appropriate staff members, the CEO, and perhaps campaign committee chairs of the various subcommittees. The executive committee will guide the campaign on a regular basis and serve as a sounding board for major campaign decisions. The executive committee will have the authority to act on behalf of the lead campaign committee. An organization might even consider moving the early campaign planning committee into this role. Certainly, some members of the early planning committee should be members of the executive committee for the sake of continuity.

The Honorary Campaign Committee

Persons close to the organization may want to participate in some way with the campaign, but they may be unable to do so because of physical impairment, inability to make meetings, geographic location, or other reasons that would deny their ongoing participation. Forming a campaign honorary committee will keep these persons involved and informed about campaign progress and serve as a way to recognize a distinct group of benefactors who are interested in the institution but are unable to participate on a regular basis.

The honorary committee can also serve as a mechanism to recognize government officials, heads of support organizations, and other important individuals who may not have the ability to make a major campaign commitment but who occupy a special role of importance in the organization.

Some campaigns will treat honorary committee members the same way they treat other committee members, inviting them to meetings and dealing with them as full-fledged committee members. In the alternative, some institutions will deal with the honorary committee separately.

It is also possible to simply name individuals honorary members of the overall lead committee. In a sense, this vests them with an honorary title but allows them to have the same duties and responsibilities as full-committee members.

Campaign Organizational Models

A plethora of volunteer organizational models exist across the country. Some smaller campaigns may depend exclusively on the lead campaign committee, breaking that committee into subcommittees for certain duties and responsibilities. In larger, more diverse organizations, two or three levels of subcommittees may handle myriad responsibilities by geographic regions, by donor level, or even by a professional categorization (doctors, lawyers, engineers, etc.).

What is most important to keep in mind is that every committee inaugurated within a campaign should have a definitive goal and set of objectives. A campaign should not organize a committee unless it has definitive objectives in mind. Volunteers need to know specifically what is expected of their respective committee, and they need to know when they have completed their task and been successful. Every committee should have a task plan and a definitive purpose *before* the committee is organized. The campaign committee should not be recruited until there are definitive plans and tasks assigned to those committees. Campaign committee membership should not be impaneled and organized until the campaign has reached the point where there are goals and objectives for that respective committee.

Organizing subcommittees or special committees without specific tasks will only lead to widespread confusion in the campaign. Volunteers will feel the campaign is not progressing and that they have been asked to participate but given no duties or responsibilities. Refrain from organizing any committee that does not have a task plan and a definitive set of objectives. A campaign committee that has been given no purpose for its existence should not exist.

Many campaigns operate subcommittees under the overall lead campaign committee. Again, this will depend on the scope and size of the organization, the number of prospects, sophistication of the organization and the volunteers, and the size of the volunteer network. There are certainly many advantages in forming subcommittees, for they can give definition to the campaign and the organizational structure. Organizing subcommittees into geographic regions, gift levels, and functional areas helps to maintain a tightly controlled organizational structure and can assist institutions—both large and small—in moving the effort forward with deliberate speed.

The other side of the coin is that multiple subcommittees can also lead to confusion and unnecessary disbursement of staff. Again, the most important element is to be certain that each subcommittee has a definitive task plan and purpose for existence. It is also absolutely vital that each subcommittee have a staff member assigned to serve the committee and assist it with its objectives and goals. Leaving volunteers to fend for themselves without proper staff assistance and support will doom the committees to failure in most cases. The subcommittees will want to be given maximum staff support and feel there are professional staff members working alongside them to achieve their goals and objectives. If an organization does not have adequate staff to serve the various committees, then the staff either needs to be increased or the subcommittee disbanded or never formed in the first place.

Decide early in the campaign how to organize the volunteer committee structure. Volunteers must be able to understand where their committee assignment fits into the overall organizational structure of the campaign, and this structure must be explainable and defensible as well as operational to one's constituency. An organizational structure that is confusing and overly complex wastes volunteer and staff time. I recommend that organizations maintain a tightly controlled committee structure and avoid creating a profusion of committees and subcommittees that have no real operating plan or objective.

A plethora of organizational structures and models commonly exist in capital campaigns. Keep in mind that many campaigns across the country use various parts of each of the models that will be presented in the following pages. These models are presented as potential models for your structure and should be considered recommendations from which an organization can pick and choose the best model or models to fit its own particular circumstances, volunteer network, and needs.

Gift-Level Model

The gift-level model creates committees according to the size of the gift solicited. Solicitations are generally performed sequentially, with the largest gifts solicited first and then down the ladder until the annual fund level has been achieved. Subcommittees under the gift-level model are based solely on gift size and do not take into consideration the type of prospect being solicited (i.e., corporate, individual, foundation, association.) Three distinct subcommittee types are presented under this model:

Principal Advance Gifts Subcommittee. Members of the principal advance gifts committee participate in solicitation at the highest gift level in the campaign. These persons solicit gift commitments before the public announcement of the campaign at significant six-and-seven figure levels. Generally, principal gifts can be defined as those at the $250,000 minimum level and above. The committee is responsible for seeking the largest gifts in the campaign from the most generous and influential benefactors of the organization.

Generally, this subcommittee is composed of a small group of principal gift benefactors who can solicit their peers at the highest possible level. The advanced principal gifts committee does not cease existing after the public announcement of the campaign, but continues to operate through the life of the effort.

Ten to 15 years ago, most professionals believed that 80 percent of the contributions to a capital campaign came from fewer than 20 percent of the donors. These numbers have changed rather dramatically, and it is now standard practice to see many campaigns where 95 percent of the contributions come from fewer than 5 percent of the donors. *Campaigns are finding in increasing numbers that the small-knit group of principal gift benefactors will make or break any campaign. Thus, this committee is vitally important to the successful operation of the campaign. As goes the advanced principal gifts committee, so goes the campaign!*

The principal gifts committee should be chaired by an individual who will make a major commitment himself or herself and is a highly respected volunteer. There is no doubt that this committee is the most important committee in reaching the goal and declaring campaign success.

Major Gifts Committee. This committee is charged with seeking gifts that typically would fall below the principal advance gifts phase of $250,000. Many of the gifts in this area will be at the $50,000 to $100,000 level, all the way up to the $250,000 level. This committee's work will continue throughout the life of the campaign.

Committee membership should be composed of persons who are most comfortable with this level of giving. Often, the major gifts committee is a separate level of the campaign and is composed of persons who do not sit on the lead campaign committee. (The theory is that members of the lead campaign committee should be contributing at the principal gifts level.)

Annual Fund Committee. As noted previously, it is most important to continue the annual fund component of the ongoing development program, even during the life of the capital campaign. Many persons closely associated with the organization may not have the wherewithal or inclination to make a major gift to the capital campaign, but will want to continue to give to the organization on an annual basis. The annual fund committee finds ways to involve these persons continually in the life of the organization as well as the campaign. As also was previously mentioned, care should be taken that this committee not seek preemptive gifts from individuals who do, in fact, have the capacity to make larger capital commitments over a multiyear period.

Functional Model

Some campaigns are organized around functional models rather than gift levels. Many campaigns organize their efforts using both a gift model and a functional model.

The functional model, unlike the gift model, concentrates on the origin of the gift. In other words, it looks to the classification of the donor and organizes around that classification (e.g., friend, board member, campaign committee member, alumnus, corporation, foundation, staff members).

Although every committee should be concerned with the dollar level of any particular solicitation, the functional model is concerned more with the entity that is being solicited as the common denominator. Principal and major gifts can still be solicited from persons, corporations, and foundations assigned to the functional model committees, and volunteers and staff should always be conscious of the gift level in any solicitation. Types of functional models are:

Leadership Gifts Committee. Some campaigns will form what might be called a "leadership gifts" committee. The responsibility of this committee is to seek gifts from the volunteer leadership of the campaign as well as the organization.

This committee should solicit every member of the lead campaign committee as well as other subcommittees as organized. The leadership gifts committee should broaden its responsibility to solicit the governing board of the organization as well as other significant advisory boards and constituent units. The committee is so named because it solicits commitments from the leadership volunteers of the institution. Campaign leaders must show strong support by contributing their own personal resources, and this committee is charged with the responsibility of obtaining these gifts from volunteers to the organization.

The primary work of this committee should be completed before the public announcement of the campaign. It is hoped and expected that the leadership gifts committee will receive 100 percent participation from lead campaign committee members as well as from governing board members.

Corporate and Foundation Gifts Committee. This committee is charged with the responsibility of soliciting gifts from corporations and foundations. Although the committee should be concerned with gift levels as just stated and solicit gifts sequentially, its functioning purpose is to concentrate on the area of corporations and foundations.

Care should be taken to recruit candidates for membership on this committee who are knowledgeable about corporate and foundation giving as well as those who have real clout in the corporate community. In the Campaign for the Twenty-First Century at the University of Arkansas, the chair of the world's largest protein producer, Tyson Foods, Inc., chaired the corporate and foundation gifts committee. Members of his committee included the president and chief executive officer of the world's largest corporation, Wal-Mart, Incorporated, and the senior chair as well as president and chief executive officer of a major national trucking firm, J. B. Hunt Transport, Inc. These are people of real clout who opened many doors to the university and the campaign.

Individual Gifts Committee. Some campaigns will choose to organize their volunteers by appointing them to a subcommittee for individual gifts. In a sense, an argument could be made that this is just another name for the principal gifts committee or major gifts committee. Basically, the campaign that organizes with an individual gift committee has made a decision to solicit all individuals at a major level under this organizational model. Generally speaking, individual gifts committees are formed in much smaller campaigns with much smaller bases of prospects.

Planned Gifts Committee. Some campaigns will form a planned gifts committee to concentrate on planned giving techniques, including charitable remainder trusts, gift annuities, life insurance, pooled income funds, gifts of property, wills, trusts, and life estates.

This may be more of an advisory committee than a solicitation committee. If the planned gift committee is a soliciting committee, there will be great overlap between this committee and the individual gifts committee, because volunteers have no way of knowing when individuals may want to use a deferred-giving technique as their commitment to the campaign. Care should be taken that this committee does not confuse volunteers in the solicitation process.

If an organization has a sophisticated planned giving staff, there may be advantages to creating a planned gifts committee that would work closely with professional staff in this defined area.

Communications Committee. All of the committees discussed thus far are designed to be involved in the solicitation and cultivation of prospects. It is often necessary to form other committees that do not have solicitation and cultivation goals. One such committee may be a communications committee. The purpose of a communications committee is to work with staff to create a solid communications plan for the campaign (e.g., campaign publications, campaign announcements, campaign gala events, and all internal and external communications.) Such a committee was formed during Pennsylvania State University's first campaign, from 1984 to 1990. It was headed by a renowned executive of Johnson & Johnson who was in charge of the corporation's communications programs. His expertise and support were most helpful as the campaign formed and implemented a communications plan.

In the most recent Campaign for the Twenty-First Century at the University of Arkansas, the decision was made to have staff members perform the communications function without a volunteer committee.

If your campaign does decide to form a volunteer communications committee, you must be prepared to listen to the advice of volunteers and respond appropriately. Be absolutely certain that you want your volunteers to be advising your organization on ongoing communications issues.

Geographic Model

Those institutions with large constituencies in multiple locations may want to consider a geographic model that creates volunteer committees on either a regional or major city basis. One advantage of the geographic model is that it uses volunteers to make calls on prospects living in their locale. Some experts believe that prospects are far more likely to respond to committee members in their locale if they know the individuals and feel a sense of community.[7]

Care should be taken in creating geographic regions that the regions be manageable. Regions can be so large that the area is cumbersome and unmanageable and thus impractical when attempting to solicit major gift prospects. Regional volunteer chairs should reside within a radius that allows for easy travel.

Managing a large network of committees with multiple volunteers and multiple regions and cities requires a tremendous amount of staff time and follow up and can be a most difficult process. It is only recommended for a sophisticated development shop with large national constituencies and large staffs that have the ability to cover regional assignments.

One potential compromise for organizations that do, in fact, want to implement a regional approach to their campaigns is to organize geographic volunteer committees in a limited number of major cities where there is a high constituency base. This strategy would create a volunteer chair and regional committee in a small number of major cities where there are high concentrations of major gift prospects. Certainly, this suggestion will not cover every prospect, but it will give the campaign a sense of national breadth and scope.

The first campaign at Penn State used 14 regional committees. They were spread all across the United States. Frankly, some operated better than others, while some didn't operate at all! It was a cumbersome model that presented many difficulties and sapped important staff time.

During the Campaign for the Twenty-First Century at the University of Arkansas, a decision was made to create better-defined regions in a relatively small number of cities with high concentrations of alumni. It proved to be the proper decision and was many times more manageable.

Academic Unit Model

Academic institutions with multiple colleges may want to consider creating volunteer committees by academic units. For large multicampus institutions that have launched capital campaigns to benefit the entire system, this model will be built around campuses. For single institutions, the model may be built around colleges and schools. Volunteers are organized into committees for each of these academic units.

Organizing committees around academic units in colleges and universities can be cumbersome and difficult to manage, but it probably is the preferred way of involving the academic leadership of an institution. Care should be taken that the academic model does not break down the campaign into competing fiefdoms and allows for a cohesive, systematic approach to major gift fund raising. Also, care should be taken that the campaign does not become a series of multiple campaigns. It should sustain a unified approach that promotes the entire university toward common objectives and maintains control of major gift prospects without a free-for-all among competing deans and development officers.

A prospect management system is the best way to manage an academic unit model. Pulling some of the principal and major gift prospects for central control and action will be necessary and is advised.

The models above should not be viewed as mutually exclusive. Campaigns generally blend all of the models in an attempt to form the best possible organizational structure.

Role of the Campaign Chair

The campaign chair is a critically important position to the campaign. As Robert Krit writes, "Obviously, the campaign chair should be someone who holds a high position in the business or social life of the community, but this in itself is not sufficient. The general chair must have the willingness and the time to work. A prominent name on a letterhead alone will not attract support."[8]

Generally, the campaign chair is an individual who has had a strong affinity to the organization and has already been a major benefactor. Organizations should look to individuals who have a passion for the mission and goals of their organization and should find someone who has already exhibited major interest in the nonprofit.

There are many elements that come together to create the ultimate campaign chair. Organizations may want to look to an individual with the credentials of a chair, president, or chief executive officer of a nationally respected company. The CEO of a major company has the advantage of a staff readily available to assist in a multitude of campaign arrangements.

Some campaigns have chosen individuals who are retired from their CEO position and, many times, they make excellent campaign chairs. However, an institution should keep in mind that a CEO's clout is diminished considerably upon retirement, and though the individual may have time to give to the campaign, he or she may have reduced leverage with major gift prospects, particularly in the corporate sphere.

Professionals such as doctors, lawyers, engineers, accountants, and money managers can make good campaign chairs if they are willing to devote the time and effort to the process. Many professionals' income levels depend entirely on their own personal billable hours, and they may not be willing to expend time on behalf of the organization if it means income loss.

The chair of the campaign should have good public speaking ability. He or she will be called on countless times in large group settings to galvanize and motivate campaign volunteers and staff members. The chair will be a major spokesperson for the campaign, and the individual who occupies this special role should be at ease with a microphone as well as comfortable in responding to tough questions from the media.

The campaign chair should be an individual who is respected by fellow committee members. The chair must be a leader and someone who other committee members are willing to follow. The committee chair must a hard driver, but this should be tempered with an ingratiating style and sense of inclusion of all committee members.

The campaign chair should be an individual who stimulates interest and enthusiasm for the entire campaign. His or her time must be devoted to policy decisions and the cultivation and solicitation of major gift commitments to the campaign. The chair will help to inspire and persuade members of the campaign committee to carry out their responsibilities thoroughly and promptly and should be a person who *leads by personal philanthropic example.*

The chair sets the tone for major campaign commitments, and if it is perceived that the campaign chair has made less than a stretch commitment, it can be damaging to the campaign's ability to garner other major gifts from committee members.

The campaign chair:

- Accepts executive responsibility for the overall successful completion of the campaign;

- Presides at all meetings of the lead campaign committee and the executive committee and is involved in every aspect of the planning and implementation of campaign objectives;

- Reports progress to the governing board of the organization as well as to campaign support groups;

- Endorses and represents the campaign goals and plans and is the primary spokesperson for the campaign along with the CEO;

- Speaks publicly on the campaign's behalf to the media and to the institution's various constituencies;

- Remains heavily involved in the advanced gift phase of the campaign in soliciting major gifts for the effort; and

- Makes a personal lead gift that is seen as inspirational and transformational to the organization.

The campaign chair must appropriate enormous energy and enthusiasm and must dedicate himself or herself to leading the campaign throughout its life. The campaign chairperson will be pivotal to the success of the effort.

Consideration of Multiple Campaign Chairs

In recent years, a number of campaigns have tapped campaign chair leadership by involving multiple persons in a leadership capacity. Often they are called presiding cochairs, and they have a definitive term whereby they preside over the committee meetings.

In the most recent Campaign for the Twenty-First Century at the University of Arkansas, the campaign used the services of four presiding cochairs. The first was S. Robson Walton, chairman of the board of Wal-Mart Stores, Inc. He was followed by Tommy Boyer, owner and chief executive officer of Micro Images. Mr. Boyer was followed by Jim Walton, chairman and chief executive officer of Arvest Bank Group, Inc. Mr. Walton was followed by Coach Frank Broyles, long-time athletic director and football coach at the university. This model worked extremely well and allowed for variety while maintaining continuity.

As was previously pointed out, it is difficult to involve volunteers for long periods of time. Asking an individual to sign on as chair of a major capital campaign for a five- to seven-year term is a huge commitment. By spreading this responsibility among several persons, your organization might be able to attract a number of high-level executives and professionals to serve in leadership capacities if they know they will not be called on exclusively and for a multiple-year period.

Job descriptions for the campaign chair can be found on the "Campaign Tools" CD.

Role of the Campaign Vice Chair

Some campaigns may want to use the title of campaign vice chair as a way to elevate certain committee members to special status. It is also important to have an individual in this capacity who can serve in the absence of the campaign chair should that become necessary at certain campaign meetings and events.

It is also possible for campaign vice chairs to head major subcommittees of the campaign.

Role of the Campaign Treasurer

The volunteer position of campaign treasurer can be a most important way to involve a volunteer benefactor in the life of the campaign. While treasurer reports are generally created by the campaign staff, the campaign treasurer can deliver the reports at all campaign meetings. The campaign treasurer can send out monthly reports to various volunteers as well as the governing board and other constituent boards, updating your organization's constituency on campaign progress.

Creating a position of campaign treasurer is another way to involve a volunteer in campaign responsibilities. This position was used for both the campaign for Penn State and the Campaign for the Twenty-First Century at the University of Arkansas. In both cases, the individuals occupying that position made gifts to the campaign totaling over $15 million each.

It can be a significant way to involve volunteers in the campaign.

Role of the Governing Board

The role of the governing board in the capital campaign will depend, to a large extent, on the type of institution that is conducting the campaign.

The governing board of a nonprofit organization or independent institution is often composed of individuals who have the potential to make major philanthropic commitments to the organization. The governing board may be an excellent source of campaign committee members, and these governing board members should be tapped for volunteer activity as appropriate. If governing board representatives serve in a volunteer campaign capacity, it will heighten the awareness, interest, and importance of the campaign not only among those on the governing board but also the entire organization as well as the public at large.

In public institutions, the governing board is often formed through political appointments, and the board members may have little or no interest in philanthropic endeavors.

Regardless of the type of institution—public or private—the governing board should show full support of the fund-raising effort by endorsing the campaign with a board resolution early in the public phase of the capital campaign. The CEO will want to keep the governing board fully apprised of campaign objectives. It is also advisable to solicit the governing board, though some members of the board of a public organization may not be able to make a major commitment. Certainly, a board member can make some level of commitment appropriate to his or her financial circumstances.

I recommend a recent book by Robert Zimmerman and Anne Lehman, published by Jossey-Bass and titled *Boards that Love Fund Raising: A How-to Guide for Your Board,* for those interested in governing board leadership and a governing board's fund-raising responsibilities. The book identifies specific fund-raising responsibilities of governing boards including financial contributions; solicitation of friends, relatives, and colleagues; and oversight of the organization's fund-raising efforts.

Development Support Groups

Many organizations already have volunteer groups in place before launching a capital campaign. These volunteer groups may be titled development councils, boards of visitors, development advisory boards, or perhaps foundation boards. In large public universities, the foundation board may have legal authority over gift assets of the institution. The foundation board may operate as a development governing board, and a chief executive officer of the foundation often is the chief development officer of the institution.

Many of these groups are legal entities created by the institution to serve as conduits for private gifts, and they may, in fact, literally guide and direct all aspects of the development program. The foundation board may, indeed, be the unit that gives authority to a campaign lead committee, and in some cases, it may become the lead committee itself. Care should be taken to ascertain there is a clear delineation of responsibilities among the various constituency volunteer groups. It is certainly possible that an advisory development board, council, or foundation may coexist with a campaign lead committee, and ways should be found to deal with all of the support groups during the life of the capital campaign.

Campaign organizational charts and campaign roles and responsibilities can be found on the "Campaign Tools" CD.

Various Campaign Volunteer Meetings

Questions that seem to dominate many discussions with development officers include: "What do we do at volunteer committee meetings? What are the agenda items of those meetings? Do they really have an important purpose, or are volunteer committee meetings just window dressing?"

There will be many opportunities for volunteers to meet both formally and informally during the life of the campaign. For the formal occasion, predominantly business meetings, development staff members are advised to use tailored agendas that cover all of the various items that need to be discussed at the committee meeting. Without firm agendas, the meetings can quickly move off track, and lack of agenda is an easy way to allow less well-informed volunteers to move the meeting in a totally different direction. Always have written agendas for any campaign committee meeting at any level.

This book has already discussed a number of different types of volunteer committee meetings. A quick review of them might be helpful:

- **Precampaign Briefing Sessions in preparation for a Feasibility Study.** These are meetings where volunteers and benefactors will be called together to discuss the campaign feasibility study that will be taking place very soon. It is a time to inform key persons of the coming campaign provided the study is positive.

- **Campaign Planning Committee or Group.** As previously stated, this small group of campaign volunteers began the process of guiding and leading the campaign early on in the process.

- **Lead Campaign Committee Meetings.** These are the meetings of the lead campaign committee and should be held on a regular basis.

- **Subcommittees by Gift Level, Geographic Region, Functional Model, Academic Unit Model.** These subcommittees will meet regularly to discuss the various responsibilities of each committee and the involvement of volunteers and the duties and responsibilities.

- **Social Occasions for Building Consensus and Support.** Be certain to involve volunteers in social occasions built around committee meetings. This is an excellent way to build camaraderie and consensus and allow committee members to get to know one another in an informal social setting. It is a very important way to build loyalty and support.

- **Prospect Identification and Screening Meetings.** There will be many opportunities for volunteers to help in the identification of prospects through appropriate screening sessions.

- **Announcement of Major Gifts.** For those principal gifts that are truly record breaking, it may be necessary to hold a press conference or general public announcement. This is a good time to bring together volunteers to hear the exciting news about campaign progress.

- **Campaign Gala Events.** Launching campaign efforts with gala events and finishing them with concluding events are excellent ways to energize volunteers and donors and capture their attention for worthwhile projects.

The above are just a few of the opportunities to conduct meetings and social gatherings for campaign volunteers.

Typical Volunteer Agenda Items

Typical lead campaign agenda items might be the following:
- Call to order
- Greeting and approval of the minutes
- Introduction of committee members
- Discussion of campaign timetable
- Campaign treasurer's report
- Introduction of campaign officers

- Discussion of campaign plan and organizational structure
- CEO's or chairman's of the campaign charge to the lead campaign committee
- Video presentation about the needs of the organization
- Benchmarking information about campaigns of other competing organizations
- Gift range chart and the importance of the chart to the campaign
- Discussion of campaign goal
- Progress report on special gifts to the campaign and announcement of gifts from committee members
- Video on campaign highlights
- Various committee chair reports such as corporations and foundations, regional committees, constituent-based committees, planned giving, annual giving, principal gifts committee, major gifts committee, leadership gifts committee, etc.
- Discussion of meeting the campaign objectives (not just the campaign dollar goal)
- Introduction of new staff personnel
- Special presentation by organization executives, faculty, students, or others benefiting from campaign gifts
- Special presentation on the importance of endowment
- Special presentation on projects contained within the campaign strategic objectives
- Discussion of what counts toward campaign totals
- Discussion of proposed campaign public announcement
- Discussion of resetting the goal

The above are some of the myriad agenda items that can be included in a lead campaign committee meeting.

Agenda items have been included on the "Campaign Tools" CD for the Campaign for the Twenty-First Century to show the evolution of the agenda items throughout the life of the campaign.

Notes for Chapter 5

1. Wallys W. Conhaim, "Virtual Volunteering," *Information Today* 20, no. 3 (March 2003): 27.

2. "Volunteer Management Capacity in America's Charities and Congregations: A Briefing Report." Washington, DC: Urban Institute, 2004.

3. Ibid.

4. Cassie Moore, "Charities Must Learn to Better Manage Volunteers, Study Finds," *The Chronicle of Philanthropy* (March 18, 2004).

5. Richard J. Pokrass, *CASE Currents*, April, 1986.

6. Richard Fox, "Your Partnership with Power People," *CASE Currents* 10, no. 20 (November/December 1984): 43.

7. Robert L. Krit, *The Fund-Raising Handbook*. (The United States of America: Scott Foresman Professional Books, 1991), 13.

8. Ibid., 35.

Campaign Details

Having gained, in a right sense, all you can, and saved all you can, in spite of nature, and custom and world prudence, give all you can.

John Wesley

Capital campaigns are enormously time consuming and complex undertakings. Good planning, with detailed policies and procedures, will help keep things from falling apart midway though the campaign. This chapter is designed to discuss the details that are critical to campaign success.

Amount Raised Before Public Announcement

Most professionals agree that a capital campaign should never be publicly announced without a major percentage of the goal already committed. Announcing a goal before a significant amount has been raised can doom the entire campaign to failure.

Some professionals will argue that at least 50 to 60 percent of a goal should be committed in gifts and pledges before the public announcement. While this is an admirable suggestion and can certainly serve as a good guideline, it may be impractical. In these days of media attention and instantaneous communication, it may be difficult to hold off on a public announcement until the campaign totals have reached 50 to 60 percent of the goal.

The real question is not so much the amount of the goal that has been committed, as the level of prospects who have the ability and inclination to make gifts and pledges to complete the entire campaign goal. In other words, as a development professional, you should want to be certain that any campaign goal that you set is entirely reasonable and attainable. Setting an unreasonable goal from the beginning creates nervousness and anxiety on behalf of volunteers and benefactors. This is not to say that the goal should be set so low that there is no room for individuals to stretch their giving, but it is important that development professionals have a fairly good sense that the goal is achievable with hard work and determination.

Perhaps a more practical aim is to achieve somewhere between one-third and one-half of the goal in pledges and commitments before announcing the campaign publicly. This is a respectable figure that shows forward momentum as well as the ability of the organization to attract major commitments.

While some may argue that a higher percentage needs to be achieved before public announcement, caution should be exercised in sending a signal to the public as well as to other potential benefactors that the achievement of the goal is too easy and has not been set high enough. This could, in fact, cause donors to lower their sights in terms of their own campaign giving. It is never wise to give benefactors and volunteers the feeling that the achievement of the goal will not require a stretch commitment on their part.

If the feasibility planning study has indicated the dollar goal you are announcing is achievable, if you can see clear to a number of major and principal gift prospects that most likely will occur, and if you have a volunteer committee or committees taking ownership and moving the campaign forward, and you have a CEO, governing board, and other senior officers of the organization who are committed to the campaign, then announcing the capital campaign once you have completed somewhere between one-third and one-half of the goal is certainly acceptable.

Creating the Campaign Budget

How many times have you heard the phrase, "You have to spend money to make money?" Well, get ready to hear it again! Capital campaigns are costly. If you are organizing the campaign the correct way, you are going to spend resources. Capital campaigns are doomed to failure when senior administrators refuse to recognize that the campaign will cost money. It is simply not possible to run the effort without an infusion of resources over and above the normal operating budget of a development office. Just count on it. Campaigns are expensive!

For some reason, this can be a difficult concept to sell to CEOs and chief financial officers. Unfortunately, there seems to be a proclivity toward asking development personnel to produce revenue but not expend it. It may be a vestige of the past when development officers and fund raisers were not considered to be in the organization's main stream, and fund-raising duties and responsibilities were added on to other assignments.

So just exactly what will it cost to run the capital campaign?

In previous chapters, we discussed the importance of conducting a planning study early in the campaign to determine the level of budget and staffing required to undertake the campaign. In fact, some consulting firms refuse to perform an external feasibility study until an internal planning study has been undertaken and concluded. One such firm is Grenzebach Glier and Associates, which believes that issues of budget and staffing are just as important and equally as critical as issues of external support capacity.

Many attempts have been made to quantify as well as qualify fund-raising costs. Most experts agree general fund-raising costs that begin to exceed 25 percent of the revenue produced are starting to be considered high expenditures. While it is difficult to make broad statements about fund-raising costs, most professionals agree that average fund-ranging costs across the country are approximately 20 cents to raise one dollar. The Council of Better Business Bureaus states that fund-raising expenses exceeding 35 percent are excessive.[1]

Principals of Grenzebach Glier and Associates have maintained for some time that fund-raising costs for major organizations such as major research colleges and universities or large agencies should keep capital campaign costs as well as overall fund-raising costs below 10 percent of the funds raised. The Association of Fund Raising Counsel recommends that capital campaign costs stay between 5 and 10 cents per dollar raised.[2]

A more reliable way to get a handle on fund-raising costs is to review a list of those items requiring an appropriation of funds for adequate coverage in the campaign. The following is a partial listing of major capital campaign expenses:

- **Additional Staff Costs.** As previously noted, there are a number of staffing issues that will need to be addressed in a capital campaign. Certain services must be covered for the normal operation of the campaign, and your institution should be ready and willing to add appropriate staff in a number of key areas in contemplation of a campaign.

- **Travel Budgets.** It is not unusual to expect a 50 to 100 percent increase in travel budgets, particularly the first two to three years of the campaign operation. Impaneling campaign committees and soliciting principal and major gifts will all require extra expenditures.

- **Volunteer Implementation Costs.** Funds will be needed for the ongoing cultivation of volunteers. Volunteer meetings will take place throughout the life of the campaign, and they will inevitably bring additional social event costs.

- **Donor-Relation Costs.** Donor-recognition costs climb markedly, particularly during the final stages of the campaign.

- **Publication Costs.** Campaign publications, including the campaign brochure and periodic public reports, require additional resources for the development office.

- **Consultant Fees.** If you decide to hire outside counsel, there may be considerable costs in engaging the services of a consulting firm. In addition to campaign consultants, you may need to employ the services of planned giving experts, which may add attorney and consultant fees throughout the life of the campaign.

- **Administrative Services Costs and Database Management.** The cost of upgrading a record system in anticipation of a capital campaign is costly—not just in terms of resources but in staff time as well.

- **Kickoff and Concluding Events.** A campaign kickoff and concluding event are not only time consuming from a staff standpoint, but also quite costly. Funds must be appropriated, as needed, for these two important campaign events.

- **Staff Training and Volunteer Training Sessions.** It may be necessary to hold training sessions for major gift fund raising for staff as well as volunteers.

- **Video and Publication Costs.** Campaign videos and publications, including the lead campaign brochure and periodic reports to constituents, will require additional resources for the campaign office.

- **Telephone, Supplies, Equipment, Furnishings, Printing, Postage.** Expect increases in normal administrative costs as the campaign moves into reality.

- **Entertainment and Cultivation Costs.** In addition to travel increases, expect an increase in the cost of cultivation of major gifts prospects, including meals and entertainment. These costs have risen dramatically in recent years, and allowances should be made for these increased costs.

- **Electronic Screening of Constituency Base.** Depending on the size of a campaign's constituency, electronic screening from major gift prospects can be a considerable cost.

- **Campaign Volunteer Screening Meetings for Prospects.** Depending on the size and scope of the organization, the number of volunteer screening sessions can add a sizeable cost to a campaign budget.

- **Campaign Feasibility/Planning Study.** The costs of undertaking feasibility planning studies can be considerable.

- **Advertisement and Promotion.** As previously discussed, the campaign may want to run a series of advertisements in local statewide and regional media outlets. These costs can be considerable.

For sheer emphasis, it is important to state again that capital campaigns do not run themselves. They are extraordinary undertakings, requiring time commitment and resource commitment. If your organization tries to "do it on the cheap," you will simply get what you pay for!

Financing the Capital Campaign

Nonprofit organizations use a variety of techniques to fund their development or fund-raising operations. As previously stated, additional levels of support will be needed for a comprehensive campaign, and organizations may want to look at different ways to fund the capital campaign.

The following are a number of alternatives for funding capital campaigns:

Line Item in the Organization's Budget

Many nonprofits fund their development operation and capital campaign directly from their institutional budget. Since the development operation of the institution is considered to be a mainstream obligation of the organization, many have chosen to fund the operation just as the institution would fund any other main functional area. This treats the development program and the capital campaign as any other important administrative unit to the organization and budgets for its operation and personnel as an ongoing operating unit of the institution.

Endowment Earnings

A number of organizations use a portion of their endowment earnings to help finance their fund raising and capital campaign operations. Basically, the organization takes a percentage or, in most cases, basis points of the earnings of the endowment for certain fund-raising costs. This method of financing fund-raising programs and new capital campaign expenditures is fairly popular among those organizations that have large endowments. Nonprofit endowment funds regularly use a percentage of the return on investments to compensate portfolio managers as well as to pay for expenditures related to the management of the endowment. Using these funds to increase the endowment principal is also a justifiable expense.

Caution should be observed in some jurisdictions where state laws regulate the use of endowment income for fund-raising expenses.

Unrestricted Gifts

Many organizations use unrestricted, undesignated gift funds to finance a portion of their capital campaign. Colleges and universities, in particular, use unrestricted annual gifts to fund their development operations on a regular basis. Since these funds have been given to the organization with "no strings attached," there should be no legal restrictions on using the revenue to pay for fund-raising costs (provided the costs are legitimate and appropriate expenditures).

Gift Tax

For lack of a better description, a number of institutions charge a gift tax to finance fund raising. Benefactors typically do not look upon gift taxes favorably. Generally, benefactors want to know that 100 percent of their gift is being expended on the project of their interest, while staff want to be able to expend all of the gift, with overhead being deducted. This method of financing fund raising is probably the least desirable and can be met in some jurisdictions with legal restrictions.

Gift "Float"

Some organizations deliberately hold funds that might otherwise be designated to particular units of the organization for expenditure for as long as 90 days or beyond. During those holding periods, the organization invests the funds and uses the interest to help finance development operations. This "float" can provide substantial resources to help defray fund-raising costs. While the term is generally in the 30- to 90-day period, some organizations will even take a float of six months to a year.

Unrestricted Bequests

With increasing frequency, organizations are placing unrestricted bequests in a special endowment fund for the purpose of financing the fund-raising program. This provides a longer-term solution for funding development operations, and once such a fund has built to a substantial level, the income can help defray much of the development operation cost.

Some organizations are also taking a major percentage of unrestricted bequests off the top and using it for fund-raising costs. At the University of Arkansas, any unrestricted or undesignated bequests will have 25 percent taken from the bequest and moved into a special fund for development operations.

The Gift Range Chart

Most campaigns develop a gift range chart early in campaign planning, which is designed to show the number of gifts required at certain levels in order to reach the goal. In other words, how many gifts of $1 million will be needed to achieve a goal of $100 million? How many gifts of $500,000 will be required?

But how does an institution know how many gifts it can attract at these various levels of the gift range chart?

A gift range chart should not be created in a vacuum. Rather, it should be tied to an institution's prospect management program. The number of legitimate prospects an institution has will have a significant impact on the creation of the gift range chart. If you create such a chart that indicates you need at least 10 gifts of $1 million to achieve your goal, do you have information based in reality to suggest that there may, in fact, be at least 10 people who will make $1 million gifts?

The number of prospects needed for the achievement of a gift in a particular category is the subject of some debate. Some professionals suggest that a rule of three is appropriate, but I believe that a rule of five is more feasible. In other words, for every $1 million contribution an organization hopes to receive, they will need at least five viable prospects to achieve that one donation.

Therefore, the conclusion can be drawn that to achieve 10 $1 million gifts in a capital campaign, it will be necessary to have a minimum of 40 to 50 viable prospects who have the potential and inclination to contribute at this level.

Obviously, development officials must labor in reality when creating the gift range chart. A number of years ago, the *New Yorker* magazine ran a cartoon in which several volunteers were sitting around a table planning a benefit. They were trying to determine how many tickets they would need to sell to raise $100,000. One volunteer explained, "I've got a good idea, let's sell one ticket for $100,000!"

If the gift range chart is tied to the prospect management program, then there is some scientific basis on which to assume gifts may fall along the lines of the chart. A carefully crafted gift range chart helps an institution track its progress toward achievement of the goal.

Using the previously stated estimate that 95 percent of the campaign gift totals will come from fewer than 5 percent of the contributors, it is easy to understand the importance of a gift range chart. The critical importance of principal and major gifts to a campaign can quickly be understood. The actual number of gifts necessary to achieve a very high percentage of the total goal will be quite low. The campaign will be made or broken by a relatively small cluster of principal and major gifts.

This concept is sometimes difficult for volunteers who have not been involved in major capital campaigns to understand. They tend to focus on the number rather than the quality of prospects.The gift range chart is essentially a campaign management tool used to show progress toward the stated goal. Naturally, it is a fluid document that may change during the life of the campaign, but it can be very helpful when the chart is exposed to major benefactors who then start to seek the level where they believe their gift might reside. Those interested in creating a gift chart for their organization might want to refer to www.campagne.com/giftrange/default.asp.

After the careful creation of the gift range chart tied to prospects in the organization's prospect management system, it is most interesting to see the reactions from lead volunteers when they first see the chart. They begin to understand the importance of major gifts in a capital campaign and the urgency of the task ahead.

Another important exercise to the campaign is to link the gift chart to appropriate campaign objectives and naming opportunities. Be certain that the gift levels in the gift chart are appropriate to the funding opportunities. In other words, if the organization wishes to create endowment funds that cost $500,000, then there should be a $500,000 gift designated category on the gift chart.

The Term of the Capital Campaign

The length of a capital campaign normally spans from three to seven years, and it is recommended that no campaign have a term longer than seven years.

The rationale for a limited term is that capital campaigns can neither sustain themselves nor sustain the enthusiasm of volunteers much longer than six or seven years.

Organizations have been known to conduct capital campaigns with a 10-year term or more, but quite frankly, these organizations are probably not conducting actual capital campaigns but rather are labeling their total institutional support over that 10-year term as a capital campaign for purposes of being able to announce a larger goal.

One well-known Eastern university wanted to compete with some of their benchmark institutions by announcing a billion-dollar goal. The only problem was their organization could not support a goal of that magnitude unless they adopted a term of more than 10 years. There are many things in a capital campaign more important than the dollar goal.

Most institutions appear to have a campaign term of five years.[3] Five years is a reasonable period in which to galvanize volunteer support and keep volunteer enthusiasm from waning. The term of the campaign will depend a great deal on the size and complexity of the institution. Larger, more diverse institutions with multiple consistencies may need longer terms to complete all of the gift solicitations required. It simply may not be possible to cover all of the bases and solicit all of the individuals, foundations, and corporations appropriately with a term less than seven years. Institutions with smaller constituencies may be able to complete the major gift process in a much shorter time period, even as short as three years.

The continuity and longevity of staff and key volunteers also affects the length of a capital campaign. It is critically important that the CEO of the organization remain in office throughout the life of the capital campaign. Changing presidents in the middle of a capital campaign can be counter-intuitive to the overall process. Similarly, losing senior development staff members can cause an institution to lose momentum in its capital campaign. Stability of staff leadership is very important to maintain throughout the life of the effort.

Similarly, key volunteers must sign on for a definitive length of time, and it is critical that the key volunteers not only maintain interest but be officially connected to the campaign throughout its term. The longer a campaign is in operation, the more difficult the continuity of staff and volunteers will be to maintain.

The real question regarding a timeline for the campaign is how long it takes to accomplish the various critical tasks associated with the solicitation process. By the time an organization impanels its lead volunteer committee and starts the solicitation process with face-to-face, one-on-one meetings designed to raise major principal leadership gifts, a five-to-seven year term begins to take on some justification.

One thing is certain. Planning and implementing a capital campaign always takes longer than expected. When dealing with major influential prospects as well as important campaign volunteers, the cultivation and implementation period often stretches beyond the original plan.

Campaign Cash Flow

It is vital to note that a capital campaign does not necessarily create significant changes in the organization's operating cash flow in the short term. Most commitments to a capital campaign are managed on a multiyear basis. It is difficult to explain to many groups, particularly internal to the organization, that a $100-million capital campaign goal will not produce $100 million in hand in the first two to three years of the campaign. The institution will receive numerous planned gifts that may pay income to a benefactor, or the organization may have to wait a period of years to receive the actual financial benefits of the gift.

Campaign volunteers and staff members should educate internal and external constituents about this issue early on in the campaign.

At the University of Arkansas, the $300-million challenge gift that was made midway though the campaign (and at the time, was the largest gift ever made to a public university) allowed for matching gifts that were of a deferred nature to be matched by the $300 million. This enabled the university to create endowments immediately and improved campaign cash flow.

Campaign Pledge Documents and Gift Agreements

While some campaigns have been known to abridge the basic rule of counting principles, I very strongly believe that campaign commitments must be in writing and formalized before they are counted. This makes the pledge form and gift agreement documents critical elements in the campaign, and their design early on should be a campaign priority.

Various types of pledge forms can be used in a campaign environment. The first is a legally binding document that literally attempts to bind the estate of the individual making the pledge. Obviously, this type of pledge form should be used for any bricks and mortar project where funds are being expended by the institution.

A second type of pledge form is used as a statement of intent by a benefactor and is not necessarily binding on the benefactor or his estate. Some donors are reluctant to sign a document that will bind their estate should they not fulfill their pledge during their lifetime.

Many institutions will also create a gift agreement that basically lays out the uses of the gift in some detail. Gift agreements are integral documents when creating endowment funds, because they serve to spell out succinctly how the income can be used and how the funds can be invested.

Samples of these pledge forms and gift agreements may be found on the "Campaign Tools" CD.

Frequency Between Capital Campaigns

Many organizations begin planning for a second capital campaign or their next campaign almost immediately after their first has concluded.

Organizations should refrain from publicly declaring a new campaign without having a sufficient interval of time between the two efforts. At least three years, and probably five years, should separate two public campaign announcements. Again, it is important to note that the planning stage of the campaign could certainly begin immediately after the conclusion of the first effort. But launching the campaign publicly, engaging the services of volunteers, and soliciting gifts from donors needs to have an appropriate amount of breathing room between efforts. Volunteer and donor fatigue are two very important considerations in deciding the frequency of capital campaigns. An organization must give donors the opportunity to pay off pledge commitments before they are asked to support another effort.

However, development officials should not wait so long that major prospects and benefactors might pledge substantial amounts to a competing organization. Prospective donors generally continue the production of wealth and the building of capital throughout their lifetimes. It is likely that they will be making major commitments to some entity, and it might as well be yours.

Policy for Naming Opportunities

Many organizations have policies for naming opportunities within their organizations. Often, the policy is created by the governing board and lists minimum amounts that are required to name buildings, offices, endowments, scholarships, and so forth.

Before the launching of a capital campaign, institutions would be well served to make certain that they have a current naming policy that has been reviewed and approved by appropriate officials such as the governing board or the CEO.

A policy guide for naming opportunities can be found on the "Campaign Tools" CD.

The Importance of Challenge Gifts to Capital Campaigns

Data from the American Association of Fund Raising Counsel (AAFRC) suggest that major challenge grants to institutions can have a dramatic impact on leveraging gifts from other friends and prospects of the organization.

According to AAFRC:

- Individual donors are many times more likely to make a commitment to an organization's capital campaign if they know their gift will be matched by another funding source.

- Challenge grants provide incentives to prospective new donors to become first-time givers.

- Challenge grants provide prior donors with incentives to increase the size of their gifts.

- Challenge grants provide a special incentive to campaign committee members to increase the size of their own gifts and give the membership leverage when they solicit others.

- The implied endorsement of the grantor who is making the challenge helps the institution secure more grants and dollars from foundations and corporations. It positions the organization as an institution worthy of investment.

AAFRC offers these examples of successful challenge gifts in recent years:

- The Kresge Foundation, well known for its support of bricks-and-mortar projects, has for many years required matching funds and issued challenge grants at hundreds of institutions across the country. These grants have spawned millions of dollars of support from individual donors, corporations, and other foundations eager to match the Kresge challenge.

- Another foundation well known for its challenge grant is the Donald W. Reynolds Foundation, headquartered in Las Vegas. This foundation, which once exclusively supported bricks-and-mortar projects in Arkansas, Oklahoma, and Nevada, had as one of its provisions the requirement that the recipient organization produce a 20 percent match in order to receive Reynolds Foundation's support.

- A $120 million challenge grant in 1996 to the Illinois Institute of Technology in Chicago was stunning in its impact. The challenge was made by the Pritzker and Galvin families and helped to transform the institute.

- Perhaps the largest challenge grant ever made is by the Walton Family Charitable Support Foundation in 2002 to the University of Arkansas for $300 million. At the time of the publication of this book, it is the largest gift ever made to a public university and the fifth-largest gift ever made to a public or private institution.

The purpose of the Walton Challenge was to inaugurate an honors college as well as to endow the graduate school. The gift challenged others to establish chairs, professorships, fellowships, and scholarships as well as research funds for every college and school at the university. The challenge grant was the primary reason the University of Arkansas was able to take its original $300 million goal and raise more than $1 billion by the end of the campaign. The endowment of the university increased from $119 million when the campaign began to more than $700 million when the campaign concluded.

A challenge gift or Challenge Grant is usually a large commitment that comes from an individual, corporation, or foundation that will challenge others to give a gift at a certain level and then will make a donation if the "challenge" is met.

Usually a Challenge Gift is made in a multi-million capital campaign by one of the Lead Gift donors. This donor will only make a large gift that is contingent on it being equally matched by another donor or number of donors by a certain date, according to profitquests.com.

The outcome is to encourage others to maximize their gift with a challenge or matching gift from a key individual in your organization. This will energize all donors to give more than they would normally, bringing in more funds for your campaign.[4]

Susan Schaefer in "The Challenge of Challenge Gifts" writes:
Challenge grants can be a simple way to give your fundraising program a boost, and yet they can be . . . well, challenging. They offer an opportunity for your organization to grow its support base, increase giving across a particular donor segment, and increase gift amounts. However, they are not a tool to be taken lightly.[5]

When executed well, challenge grants can give your campaign renewed momentum and a sense of urgency without creating a new campaign. Ideally, donors get so energized that match totals often exceed the amount of the challenge.[6]

Campaign Counting

Capital campaign fund raising is a way of life for thousands of charities and philanthropic organizations throughout the country. These campaigns do much good for their respective organizations and have raised millions of dollars for very worthy causes. The capital campaign is a symbol of the generous American spirit that has literally transformed many organizations, institutions, and worthy programs and projects.

In announcing mega campaign goals, some higher education institutions, in their enthusiasm to report the largest possible number, use various assumptions rather than consistent reporting rules. This practice sometimes results in numbers that may be inflated rather than actual.

Unfortunately, this reporting inflation has fueled a public perception of institutional greed and overreach, particularly as regards the very large goals that have become commonplace.

Because of this public perception, philanthropic organizations have been cautioned for years to adhere to commonly accepted reporting standards or guidelines promulgated on a national basis. Both the Council for the Advancement and Support of Education (CASE) and the National Committee on Planned Giving (NCPG) has responded to this need, with each organization issuing new standards in 2004 and 2005, respectively. More recently a group of primarily research universities has developed National Capital Campaign Counting Guidelines.

CASE Guidelines

The Council for Advancement and Support of Education (CASE) has worked diligently over the past 25 years to create guidelines for counting philanthropic support to colleges and universities both on an annual basis as well as capital campaign counting. Although the guidelines technically apply only to educational institutions, many nonprofits adhere to the policies or adapt them to their campaigns.

The first committee appointed by CASE to address campaign counting was created in 1982, and produced management reporting standards for educational institutions. This committee was subsequently followed by five more committees in an effort to adopt standards for the fund raising profession. The most recent effort resulted in the Third Edition of the *CASE Management and Reporting Standards for Annual Giving and Campaigns in Educational Fund Raising*, published in 2004. The publication is available from CASE (www.case.org).

While CASE should be highly commended for its work to create a standard campaign and annual fund counting process, the 2004 guidelines have not been fully accepted by some institutions.

The latest round has sparked both controversy and frustration among some college and university fund-raising officials. At the time of publication a number of major consortia are not following the new guidelines, including the majority of institutions in the Big 10 and the Southeastern Conference (SEC).

Historical Context. Some industry professionals believed that the 1994 publication of the *CASE Campaign Standards: Management and Reporting Standards for Educational Fund Raising Campaigns* was a definitive document that had been adjudicated by many and was widely accepted in the profession. The standards were subsequently endorsed by 18 national and international fund-raising organizations.

The 1994 guidelines created a compromise position on counting deferred gift commitments. The committee recommended that deferred gifts be reported annually to CASE at both face value *and* discounted present value. This compromise was made in the final negotiation process when the committee met on December 9, 1993. The original draft required that all deferred gifts be discounted to present value but this caused an uproar in the profession. Surveys conducted at the time indicated that well over half of the development professionals in the country believed that discounting deferred gifts to present value was not an acceptable way to proceed, and the committee felt that this threatened the survival of the document. The committee decided that a compromise was important in order to resolve the issue and receive maximum acceptance of the campaign guidelines from professionals throughout the country.

The 1994 guidelines proposed that each college or university conducting a capital campaign would be asked to file a report annually with CASE. This information would then be compiled and published annually by CASE as a service to its membership and the public. The report would provide professionals with a common language for discussing the progress of their capital and major gift campaigns. Institutions were asked to report their campaigns financial results in basically three distinct columns. The first was a reporting of *current* gifts and pledges at *face value*. The second was a reporting of *deferred* gifts and future commitments at *face value* for featured objectives and other objectives. The third column was to be a reporting of *deferred* gifts and future commitments at the gifts' *discounted present value* for featured objectives and other objectives.

The 1994 document was created after an exhaustive study and intense vetting among many persons. It was endorsed by some of the leading educational organizations in the nation, and it has been in operation the past 10 years.

The 2004 Standards. CASE indicated that "over time…it became apparent that the standards required updating to account for new fund-raising practices and circumstances and to clarify issues that arose over the years."[1]

Another committee was formed to focus on four broad objectives:

- "To provide expanded definitions and explanations for existing elements of the standards—for instance, clarifying the difference between gifts, grants, and contracts for reporting purposes.

- To confirm and/or expand the list of exclusions from gift totals—for example, reaffirming the exclusion of funds from all government sources and adding the cost of appraisals to the list of exclusions.

- To add definitions for certain types of gifts not previously covered in the standards, such as "mega" gifts of software.

- To determine the best means of valuation of deferred gifts of various types for purposes of reporting to CASE and CAE, an issue on which has been difficult to find consensus."[2]

The final objective has caused discussion within the profession. While no one can doubt that some tweaking of the 1994 standards was probably necessary and advisable, the real sticking point in the 2004 report is the issue of counting deferred gifts.

Another special subcommittee was formed in late 2002 to take up the difficult issue of counting deferred gifts in an attempt to resolve the controversy. That subcommittee recommended discounting deferred gifts and that recommendation was ultimately accepted and became part of the 2004 standards. Fund-raising leaders recommended the counting of deferred gifts at present value as the best way to ensure apples-to-apples comparisons in national surveys, given the "time value of money," according to CASE. The decision was made following two public comment periods and thorough review by the CASE Board of Trustees and the CASE Commission on Philanthropy. At least eight organizations have endorsed the 2004 standards, including the Association of Governing Boards and the Council for Aid to Education.

CASE suggests that the 2004 standards are not intended to be used for donor recognition purposes. The introduction to the 2004 standards state "…. these standards relate only to the amounts that an institution should report in its fund-raising management reports submitted to CASE and CAE. These amounts may differ from the values of the charitable deductions taken by the donors as well as the amounts used for donor recognition purposes."

Observations about the 2004 Standards. The new guidelines may confuse practitioners and volunteers when they find it necessary to report two conflicting campaign total figures, one to CASE and CAE and one for public consumption when promoting campaign success. Lay people, including campaign volunteers and governing board members may not understand the difference.

The blending of annual gift reporting with capital campaign reporting has caused confusion. By merging the definitions and two concepts, practitioners are now confused about applying the guidelines to counting policies in their capital campaign.

By eliminating the dual campaign reporting of face value and discounted value (that came out of the 1994 standards) the profession is left with only one choice of discounting and some institutions will choose not to follow the recommendation of discounting deferred gifts when counting campaign totals. This will make campaign comparisons from institution to institution more difficult.

NCPG Standards

Unlike the CASE guidelines, the NCPG Guidelines for Reporting and Counting Charitable Gifts, released in March 2005, were not primarily crafted for colleges and universities. The NCPG guidelines provide a tool for all types of charitable organizations to use for reporting and counting fund-raising activity. According to NCPG President and CEO Tanya Howe Johnson, "The new guidelines broaden the counting and reporting options available to organizations, so that they can choose a sound and straightforward methodology that best supports their organization's campaign goals."

Developed by a task force of NCPG members, the guidelines were published following a year of research and development, a six-week comment period, and final revisions. The guidelines are designed to complement NCPG's Valuation Standards for Charitable Planned Gifts, published in April 2004. The valuation standards are for internal use, helping organizations understand the future purchasing power of a planned gift. The reporting guidelines are externally focused.

To learn more about the NCPG guidelines, go to www.ncpg.org and click on Ethics & Standards.

The National Capital Campaign Counting Guidelines

In an effort to provide practitioners with alternative guidelines for campaign counting in their capital campaigns, a group of development officials from institutions across the country, including the author, have created the National Capital Campaign Counting Guidelines. Preliminary endorsees of the guidelines include development officers at University of Arkansas, University of South Carolina, University of Michigan, Penn State University, Ohio State University, University of Southern California, University of Pittsburgh, University of Florida Foundation, Defiance College, Iowa State University Foundation, Minnesota Medical Foundation, and others. The relatively simple, direct guidelines provide development officials, not only at colleges and universities but other philanthropic organizations, guidelines in how to count campaign gifts.

Recently, this group has been collaborating with the National Committee on Planned Giving (NCPG) in an effort to create one set of guidelines for the profession to use.

Notes for Chapter 6

1. Jon Van Til and Associates, *Critical Issues in American Philanthropy: Strengthening Theory and Practice* (San Francisco: Jossey-Bass Inc., 1990), 56.

2. James M. Greenfield, "Fund-Raising Costs and Credibility: What the Public Needs to Know," *NSFRE Journal* (Autumn 1988).

3. "Capital Campaigns 1991-92," *Capital Campaign Report,* Brakeley John Price Jones, Inc., Spring 1992.

4. "Challenge Gifts," *Profit Quests Fundraising*, December 17, 2004.

5. Susan Schaefer, "The Challenge of Challenge Gifts," *Grants & Foundation Review* (August 20, 2004).

6. Ibid.

7. *CASE Management Reporting Standards: Standards for Annual Giving and Campaigns in Educational Fund Raising, Third Edition*, (2004 by the Council for Advancement and Support of Education), p. 12.

8. Ibid.

seven

Asking for the Gift— Motivations for Giving

He who gives while he lives also knows where it goes.
Percy Ross

Stewardship, Donor, and Constituent Relations

This chapter focuses primarily on the major gift solicitation process as well as motivations for giving and, finally, on the important issue of stewardship and donor/constituent relations.

The solicitation process—asking for a major gift—takes patience and persistence. Process, patience, and persistence all are key words to describe major gift fund raising.

A campaign can have the best organizational structure in the world. It can have the best campaign publications, the best timeframe, the best case statement, the best funding opportunities, and an organization that is deemed highly worthy of support. But nothing will really happen until the process of major gift solicitation is put in place. The process of asking for the gift, preparing for the solicitation, is what will ultimately bring major commitments to your organization.

The cultivation and solicitation of individuals, corporations, foundations, and associations is a careful step-by-step endeavor that culminates in convincing the potential benefactor that his or her support is critical to your organization. The process can take months—or even years. Rarely, if ever, is a major gift made to an institution without careful and deliberate planning by staff members and volunteers. Surprise gifts do happen, but they are uncommon. They are wonderful when they occur, but they can never be counted on and should never be included in campaign strategy. Through the years, authors have formulated many strategic steps to a major gift. Almost all of them have the three key words in common: process, patience, and persistence.

Constituent and Donor Relations

A critical component of any major gift operation is appropriate stewardship of an organization's major gift benefactors. Attracting major gift benefactors to one's organization is a time-consuming process that takes hours of hard work and extraordinary patience. Once the donor has been attracted to the institution, the challenge is to keep him or her engaged and involved. Engagement and involvement begets support and is as much a part of the cultivation process as any step in the major gift continuum.

Many more sophisticated development operations have created donor relations or constituent relations offices designed to ensure that major benefactors are appropriately stewarded.

The purpose of a constituent or donor relations office is to enhance the relationships between your organization and your benefactors, encouraging lifetime support. A good donor recognition program exists to ensure that the organization's donors are recognized appropriately and engaged with the philanthropy throughout their lifetime.

The duties of a donor relations or constituent relations program include the following:

- Contribute to the positive experience that the donor feels from giving to the organization

- Increase familiarity with the donor's areas of interest and with the organization

- Prepare donors and prospects to consider giving to university priorities, endowments, and so forth

- Provide stewardship by giving donors opportunities to meet recipients benefiting from their support, such as students for scholarships and faculty for professorships

- Provide annual endowment reports to donors to establish or make major gifts to endowed funds

- Support key development strategies for individuals, foundations, and corporations in an effort to inspire increased gifts for a donor's lifetime

- Honor donors appropriately who make gifts at major levels by recognizing them in a cumulative gift society

- Monitor the appropriate use of gifts to reward donors of extraordinary support

Recognizing benefactors is an extremely important activity. The "Campaign Tools" on CD includes several documents that relate to donor relations or constituent relations.

There is even a donor relations professional society, Association of Donor Relations Professionals. For more information, contact their Web site at www.adrp.net.

Strategic Steps to a Major Campaign Gift

1. **Identifying the Prospect.** Does the prospect have the financial capacity to make a major gift to your organization? Do we know the prospect's financial base? Do we know the prospect's standard of living? What causes us to believe that the prospect in question can make a six- or seven-figure gift to your organization?

2. **Researching and Qualifying the Prospect.** What are the prospect's potential interests and priorities? Does the prospect have a relationship with our organization? What form of assets make up the prospect's wealth? Is the prospect known as a philanthropist? Has he or she made major and principal gifts to other philanthropic endeavors? Is his or her philanthropy well known in the community? Who are the prospect's best friends? What information do we still need to be able to build a cultivation and gift strategy for this particular prospect?

3. **Developing a Cultivation and Solicitation Strategy.** What kind of contact has the organization in question had with the prospect? Has the prospect met the CEO or other senior officers of the organization? What are the prospect's interests and do they match the interests of the organization? What does the prospect need to know, feel, and experience to bring about a major gift commitment? Who would need to be involved—inside or outside the organization—in cultivating and finally soliciting the prospect? Who can best open the door to the prospect? How long of a period of cultivation will be needed before the gift ask can be made? Is the prospect close enough to the institution to receive a major gift ask?

4. **Involving the Potential Benefactor in the Life of Your Organization.** How does your organization go about building a bridge to the prospect? What appear to be important factors in why this particular prospect might make a major gift to your organization? How can we meaningfully involve the prospect in the organization's programs and interests? Who at the institution is most respected by the prospect? What are the interests of the prospect's spouse, and can we engage the spouse in the cultivation process?

5. **Finalizing the Evaluation, Size of the Request, and the Proposal.** Do we know that the prospect is ready to be solicited? Are we sure of the size of the gift request and completeness of the proposal? Who will be involved in making the ask? Have we agreed to the size of the request? Have we prepared a high-quality proposal, and do we believe that the prospect will respond favorably to the request and the specific project in the proposal?

   Has a formal appointment been made for the solicitation? Are those who will be making the solicitation adequately prepared for what will happen in the solicitation environment?

   Do the solicitors understand the nature of the proposal and how it will affect the organization? Can they answer questions about the proposal and do they understand how it will contribute positively to the campaign? Who will be responsible for outlining and presenting the proposal in the solicitation environment? What if the prospect rejects the proposal? Do we have a fallback position?

6. **Making the Ask; Soliciting the Prospect.** Is the ask formalized in writing? Are the nature and size of the gift invitation clear to the prospect? Are there any crucial objections or concerns that have been voiced by the prospect after the solicitation has been made?

7. **Closing the Gift.** How close are we to getting the prospect to actually making a commitment? What further concerns by the prospect need to be addressed by the organization? Does the original proposal need to be changed in a way that would be more acceptable to the prospect? Do we need additional professional help such as planned giving experts to become involved in the solicitation? How long are we going to wait to get back to the prospect in a timely fashion in order to follow up on the proposal and the gift invitation?

8. **Ensuring Acknowledgement, Stewardship, Recognition, and Follow Through.** Has the organization decided who will express appreciation, thanks, and gratitude to the benefactor? Will the gift be announced and has permission been received from the benefactor to announce his or her commitment? Is there personal attention that must be shown to the benefactor, and are there opportunities for strengthening the benefactor's ties with the organization? Is permanent recognition being discussed with the benefactor? Is the benefactor a prime prospect for another major gift to your organization? Who is actually charged with the responsibility of stewarding the gift and staying in touch with the donor after the gift has been made?

Critical Factors in Successful Major Gift Solicitation

Volunteer leaders in partnership with staff members are the key to success in any major capital campaign. There can be no substitute for peers soliciting peers. Success in getting big gifts often has as much to do with the volunteer's influence as the organizational quality or characteristics of any particular program or cause. Do not underestimate the ability of volunteers to make a huge difference in the process of major gift fund raising.

A successful major gift campaign has a number of requirements, including: the right volunteer leadership, an effective organizational structure, specific goals and objectives for each campaign committee, a compelling case for support, a favorable economic environment, and strong staff support. When it comes to asking for the gift, the importance of the following factors cannot be overlooked:

- **Lead Principal and Major Gifts in the Six- and Seven-Figure Range.** As has already been mentioned, 95 percent of the dollars contributed to any capital campaign is raised from fewer than 5 percent of the donors. The importance of major gifts cannot be overemphasized. Those commitments must be made early for the campaign to be truly successful.

- **The Influence of Peers.** A compelling case for financial support is important, but people do indeed give to people. Major donors are more likely to give at higher levels when they are invited to do so by their peers. Although staff members are very important to moving the solicitation process forward, many times only a peer can convince a particular donor to give in a very significant manner.

- **Sequential Giving.** The largest gifts should be solicited first. Success at this level sets the pace for those with smaller giving capabilities and unquestionably establishes the level of giving for the rest of the campaign. Because the number of any institution's major prospects is limited, great effort must be expended to persuade these initial major prospects to give in proportion to their capacity.

  Every campaign should move its gift process forward sequentially, allowing the successful solicitation of the largest gifts to influence the level of the next largest gift and so on. The successful achievement of any campaign goal is most often dictated by how well this early stage of advanced gift solicitation proceeds.

- **Formal Solicitations.** Major gifts almost never result from letters, phone calls, or casual requests. If a prospect feels that the campaign is not worth more than a letter or phone call from a volunteer or staff member, he or she is likely to decide it is not worth the gift either. It is vital that key prospects receive specific written proposals followed by, or in conjunction with, face-to-face meetings. When possible, solicitations should be conducted on a two-on-one basis, as this type of team effort has proven to be most effective. Typically the team might include the CEO or a senior officer of the institution along with a volunteer leader who is acquainted with the prospect. Teams reinforce one another, and it shows the importance of the solicitation.

  It is the development officer's responsibility to provide the team with cohesive, well-written proposals tailored to the prospect for presentation during the solicitation visit.

- **Cultivation.** Major gifts frequently require months—or even years—of cultivation before being realized. In fact, John Glier, president and chief executive officer of Grenzebach, Glier, and Associates in Chicago, Illinois, says that the average principal and major gift requires a cultivation period of 18 to 36 months.

  Campaign leaders are in a position to conduct informal cultivation activity by entertaining at their homes, hosting small luncheons, or talking with likely prospects at social events.

  Cultivation is part of the early leadership phase of the campaign, although a volunteer's first visit to a prospective donor will probably not be a solicitation call. Most major gifts are made by individuals who are significantly aware and vitally involved in the activities of the organization. Cultivation is the process that brings prospects closer to the organization.

- **The Difficulty of Preemptive Gifts.** Allowing prospects to establish their own gift levels without the benefit of focused cultivation and formal solicitation almost always produces gifts that most campaign leaders view as less than total commitment. To ensure the success of the capital campaign, the solicitation teams must be able to propose the right program opportunity at the right level of giving for each campaign prospect. A campaign must try to avoid allowing a donor to make a gift or a pledge before the actual proposal is formally made. Preemptive gifts can destroy a campaign.

- **The Volunteer's Gift First.** A volunteer's confidence in the validity and urgency of the campaign will be a major factor in persuading others to make a significant gift. The best evidence of this confidence is a volunteer's own generous participation at the highest possible level. If you're going to be a part of a solicitation team, make your own gift first. It will make it much easier to ask if you have made a commitment yourself.

- **Knowing the Prospect.** Volunteers should work with the development staff to know as much as possible about a prospect before the visit. In all cases, a prospect should not be visited by a volunteer until the volunteer has enough background to ask for the right gift for the most appropriate program in the campaign. Volunteers should look for ways in which the prospect's investment can allow for greater participation in the program or in the institution as a whole.

- **Recognizing Institutional Needs in the Campaign.** A volunteer or staff member must be ready to answer questions about both the institution and the campaign needs. Volunteers cannot be expected to know every minor detail about the needs in every area of the organization. However, a general understanding of the main goals of the campaign and what the funds will be used for is most important when soliciting a prospect.

- **Personal Solicitation—An Absolute Priority.** Major gifts require personal contact. Phone conversations should only be used to discuss the campaign in general terms. A volunteer must find a time and place when the prospect can give full attention to the presentation.

- **Soliciting the Best Prospects First.** As has been previously mentioned, solicitations should proceed sequentially, soliciting the best and largest prospects first and so forth down the line. This will give volunteers more confidence for calling on other prospects who may be more difficult.

- **The Case for Clear and Understandable Support.** The volunteer or staff member should first explain the campaign goals and explore areas of interest. The volunteer should talk about why the institution is worthy of the prospect's time and resources. Discussion allows a prospect to develop enthusiasm and interject personal interests and inclinations into the environment. The volunteers and staff members must be equally enthusiastic about their own personal interests.

- **A Clear Ask.** At the appropriate time in the gift solicitation process, the potential benefactor should be encouraged to make a stretch commitment. The solicitation team should discuss designated gifts, pointing out memorial or tribute opportunities to indicate the level of gift the institution is hoping to receive from the prospect.

   In a face-to-face solicitation environment, perhaps the most difficult part of the solicitation is looking the individual in the eye and asking for an actual amount. It is also the most crucial part of the process.

From the moment a volunteer and staff member make the call, the prospect is waiting to hear the dollar amount that will be requested. Asking for the gift is the key element of the solicitation. It cannot be left hanging in some vague, misunderstood language. The amount must be stated clearly and definitively, and the prospect must realize that a solicitation for a specific dollar amount has taken place and an appropriate answer at some point will be required.

Knowing the right way to ask for a gift is something that will come only with practice and experience. The most seasoned development officers who have asked for a gift literally hundreds of times still have difficulty when it comes to requesting a dollar amount. A volunteer, or for that matter, a staff member, should not feel inadequate simply because he or she finds this extremely important part of the solicitation difficult. The bottom line is that it is difficult, but it is essential.

The gift amount should always be decided in advance and supported with a specific written proposal provided by the staff. Prospects will appreciate being asked to consider a targeted program or programs and a specific dollar amount. The proposal should be tailored to a prospect's personal interests and needs. The solicitation team should always keep the discussion focused and seek resolution. Initially, negative responses are common, and a volunteer should not back away from the solicitation if the prospect does not respond positively.

A lower gift should be negotiated only when the target ask is clearly beyond the reach of a prospect. Stories are legendary of prospects who have rejected initial proposals only to make much larger gifts later in the campaign—after a lengthy period of cultivation and involvement.

Exploring Ways to Give

Volunteers and staff should remind the prospect that gifts can be made with a variety of assets, including stocks and securities, real estate, insurance, as well as in certain cases, inclusion of the organization in one's estate plans. Cash, of course, is always an option.

If an outright gift is simply not possible, then the solicitation team should explore the possibility of a planned gift. Although tax incentives are generally not seen as the primary motivation for making a contribution, it is still important to emphasize the tax advantages of giving.

Mentioning Gift Recognition

Naming opportunities can provide an important motivation and should be mentioned in the major gift solicitation environment as well, of course, as in the written proposal.

Pledging Opportunities

The solicitation team should always encourage potential benefactors to give the largest gift possible by extending payments over a period of years. Pledges can generally be paid over a five-year pledge term, and this allows benefactors to stretch their commitment to a higher level.

Many times the solicitation team will need to leave pledge forms along with the written proposal in the hands of prospects, because the prospect may resist making a commitment and signing the pledge immediately. It is important to keep in mind that when asked for a major gift commitment, the prospect will probably need time to consider the proposal and will want to talk with other family members. Pushing a prospect for a gift decision during the solicitation may cause the prospect to make a smaller gift than might otherwise be considered upon reflection. Prospects should be allowed to discuss pledge forms and proposals with family members and given time to think about the proposed gift's impact on the institution. Major gifts are generally always made after much deliberation and thought.

A commitment should always be made in writing. This will allow your organization officially to count the gift toward the campaign goal and to recognize it appropriately.

Showing Restraint

Major gifts take time. They cannot be hurried. As gift size increases, the time required to reach a decision is longer. The prospect may want to consult with his or her family or personal staff and possibly a financial or legal advisor before deciding upon the size and method of giving. Always encourage such consultation. You want the prospect to make the pledge commitment freely and enthusiastically.

A member of the solicitation team should follow up with the prospect and even set a date in the future to discuss the pledge. Be certain that the prospect knows you will be back in touch with him or her in a reasonable period of time to seek closure on the gift. It is crucial, however, to be sensitive to the prospect's need for adequate time to genuinely reflect on the gift decision.

Thinking Positive

Volunteers and staff will receive many turndowns. Do not become discouraged. The job of solicitation is a difficult one. Keep in mind that the benefits to your organization are immense. You are helping to change the institution for the better and positioning it for the future. The gifts that you secure will make all the difference.

The Written Proposal

The written proposal is extremely important to the solicitation process. Many development directors have failed because of their inability to reduce the gift ask to a written proposal. Often the written proposal is the last thing to be pulled together prior to the solicitation.

The written proposal should be neither complex nor difficult to produce nor should it be too lengthy for the prospect. The proposal is simply a statement in writing of the most critical reasons why the campaign must be successful and how the prospect's gift support will lead to a better organization. A brief proposal, is preferable— no longer than two to four pages. This is entirely adequate to delineate the needs of the campaign and the specific gift proposal amount for the individual prospect. Prospective benefactors are looking for substance.

Proposals should always state an amount and a pledge term so that benefactors are clearly aware of the expectation of the organization. The gift ask should be clearly delineated in the letter or proposal.

Many development officers have asked what kind of format will get a better reception—a proposal format or a letter format. I believe that a letter format is a much warmer communication. A proposal printed on campaign letterhead or the CEO's letterhead may be preferable to a multipage proposal that does not have the warmth of a personally directed letter.

It should be noted that many corporate entities and foundations may require more formal proposals of considerable length. Guidelines should always be consulted before submitting a proposal to a corporate or foundation entity. The two- to four-page letter format suggested above may not be appropriate in a corporate or foundation environment.

There also may be times when a lengthier proposal is necessary to explain the program in greater detail. Suffice it to say that a two- to four-page format should be considered a guideline, and the length of the proposal will always depend on the project and the person or entity being solicited.

Motivations for Giving

There are many reasons why a benefactor makes a gift to your organization. I have accumulated a list based on 28 years of major gift solicitation experience.

- **Altruism.** Do not assume there are hidden agendas and motives for giving. Many benefactors genuinely are concerned about the welfare of your institution. Philanthropists are often motivated by a sincere desire to help humankind. They are unselfishly concerned about the welfare of others. Major benefactors hope their efforts will lead to the improvement and betterment of the organization that they have adopted.

  Million-dollar-plus gifts are generally made because a benefactor sees an opportunity to shape and mold the future of the organization. Indeed, nonprofits have been transformed literally overnight because of the altruism of generous benefactors.

- **Immortality.** Many people want to be remembered and to make their mark on the world. The quest for immortality can play an important role in major gift fund raising. Many institutions in the United States were named for philanthropists who injected massive resources into the institutions. Benefactors want to be remembered and are willing to make six- and seven-figure contributions so that they or their loved one is forever intertwined with a particular cause or social concern.

  Do not mistake a donor's shyness or lack of insistence on naming opportunities as being disinterested in immortality. Many benefactors do not actively seek publicity, and it is the development officer's job to ferret out a donor's real thoughts and inner feelings about perpetual naming opportunities. It is my experience that the vast majority of major benefactors do want to be recognized, if only modestly, for what they have done to enhance a particular program or project through their giving. Pursue naming opportunities with a benefactor until you are absolutely convinced that the benefactor sincerely wishes anonymity.

- **Peer Pressure.** The old adage, "people give to people," continues to have some validity. While the concept has changed through the years and is not as definitive as it perhaps once was, the whole concept of volunteerism is built around the premise that one's peers are more successful in soliciting a gift from associates than a disassociated third party.

  Human nature is such that it is difficult to turn down the request of a colleague or business associate. This is not to say that a benefactor will support any cause, regardless of its stated purpose. Certainly, benefactors must recognize and appreciate the importance of the philanthropic endeavor. But experts in the field frequently have discovered that it is the volunteer who can exercise a degree of peer pressure that, when coupled with a sincere and worthy cause for support, will convince a prospect to step forward and be counted as a major contributor. Wise development officers use peer pressure to their advantage. Be alert for opportunities in matching the right volunteer to the right prospect.

- **Control.** All experienced development officers have witnessed benefactors wanting to exercise a level of authority and control over an organization because of their gift support. This desire for influence can range from benefactors wanting choice athletic tickets to those asking that their son or daughter be given preference for admission to a college or university. In fact, around March or April, many development officers become de facto admissions officers, because some benefactors attempt to exercise their influence to get their sons and daughters and the sons and daughters of friends and business associates into the institution.

  Many major donors will come to feel an ownership of the institution and will want to exercise control and authority over the management of the organization. Their interests may indeed be beneficent, and they may truthfully be philanthropists in every sense of the word; however, their interest and their financial support extend much further than a true philanthropic spirit. No institution should compromise its basic integrity for any benefactor, large or small.

- **A Desire for Inclusion.** Benefactors of all ages and philanthropic levels genuinely want to be a part of a successful enterprise.

They will make a decision on gift support because they want to be included among those who have supported a successful endeavor.

Some gift programs are designed around gala dinners and other events that list benefactors in programs and brochures. The benefactor is listed by levels according to the degree of support, and the classifications are as broad as the gifts themselves. Individuals will invariably turn to the page where they expect to be listed to be certain that they have been included at the appropriate level.

Practically everyone wants to be part of a successful ongoing endeavor. Sometimes it can be a primary motivator for major gift support.

- **Transformational Change.** Experience has shown with increasing frequency that a number of wealthy benefactors want to make transformational gifts that will truly shape society. This is a desire to use their wealth to make a difference and literally change the social and educational underpinnings for the better. In a sense, this is a new paradigm defined by the Baby Boomer generation. This new paradigm will be discussed later in this chapter.

- **The Passing of Wealth from One Generation to the Next.** Many benefactors have come to realize that great wealth passed on to children can have a deleterious effect on their lives. They may, in fact, want their children to be "comfortable" and receive an inheritance that will make life's pleasures more possible, but they are not intent on leaving massive wealth to their children. They worry that their children will have a less disciplined and less honorable life if they inherit great wealth. A wonderful article by Richard Kirkland written a number of years ago titled "Should You Leave It All to the Children?" in *Fortune* magazine summed up the issues quite succinctly.[1]

In today's society, it is not unusual for a corporate executive to amass a fortune above $100 million by the time of his or her retirement. Some individuals who have remained with a single company their entire life and have accumulated stock and risen to the highest levels of the corporation are able to accumulate estates worth $300 to $500 million.

The decision about what to do with an estate of this size is a major issue in today's society. The intergenerational transfer of wealth will affect every level of society during the next 15 to 20 years and beyond.

- **Tax Considerations.** Experts in the business as well as commentaries in major trade journals have almost unanimously suggested that tax deduction is not a primary motivator for philanthropy. While this may, in fact, be a true statement with the vast majority of major philanthropists, it certainly can have a deleterious effect on giving. Often donors will use the excuse "I have used up my tax deduction" as a primary reason why they should not give to your program. Taxes do appear to still play a role in decision making on both sides of the giving equation.

Stumbling Blocks to Giving

Prospects have a plethora of reasons for withholding contributions to philanthropic organizations. Seasoned development officers have heard hundreds of excuses—the reasonable, the unreasonable, the palatable, and sometimes the just plain bizarre. Here are some of the more common ones:

- **Funds Tied Up in Investment.** How many times have we had a benefactor suggest that he or she could not make a gift to the campaign because his or her assets are "tied up in investments"? Donors will claim they are on a fixed income and that their funds are tied up in trusts, certificates of deposit, stocks, and bonds that do not allow for ready accessibility.

- **Out of Touch, Out of Mind.** There are literally thousands of philanthropic causes in the United States, and philanthropists develop loyalties to a host of community causes over a period of years. Development officers will hear potential benefactors exclaim many times, "I've been right here in your backyard, and where have you been all these years?" Many prospects are already giving to a multitude of philanthropic endeavors and adding your organization to the list is simply not a priority. Institutions may find it difficult to gain the loyalty of a prospect, realizing that his or her principal philanthropic interests lie elsewhere.

- **Ultimate Benefit to Family.** Although some benefactors wish to refrain from leaving a substantial estate to their children, most often the reverse is the norm. Most prospects do indeed want to pass their life's labor on to their children. They have worked hard to build a considerable estate and want their children to have the benefit of their labors. Family interests can be tough competition for nonprofit organizations.

- **The Greatest Generation.** Tom Brokaw referred to it as "The Greatest Generation," those persons who lived through a world war and the Great Depression and often were literally concerned about the next meal on the table. It certainly must be said that the "greatest generation" is a generous one. Although many magnificent gifts that have transformed organizations have come from this generation, there are prospects among them who find it extremely difficult to part with capital, fearing that history might repeat itself and they might not be able to take care of themselves or their family. This line of thinking is a very real phenomenon and difficult to overcome.

  A depression-era prospect at a large land-grant university was cultivated for a number of years by the institution. The prospect made small gifts to the organization but never a major gift, although she was encouraged to do something in her estate plans. She insisted that she was afraid she would become ill and not be able to afford paying her health bills, although she was well known in the community as a person of means. When she died intestate, it was discovered that she had an estate of more than $13 million. At the time of her death, in her regular, no-interest checking account, she had a balance of $210,000.

  Federal and state taxes took more than half of her estate. The rest was distributed to second and third cousins, some of whom she had never met.

- **The Cultivation Game.** Some donors actually enjoy the cultivation game, which we might call the game of "cat and mouse." They thrive on the attention of presidents, development officers, and volunteers visiting them on a regular basis. These prospects reason that if they make a major commitment to your organization, you will forget about them and stop coming to see them on a regular basis. Early in my career, a wealthy widow, when asked to make a major gift exclaimed, "If I go ahead and make a gift, will you still come to see me?" Many prospects enjoy visits by professional staff and volunteers.

- **Philanthropy as a Habit.** Many prospects have never enjoyed a true spirit of philanthropy as a part of their daily life. They simply have not acquired a habit of giving and do not understand the nature or value of giving. Generosity is a learned behavior.

What Makes a Successful Major Gift Fund Raiser?

Successful fund raising requires the ability to:
- Identify the prospect.

- Qualify the prospect as someone with legitimate interest in the organization.

- Develop a cultivation and solicitation strategy.

- Execute a plan and involve the prospect in the organization.

- Assess the prospect's readiness for solicitation, the size of the gift request, and the completeness of the proposal.

- Make the ask.

- Close the gift and lead the prospect to a real commitment.

- Express appreciation and sincere thanks, and articulate the importance of the gift to the organization.

- Patiently articulate in writing the reasons why gift support is necessary to the organization. (If you can't write it, you can't do it!)

- Understand the importance of philanthropic endeavors and appreciate a valid commitment to a philanthropic organization.

- Understand his or her role in the solicitation, purpose, and goal, and appreciate the cause to which he or she is committed.

- Make his or her own commitment first, before asking others to do so—regardless of the size of the commitment. The best evidence of a major gift fund raiser's confidence in the validity and urgency of a major gift program is participation at the highest possible level.

- Possess the patience to realize that major gifts frequently require weeks and months—or even years—of cultivation before being realized.

- Be willing to travel and meet face-to-face with major gift prospects. Staying in the office is the death knell to major gift fund raisers. You must be on the road, face-to-face with the prospect to raise big gifts.

- Know the right way to ask for a gift, stating the amount clearly and definitively. Asking for the gift is the key element to any major gift solicitation.

- Possess a working knowledge of planned giving, charitable remainder trusts, the pooled income fund, gift annuities, bequests, the use of real estate, insurance, and gifts of securities.

- Stay up to date on the latest tax techniques.

- Understand donor recognition and gift-naming policies and quickly articulate them to prospects.

- Work well and collaboratively with others.

- Involve the right people in the solicitation.

- Believe that he or she is not the most critical factor in the solicitation. Major gift officers must use the chief executive officer, volunteers and others in closing a gift. It is not always likely that the development staff can do it alone.

- Remain enthusiastic and nonapologetic, believe in winning causes, and present the institution in the most favorable light.

Major Gift Fund Raising—New Paradigms

As previously stated, it is a widely accepted fact that there will be a tremendous forthcoming wealth transfer in this country. Some have estimated the transfer to be as low as $10 trillion, while others believe it could be as high as $136 trillion.

The July 29, 2004, issue of *The Economist* predicts that another golden age of philanthropy and charitable giving will occur in the United States and around the world in the next few years. The report cites global trends and the increasing wealth base and aging population. The article goes on to suggest, however, that this major new focus on giving will concentrate on pragmatism rather than altruism. Philanthropy will become more directed, and philanthropists will be more engaged in their projects. Accountability will become the name of the game, and institutions will be required to show that the major gifts they are receiving are being spent properly and are effectively changing their organizations for the better.[2]

Donors today, particularly young donors, are interested in systemic change at the organizations where they contribute. They are young enough to see the long view and want their gifts to have a transformational impact on the organizations they support. They want to be closely engaged in the organization and, to a certain extent, help to direct the implementation of programs and projects that their philanthropy brings about.

A recent article by Judith E. Nichols, a development practitioner, author, and consultant, makes a strong case for repositioning fund raising in the 21st century. Nichols makes a number of observations about the paradigm shift in major gift fund raising:[3]

- Fund raisers continue to use old methods in raising funds. The old ways of raising dollars aren't working.

- Today, donors demand that they, in fact, guide the giving process, not the organizations to which they give.

- Today's donors are more diverse and tuned in to societal needs.

- Increasingly, adult populations that make major gifts have no memories of the first half of the 20th century. Their thinking processes are much different than the "greatest generation."

- Younger and more diversified donors are now focusing on addressing societal concerns and not necessarily sticking to the all-blind funding objections of religious organizations, educational institutions where their family matriculated, and social service organizations where they themselves or their families receive care.

- The coming generation does not look to nonprofits as authority figures, and there is a great deal more questioning and healthy discourse about the objectives of philanthropic organizations.

- The older donor generation waited to be contacted by philanthropic organizations whereas the new generation is more proactive and much more likely to initiate a relationship with a philanthropy.

- A donor's loyalty to a particular organization simply because he or she has historically been a contributor is shifting dramatically and is no longer a major motivating factor for contributing.

It appears that there is a major shift in donor attitudes taking place in this country in recent years. Old motivations for making gifts included a commitment to an institution's mission, gratitude, spiritual beliefs, community responsibility, a desire to memorialize or honor a benefactor, personal or civic pride, guilt or obligation to the solicitor, and in some cases, true benevolence. The new paradigms of giving and the new face of philanthropy is much more strategic, ambitious, and global—and demands results. John A. Byrne, senior writer at *Business Week* writes in the December 2, 2002, issue of the magazine that "This new philanthropy displays an impatient disdain for the cautious and unimaginative check-writing that dominated charitable giving for decades."[4]

Bryne also makes the following important observations about this new face of philanthropy:

- Philanthropy is more ambitious: Today's philanthropists are tackling giant issues, from remaking American education to curing cancer.

- It's more strategic: Donors are taking the same systematic approach they used to compete in business, laying out detailed plans that get at the heart of systemic problems, not just symptoms.

- It's more global: Just as business doesn't stop at national borders, neither does charitable giving. Donors today have sweeping international agendas.

- It demands results: The new philanthropists attach a lot of strings. Recipients are often required to meet milestone goals, to invite foundation members onto their boards, and to produce measurable results—or risk losing their funding.[5]

Notes for Chapter 7

1. Richard Kirkland Jr., "Should You Leave It All to the Children?" *Fortune* 114 (September 29, 1986): 18–26.

2. "A Golden Age for Philanthropy Ahead?" *Economist*, July 29, 2004.

3. Judith E. Nichols, "Repositioning Fundraising in the 21st Century," *International Journal of Nonprofit and Voluntary Sector Marketing* (May 2004): 163.

4. John A. Byrne, "The New Face of Philanthropy," *Business Week* 3810 (December 2, 2002): 82.

5. Ibid.

eight

Campaign Communications

*When asked by a prospective donor how much he should
give, the best reply is, "give until you are proud."*
Paul Ireland

Defining Communication

Communications might well be defined as a broad, strategic management
function that seeks to generate, through effective public relations, marketing,
and communications programs, the degree of attitudinal and behavioral support from key publics that is needed for the organization to attract resources
and attain its many goals.

Professionals in communications do this many ways, but generally by positioning their institutions as singular, high quality, well-run organizations that
fulfill an important societal purpose. Communications professionals promote
the organization's achievements and contributions to society and the community. They attempt to protect the organization's reputation through crisis
management and maintenance of high-quality standards in all organization
communications. Finally, the communications professional will market the
organization and its various programs and components.

The communications function of any organization must have an overriding emphasis on image and reputation building, realizing that resources
will follow reputation. Communications programs must focus on helping the
nonprofit to realize its overarching strategic goal of securing its status as a
premiere organization.

Unfortunately, many people, including staff members, volunteers, benefactors, and even senior officers view the communications function of their
organization as a tactical unit that writes press releases or produces nice
publications at the request of the organization.

In reality, communications programs must devise operations to support
the strategic goals of the organization. Although communications may, in
fact, be a service unit, it is more than that. It does not exist to manufacture
communications artifacts according to the whim of an internal customer. It

must be a unit that provides strategic public relations, marketing, communications, and relationship management programs in support of institutional goals and objectives.

The day is long over when organizations can naïvely presume to send their message or tell their story on their own terms, expecting a credulous public to react favorably. This is not to denigrate the importance of sending compelling messages. In fact, organizations need to enhance their capabilities to do so. But communications efforts, particularly for a capital campaign, must do a first-rate job of cultivating relationships with audiences and creating a climate of receptivity for messages.

Fund Raising and Communications: A Collaborative Effort

Fund-raising and communications experts must find ways to collaborate when organizing a communications plan for a capital campaign. According to a 1989 *CASE Currents* article by Dr. Roger Williams, who headed university relations and campaigns communications for Penn State University and the University of Arkansas, a major trend began in the late 1980s: "Public relations and development, once the surly partners of a shotgun marriage, have learned to get along famously. The main reason: the many capital campaigns that colleges and universities have launched."[1]

Williams surveyed 12 organizations that were involved in capital campaigns and discovered that both fund-raising and public relations officials recognized the importance of the public relations function in their campaigns.

The organizational structure of the nonprofit's communications program will heavily influence how campaign communications will be organized in a capital campaign. In some larger organizations, the communications function is separate and apart from the development function and both report to the chief executive officer. In an integrated system where all advancement personnel report to one officer, the development campaign function and the communications function may be more closely aligned. It is important, however, with any organizational model, that the communications personnel and development personnel work in tandem to create the best communications plan possible for the capital campaign.

Institutional Communications and Campaign Communications: Sharing a Common Purpose

Delivering campaign messages, while at the same time trying to promote an organization to its publics, can send confusing messages if not closely coordinated. A campaign must present a clear, focused, and consistent communications program and must allow the organization to communicate its cohesiveness, while giving the public a sense of direction and leadership. If properly coordinated, the communications plan for the campaign can have an enormous impact on the entire institution, lifting the organization to new heights of awareness among its constituents.

Capital campaigns are not just about raising funds but also about lifting the reputation of the nonprofit to a whole new level. Catherine B. Ahles of Florida International University's School of Journalism and Mass Communication stated it very well in a 2004 *CASE Currents* article:

> Campaigns are a fact of life for institutional advancement professionals. Reaching a multimillion- or billion-dollar goal has practically become a competitive sport. The nature of campaigns continues to evolve and with it, the nature and purpose of their communications. The tried-and-true methods of communication before, during, and after a campaign are changing faster than you can say "major gift prospect."
>
> Campaigns traditionally have existed to increase the financial assets of institutions through the achievement of a dollar goal. Today advancement professionals define the role and function of campaigns in a much more sophisticated way. Campaigns help institutions achieve their missions, not just reach their dollar goals. As a result, campaign communications have evolved from defending the need and use of the solicited funds to fostering an understanding among stakeholders of the institution's mission, vision, and values.
>
> Campaign communications plans offer a strategic opportunity to build higher levels of understanding and involvement among the stakeholders of the institution.[2]

The Campaign Communications Plan

Early on in campaign planning, an organization should create a communications or public relations plan as part of the overall campaign plan. The plan should have definitive goals and objectives and describe the purposes of the plan and the targeted audiences.

Dr. Williams believes that a good communications plan can contribute measurably to the overall fund-raising plan on three basic levels:

1. Contextual, creating visibility for the institution and enhancing its reputation with a variety of constituencies so that fund raising can succeed

2. Strategic, helping to resolve the what and why issues of fund raising

3. Tactical, determining how to fulfill goals and objectives with specific events and activities[3]

The general purpose of the communications plan is to create expectations of success among key constituencies and to lift the awareness of the entire organization through the success of the campaign. The plan should be designed to keep the various publics informed about campaign progress and to create a mood of forward movement and institutional success, not just campaign success.

Four Phases

A communications plan will generally fall into four distinct phases:

Phase I: Precampaign Publicity. Phase I is designed to create excitement about the campaign and the coming announcement of the goals and objectives. This phase must be delicately handled so as not to abridge the confidentiality of the targeted goal prematurely. Discussion of the campaign in undefined terms, indicating that the effort is in the planning stages, is entirely permissible and will be expected by media outlets.

It is possible that in this phase the announcement of the campaign chair as well as the lead campaign committee, or at least the planning committee, can be made.

Phase II: Announcement of the Campaign. At some point in the campaign plan, the goal as well as the progress toward reaching that goal will be announced publicly. During this phase, a number of principal and major gifts will no doubt be announced as well as the formation of the major committees of volunteers that will help garner support. A sample gift announcement policy can be found on the "Campaign Tools" CD.

Institutions may want to give consideration to a major public event to announce the goal of the campaign.

Phase III: Informational Phase. During this phase, the communication effort centers on announcing major gifts that will create a sense of momentum and will energize the campaign's key constituents.

Care should always be taken to secure the permission of the benefactors in the announcement of gifts.

The staff, in consultation with volunteer leadership, should decide early on in campaign planning the level of campaign gifts that should be publicly announced. This gift level will depend a great deal on the scope and size of the campaign, but campaign officials should be sensitive about the size of the gifts to be communicated publicly. Communicating smaller contributions could set a tone for the campaign at a level that will not help position the campaign as a major gift effort. At larger institutions, gifts below $100,000 are generally not publicly announced. Naturally, flexibility must be maintained, because there certainly are some situations where gifts of any size may require publicity, but generally speaking, announcing gifts below a predetermined threshold could be deleterious to campaign effectiveness. You want campaign constituents to be thinking about their own philanthropic support at the highest level possible. Publicizing smaller contributions can detract from the campaign, especially in the early stages.

Phase IV: Concluding Campaign and Post-Campaign Phase. Moving toward the successful conclusion of the campaign and attainment of the goal comprise the post-campaign phase of the communications plan. This phase focuses on the success of the campaign and points to the achievements of the effort toward strengthening the nonprofit's programs. An organization's constituency is interested in what happens immediately following the successful conclusion of the campaign, and a carefully structured communications plan to inform volunteers and other constituents is essential.

Some organizations will want to hold a concluding campaign event to thank volunteers and benefactors and signal the success of the program.

This is also an excellent time to boost the achievements of the campaign and how it has changed the organization for the better. Announcement of strategic objectives that have been fulfilled during the campaign and how they are benefiting the organization are all important components of this phase.

Elements of a Campaign Communications Plan

The major elements of a campaign communications plan are as follows:
- **Purpose and Objectives.** Any good communications plan should have a listing of purposes and objectives. These might include:
  - informing the organization's constituency of the case and goals in the campaign
  - motivating prospective donors to identify their interests and loyalties among the campaign priorities and to commit their resources
  - recognizing the important contributions of campaign donors and leaders
  - enhancing the organization's public image

- **Campaign Name and Logo.** As previously discussed, most campaigns have a campaign name and logo, or institutional identity, that are used during the years of the campaign. This can be used on all materials, including proposal letters, letterhead, brochures, and so forth.

- **General Messages.** Organizations may want to create general messages around the institution's case statement and strategic planning process consistent with the communications planning process. These messages and the communications plan should have a unifying theme that should run throughout the life of the campaign.

- **Focus Group Meetings.** Previously, the use of focus group meetings in feasibility planning was discussed. In a sense, these focus meetings are designed to inform a small group of benefactors and volunteers about campaign priorities. Since it is a form of communication, it might be important to list the meetings in the communications plan.

- **Campaign Public Announcement and Kickoff Event.** Most campaigns have a campaign kickoff event to announce the campaign publicly. The purpose of the event is to help motivate prospects, volunteers, and others about the importance of the campaign as well as to announce the goal and the progress to date. The campaign kickoff serves as a psychological milestone.

- **Internal Organization Publications.** Your organization will want to communicate information about the campaign in its internal newsletters, pamphlets, and so forth.

- **Existing Communications Vehicles.** You will no doubt want to use existing communications vehicles to promote the campaign, particularly when the public phase has been reached.

- **Media Announcements.** Another important component of the communications plan is the announcement of gifts at certain levels.

- **Campaign News Publication.** Many campaigns create a new publication that sends out information to constituents—both internal and external—about campaign progress.

- **Paid Advertising.** Organizations may want to consider purchasing advertising when announcing major milestones within the campaign. A number of institutions have taken out full-page advertisements in their local newspapers listing the campaign committee members and chair and announcing the campaign as publicly under way.

- **Web page.** Design of a new campaign Web page is an important consideration.

- **Campaign Case Statement.** As previously discussed, the creation of a case statement early on in campaign planning is most important.

- **Lead Campaign Brochure.** A full-color brochure that makes the case for the campaign, its priorities, and significant giving opportunities can serve as a lead document for the campaign and can be used in the major gift solicitation process.

- **Use of Video.** Video can be used for myriad purposes such as an inspirational film to be shown at the campaign kickoff event or an educational film emphasizing the themes and messages of the campaign. Videos can also be used quite effectively at campaign committee meetings.

- **"How To Give" Piece.** An organization may want to develop a separate brochure from the lead campaign brochure that describes how gifts of cash, securities, real property, deferred giving vehicles, and so forth, can be made to the organization. It is possible to include this information in the lead brochure as well.

- **Training Materials for Volunteers.** Consideration should be given to the creation of a volunteer guide to be used during the campaign so that volunteers will have a sense of solicitation do's and don'ts.

A marketing/communications plan can be found on the "Campaign Tools" CD.

Campaign Publications

It is most important to keep the internal institutional community apprised of campaign planning and direction. Often the staff outside the development office are not directly related to the campaign and can lose track of the campaign's progress without a carefully structured information network. The use of internal organization publications such as an administrative informational newsletter and CEO staff letter can help to keep internal constituents informed about campaign progress.

A good campaign communications plan should also include the use of all appropriate external publications as well as the creation of new publications designed specifically for the campaign. There is no reason why existing publications cannot be used to carry campaign themes and messages. A review of current institutional publications and how they might be used in a campaign is an important first step in a communications plan.

The creation of new external publications to keep top volunteers informed on a regular basis is also something to be considered.

The Lead Campaign Brochure

Most campaigns of any note will publish a lead campaign brochure. The purpose of the brochure is to lay out the case for support of the campaign as well as giving opportunities, naming opportunities, and general information about the organization. The lead campaign brochure is used both as an informational piece and a solicitation piece and, often accompanies the presentation of a tailored proposal on a major or principal gift solicitation.

Frankly, the use of a lead campaign brochure in a capital campaign is not absolutely vital to the success of the campaign. Some institutions have preferred not to use a lead brochure, seeing it as a waste of institutional funds. The argument is that the promotional piece looks good but is seldom read and that most copies end up on a shelf in the basement of the development office.

While it is true that lead campaign brochures probably will not cause an individual to make a gift or a larger gift to your organization, they are important pieces and serve to validate the campaign from an historical perspective.

The following are some key components of a lead campaign brochure:

1. **Opening Statement by the CEO of the Organization.** Launching a campaign is a very significant event in the life of a nonprofit organization. A statement by the CEO noting the importance of the campaign is a fundamental element in the lead brochure. Consider using a photograph of the CEO to accompany his or her statement.

2. **Statement by the Chair of the Campaign.** The chair of the campaign is a high-visibility individual who is helping to lead the overall effort. A statement or letter in the brochure from the campaign chair is most important.

3. **Statement from the Chair of the Governing Board.** Tying the governing board closely to the campaign is essential.

4. **Potential Profiles of Benefactors.** It is also important in the lead brochure to profile previous major gift benefactors, discussing the reasons for their giving and the importance of the capital campaign to the organization. These profiles can be effective fund-raising testimonials.

5. **Information About the Campaign Goal.** Campaign goals should be mentioned frequently throughout the brochure and broken down into categories of support.

   Brochures should address in detail the strategic objectives of the campaign and the various giving opportunities that might include bricks and mortar projects, scholarships, endowment, program initiatives, and so forth.

6. **Specific Way to Give.** The lead brochure should list specific categories with appropriate language so that benefactors can choose the area they wish to benefit. These might include named chairs, professorships, fellowships, scholarships, and so forth.

7. **Pledge Form.** The lead brochure should also include a pledge form or at least a pocket or foldout in the back of the brochure where a pledge form could be placed.

Concluding Campaign Brochure

A number of organizations also create a concluding brochure at the end of the campaign as a retrospective and historical document on the success of the campaign. This publication outlines the various successes of the campaign, providing information on major gift support, attainment of the goal, the listing of lead volunteers, and the campaign objectives that were funded.

Use of Advertising

With increased frequency, organizations are carrying the message of their capital campaign to their key constituents through paid advertising.

At both Penn State and the University of Arkansas, the campaign used paid advertising on several occasions.

When the original goal was announced, a full-page advertisement was carried in statewide newspapers. Space was also purchased in statewide papers that listed the major lead campaign committee.

At the conclusion of the campaigns, advertisements were placed in statewide newspapers, touting the success of the campaign and what it meant to the organizations. The advertisements gave a sense of accomplishment to the immediate community.

Campaign Speakers Bureau

One of the most effective ways to spread the word about a campaign once it reaches the public phase is through a campaign speakers bureau. The speakers bureau puts top officials and volunteers in front of service clubs, constituent groups, membership organizations, and other constituents as a way to herald the success of the campaign and involve others in the effort.

Local service clubs and other groups constantly request speakers for their organizations, and an institution should consider designing a speakers bureau that can accommodate these requests during the life of the campaign.

Campaign Videos

The use of video in a capital campaign has become much more prevalent. While the cost of producing videos can be expensive, videos or film do serve a most useful purpose of exciting and informing key constituents.

Videos or film can be used in the communications plan to inform various constituents about campaign progress. Generally, these videos are short (7 to 10 minutes), they are uplifting, exciting, and tug at the hearts of donors and constituents.

Video can be used very effectively at the campaign public announcement as well as at the concluding event.

During the campaign for Penn State, President Ronald Reagan agreed to send video greetings, which congratulated campaign volunteers for launching the effort and wishing them success. The video was played at the first campaign committee meeting.

Almost 15 years later, the same scenario was used with a different president. President William Jefferson Clinton appeared in a video to congratulate the campaign steering committee on launching the campaign at the University of Arkansas.

Videos can also have tremendous value as keepsakes and cultivation tools for major benefactors.

A Word About Video Fund Raising

For some time, nonprofits have been using video or film in their fund-raising efforts. The use of video for fund raising was pioneered about 20 years ago. Ohio State University and Penn State University are two institutions that used it very effectively in raising funds for specific projects.

In the early 1990s, Penn State University used a video presentation to help raise $20 million for a new athletic facility. A seven-minute video tape was mailed to approximately 20,000 prospects, informing them that they would be contacted by a student from Penn State who would be talking about the campaign for the new facility. The video tape outlined the various gift packages.

The response was overwhelming. The total cost of the project was approximately $182,000, but the total raised through the use of the video was $3.4 million, which exceeded staff expectations.

Video presentation, when combined with telemarketing, can have a dramatic impact on any campaign, providing the audience has been carefully screened and targeted.

The cost of video production has been drastically reduced, particularly now that CDs can be produced so cheaply.

The Campaign Kickoff Event and Campaign Concluding Event

The campaign kickoff event and campaign concluding event are celebratory functions important to any campaign. Most volunteers and benefactors want to see a beginning and an ending to the campaign, and these events serve that important purpose. Roger L. Williams, currently the executive director at Penn State Alumni Association, writes:

> Special events can inject excitement, spark enthusiasm, and generate momentum in a way that nothing else can approximate. They can introduce, recognize, thank, and motivate volunteers and major donors, communicate key messages about your institution, and dispel myths and misinformation. They can exhilarate participants—and they can be designed as creatively as the imagination will allow.[4]

Campaign events bring together volunteers and major gift benefactors in a special and memorable way. If an event is successful, benefactors will remember it as an important time to pause and assess the strengths of the organization. Events are marvelous occasions to promote good will among internal and external constituents.

Cost is always a factor, and extravagance must be avoided, but it is important to bring together the organization's internal and external family to experience a cohesiveness of purpose. If properly staged, the campaign opening and concluding events can be important occasions to promote your organization as well as its capital campaign.

Governing Board Communication

As previously noted, it may be advantageous to the campaign to have the organization's governing board adopt a formal resolution signaling the importance of the campaign and lending their enthusiastic support. This is a worthy communications device that may receive wide attention among an institution's constituent groups.

Notes for Chapter 8

1. Roger L. Williams, "They Work Hard for the Money," *CASE Currents* (June 1989): 36.

2. Catherine B. Ahles, "The Right Shift," *CASE Currents* (March 2004).

3. Roger L. Williams, "The Role of Public Relations in Fund Raising," in *Educational Fund Raising: Principles and Practice* (Washington, D.C. The American Council on Education/Oryx Press, 1993).

4. Ibid.

nine

Post-Campaign Planning

We make a living by what we get, but we make a life by what we give.

Winston Churchill

Let's hope that we have arrived at this chapter having conducted a very successful campaign. Perhaps the campaign is winding down and close to conclusion. Perhaps the dollar goal has been met and the volunteers and staff are feeling very good about the success they have achieved. The concluding gala is in the planning stages, and we can hope that the campaign has galvanized the organization for the future.

The Challenge Ahead

When the campaign enters its final phase, it is very important to undertake an evaluation of the development program and determine its direction during the immediate post-campaign period. The overriding challenge will be to continue the momentum that has been attained in the campaign and sustain the level of private gift support without a campaign context. When your major capital campaign concludes, the focus and visibility provided by the campaign will inevitably change. The case for major gift support for your organization may be more difficult to make with some potential benefactors after the campaign concludes, because many donors will believe that with the successful conclusion of the campaign, programmatic, capital, and endowment needs have been met.

The creation of a *post-campaign planning document* is an important final step in the capital campaign process. Some professionals might even conclude that it is the most important step of all in that it sets the agenda for the future of major gift fund raising for your organization.

Before a general discussion of the post-campaign planning document, it is important for any campaign to take stock of its accomplishments and to be certain that the campaign was, in fact, successful and accomplished most of the strategic objectives originally set out by the organization.

What are the characteristics of successful campaigns? How do you know if your organization has actually achieved campaign success other than reaching the dollar goal of the campaign? The following are important hallmarks of successful campaigns:

- Were the strategic objectives of the campaign closely linked to your organization's long-range strategic plan? Has your strategic plan been bolstered because of the campaign?

- Has your organization made a significant investment in the cultivation of major gift benefactors who will carry the institution long term?

- Have you maintained an experienced professional staff that will continue to work on behalf of your organization, or do you suspect that a number of your development staff members may move on to other positions?

- How effective was your organization in involving volunteer leadership? Do the volunteer leaders want to continue to be a part of your organization in some capacity and role?

- Was there consistent and thoughtful participation from senior staff members of the organization and from other employees, faculty, and persons internal to the organizational structure?

- Have you been successful in raising the sights of your largest benefactors?

- Have you broadened considerably the prospect pool during the campaign?

- Have you been constantly evaluating staff resources, budget, and infrastructure for the development program? Have you convinced the senior officers of the organization and the governing board that an investment in the development program is an investment in the long-term welfare of the institution?

- Have you increased annual fund raising for the organization during the life of the campaign?

- Do you have a major gift culture among volunteers and benefactors who understand that big gifts make all the difference in the welfare of the organization?

- Have you grown the level of unrestricted annual support that is so important to your organization?

- Do you have a strong management structure for ongoing fund-raising success?

- Has the campaign improved the cost effectiveness of fund raising? Do you know how much it takes to raise a dollar for your organization?

- Has the campaign enhanced the public image and stature of your organization?

Your answers to all of these questions will help you in formulating a post-campaign plan that will carry your organization into the future.

Some in your organization may believe that the level of resources dedicated to the development office is no longer necessary now that the campaign has concluded. A few individuals may assume that the development program as a whole is no longer necessary and can be dramatically downsized. And still others may be jealous of the resources that have been given to the development program and anxious for the organization to redeploy resources to other areas.

For all of these reasons, it is important to create a post-campaign planning document before the conclusion of the campaign so that all stakeholders, volunteers, board members, the CEO, senior officers, staff, benefactors, and all others who are associated with your organization understand and appreciate the direction that the development program will take in the post-campaign environment.

Post-Campaign Objectives

Sustain and Increase Private Giving

To sustain and increase your organization's level of external philanthropic support, the internal and external communities must understand that the efforts and pace of the development program should not decrease just because the campaign has concluded. Post-campaign planning should be based on the assumption that the primary goal is to sustain and even increase the current level of support in the final year of the campaign while preparing for the next capital campaign three to five years into the future.

There may actually be a feeling among some development staff members that the campaign never concluded! Development staff members, along with volunteers, will continue to direct, guide, and participate in the identification, involvement, cultivation, and solicitation of friends, corporations, foundations, and organizations. Although it is not business as usual, the development program is still charged with the responsibility of raising private support and should put into place structures and programs that keep the flow of private giving as high as possible.

Even though the hope is that the organization will be able to sustain the level of support that was achieved during the campaign years, an organization should anticipate that total gift support may decrease in the immediate years following the campaign. It is likely that the number of major gifts flowing to the organization could diminish and, as pledge commitments are paid off and not replaced with new capital campaign gifts, the organization may show a dip in overall giving. Expect this; it is not an unusual phenomenon, and preparing CEOs and boards for this eventuality is crucial.

The key point is to keep in place the staffing, resources, and programs to maintain total gift support at the highest possible level.

Evaluation of Strategic Objectives

The campaign will likely achieve only a percentage of its strategic objectives. Though the dollar goal may be surpassed, it is not likely that every need determined early in the campaign will have been met. A strategic objectives achievement of 60 or 70 percent is a most successful accomplishment. Institutions that have achieved the funding of these percentages in the campaign should feel a sense of major accomplishment.

The organization must now initiate a process for a new set of strategic priorities to help direct the fund-raising agenda once the campaign has concluded.

I suggest that the establishment of the new strategic objectives take a two-pronged approach:

1. A review of goals and objectives that were *not* met in the current campaign; and

2. The establishment of a new long-term listing of strategic objectives as determined by the leadership of your organization.

As we all know, needs in a campaign evolve throughout the campaign years. If a campaign runs for five to seven years, it is natural that some of the strategic objectives are no longer a priority for the organization and other objectives are of more importance.

Initially, the leadership of the organization should submit a list of strategic priorities that were not met in the immediate past campaign but are still priorities for the organization. These existing unmet needs form the basis for a revolving needs statement that will be a fluid document reviewed on an ongoing basis and subject to regular change by the leadership of the organization.

Secondly, chief officers should request that a new strategic objectives list be promulgated. Those compiling the new strategic objectives should take into account the organization's strategic long-term plan and should continue to focus on the need to move the organization ahead in every area.

Need for Feasibility Study

In some cases, new institutional objectives for fund raising may require that a formal feasibility study be undertaken to determine the likelihood of success of the new project immediately following a major capital campaign. Keep in mind that there may be some "donor fatigue," and donors may still be paying off pledges they made in the immediate past capital campaign. Organizations should be conscious of donor fatigue and be careful about launching any major effort too soon after the conclusion of the major capital campaign.

Focus or Boutique Campaigns

It is possible that a natural result of an evolving needs statement will be a decision by the leadership of the organization to undertake a limited number of smaller-focus or boutique campaigns. A focus or boutique campaign may be a project left over from the major capital campaign that was not funded or maybe one that was not even pursued in the campaign for various reasons. Focus campaigns are generally efforts that involve the entire constituency of the organization and are built around a project that will benefit that total constituency. Examples could include a new building project or major endowment effort.

Again, donor fatigue figures largely in the decision to conduct focus or boutique campaigns. One of the advantages of launching such efforts during the off years of a capital campaign is to continue to involve important volunteers and benefactors in the organization and its development program. At some point, benefactors will have concluded their campaign pledges and may be ready to make an additional commitment and will be looking for appropriate projects in which to channel their giving.

Creation of an Ongoing Volunteer Development Committee or Board

One of the most important benefits resulting from a major capital campaign will be the development of a network of volunteers. In a large, complex organization, these volunteers were most likely recruited from throughout the United States, and the participation of new friends and benefactors in the organization's affairs is at an all-time high. The organization must develop a program to continue involving the most effective of these volunteers once the campaign concludes and the volunteer network is disbanded.

If your institution does not have an ongoing volunteer organizational structure such as a development council, development committee, board, board of visitors, or foundation, give serious consideration to establishing such an organizational structure. Membership could be composed of key campaign volunteers who demonstrated their commitment to philanthropy during the major capital campaign. It is most likely that a predominant number of these volunteers will continue their volunteerism somewhere, and it might as well be with your organization. It would be a mistake to disband all campaign committees without forming another group that can tap into volunteer leadership.

Maintenance of Development Resources

In the beginning of the campaign, your organization's administration more than likely provided increased funding for the development function to carry out the myriad details of the campaign. This investment of resources helped to move the campaign forward and most likely resulted in an increase in gift support. Without this infusion of funds, the campaign would not have been a success.

To maintain the current level of support as well as to increase private giving in a noncampaign environment, I recommend that current staffing levels be generally maintained, including maintaining the budget of the development office. Governing boards and chief executive officers should not decrease the funding of the development office simply because the campaign has concluded. Now, more than ever, the development office will need the resources to continue and hopefully increase major gift support in the coming years. The campaign has allowed your organization to reach a new level of private gift support, and you want to do everything possible to sustain this level of giving. To do that, it will require resources and staffing on a continuing basis.

Too often, institutions tend to cut the staff of the development office and their annual maintenance budget simply because the campaign has concluded. This is terribly shortsighted and will only lead to a decrease in philanthropic giving over the long term.

There may be some positions that will change or evolve now that the campaign has concluded. A development program should certainly be willing to evaluate its resources and, if not cut back, at least justify their continuation once the campaign has concluded.

Stewardship and Donor and Constituent Relations

We have previously discussed the importance of stewardship and good donor and constituent relations. Now that the campaign has concluded, good
stewardship is more important than ever. Keeping donors informed about
the impact their major gifts have had on the institution and informing them
regularly about endowment levels that they may have created will be extremely
important. Holding regular donor recognition events for benefactors at various
levels is always a vital activity. Benefactors must be honored appropriately
for major gift support. Continued cultivation is essential to an ongoing development program. After the campaign has concluded, benefactors must
be made to feel that their gift is critically important and deeply appreciated
outside the context of a capital campaign.

Assessment of Development Procedures and Policies

The post-campaign environment is a good time to reassess development office
procedures and policies, looking at all aspects of the development program.
Do endowment gift levels need to be changed? Should they be increased or
lowered? Should the endowment spending policy be reviewed? Are you putting enough resources into planned giving? Are your gift recording policies
sound? All of these issues can now be addressed adequately.

The Inevitable Planning for the Next Campaign

Some institutions conclude their campaigns and immediately begin planning
a second effort to commence in four to six years. Planning toward that eventuality should begin immediately once the campaign is in the final stages.

I recommend that a post-campaign committee be appointed to work with
key development personnel to verify and draft the post-campaign plan. This
committee will assist and evaluate the success of the last capital campaign
and begin anticipating those elements that will need to be put in place for
the next one.

If your capital campaign was successful, then it is axiomatic that there
will be another one, probably sooner rather than later!

Afterword

I am approaching my 30th year raising funds for nonprofit organizations. It is hard to believe it has been that long. The years go by quickly. One day, you're the youngest person on the staff and the next you have somehow become the oldest. The institutions where you have worked begin to blend together and some old war stories start taking on bits and pieces of different organizations, not any one in particular.

Over the past 30 years, much has happened on the philanthropic scene. The economy and stock market have risen and fallen and, in some cases, plunged. Wars have been fought, terrorism has been rampant, and philanthropy in general has seen an ebb and flow, particularly in this century.

With all that has happened on the American and world scenes the past 30 years, one thing has remained constant. The American people are the most generous people in the world. Not only do we support our own philanthropic organizations very generously, but we also have been a beacon to the world in providing resources, people power, and other support to so many international charitable causes. This truly American giving spirit is what propels so many worthy organizations and causes in hopes of improving the human condition. Without philanthropy, the world would be a dismal place. Without a true benevolent giving spirit by hundreds of thousands of people supporting literally hundreds of thousands of worthy causes, many people would go wanting and many extraordinary programs would cease to exist.

Those who practice the art and science of fund raising are involved in a worthy profession. No one should ever have to apologize for being a fund raiser. The world could not operate without you. Literally, life as we know it could not function without philanthropy.

So, when things don't seem to be going your way and you are tired of getting rejections or simply exhausted from the constant pressure of this profession, try to keep in mind your noble cause and your noble profession. Just pause and look around you everywhere. Hospitals, health agencies, libraries, arts centers, human service organizations, colleges and universities, art agencies, civic responsibilities, scholarship opportunities, health care for the elderly—none of this would be possible without your work. Philanthropy has built America and will continue to do so long into the future. Take solace.

Bibliography

"A Golden Age for Philanthropy Ahead?" *Economist*, July 29, 2004.

Ahles, Catherine B. "The Right Shift." *CASE Currents* (March 2004).

Allen, Nick. "Using E-Mail and the Web to Acquire and Cultivate Donors." *Nonprofit World* (January/February 2003): 27.

Ambler, Patricia. "Getting to Know Them." *Connections* (Summer 2003).

Asp II, James W. "Pay for Performance." *CASE Currents* (July/August 1999).

Association of Fundraising Professionals. "Stressed But Coping: Nonprofit Organizations and the Current Fiscal Crisis." (January 19, 2004).

_____. "Confidence in U.S. Charitable Organizations Remains Unimproved." (September 27, 2004).

Bass, David. "Protecting Donors Privacy Is a Matter of Good Ethics and Good Business." *The Chronicle of Higher Education* 50, no. 3 (April 23, 2004): B15.

Batchelder, Duff . "Evaluating and Choosing a Fund-Raising Database Program." *Fund-Raising Management* (October 2002): 4.

Beagle, Robert M. "Competing Interests." *CASE Currents* (October 2003).

Begin, Sherri. "Support System: Online Fund Raising Grows, but Nonprofits Say It's Still a Long Way from Being the Main Avenue." *Crain's Detroit Business* 20, no. 46 (November 15, 2004): 11.

Blanton, Thomas. "The World's Right to Know." *Foreign Policy* (July/August 2002)

Boice, Jacklyn P. "Achieving Dreams Through Strategic Goals." *Advancing Philanthropy* (May/June 2003): 14–18.

Bongiorno, Deborah. "Globe-Trotting, the Functions of Advancement Go Global," *CASE Currents* (July/August 2003).

Bornstein, Rita. "The Capital Campaign: Benefits and Hazards." in *The President and Fund Raising*. Editors James L. Fisher and G. H. Quehl, 203–4 (New York: American Council on Education and Macmillan Publishing Company, 1989).

Brenna, Susan. "Buddy Systems?" *CASE Currents* (September 2004).

Brenna, Susan. "Diamonds in the Rough." *CASE Currents* (December 2004).

Burlingame, Dwight F. *Philanthropy in America: A Comprehensive Historical Encyclopedia.* Santa Barbara, California: ABC-CLIO Inc, 2004.

Byrne, John A. "The New Face of Philanthropy." *Business Week* 3810 (December 2, 2002): 82.

"Capital Campaigns 1991-92." *Capital Campaign Report,* Brakeley John Price Jones, Inc., Spring 1992.

"Capital Campaign/Venture Philanthropy." *Professional Fundraising Magazine.* (November 2002).

Carabelli, Paula. "Managers Portfolio: What Great CAOs Are Made Of," *CASE Currents* (September 2000).

CASE Management Reporting Standards: Standards for Annual Giving and Campaigns in Educational Fund Raising, Third Edition, (2004 by the Council for Advancement and Support of Education), p. 12.

Causer, Craig. "Special Report: Technology Spending Is Picking Up." *Non-Profit Times* (November 1, 2004).

"Challenge Gifts." *Profit Quests Fundraising*, December 17, 2004.

Cohen, Rick. "Donations to Public-University Foundations Ought to Be Matters of Public Record." *The Chronicle of Higher Education* (April 23, 2004).

Collins, Mary Ellen. "Campaign Strategies: Orchestrating a Harmonious Campaign." *CASE Currents* (April 2001).

Collison, Michele N-K. "Collision: Where the Color Line Yields to the Bottom Line." *Black Issues in Higher Education* (May 25, 2000).

Conhaim, Wallys W. "Virtual Volunteering." *Information Today* 20, no. 3 (March 2003): 27.

Covaleski, John. "Getting Value from Application Resellers." *NonProfit Times* (October 15, 2003).

Dickens, Andrea G. "Getting Ready for the Data: Preparing an Implementation Plan." *Connections* (Summer 2003).

Dietz Jr., John L. "University Fund Raising: Is There an Ideal Management Model for the Development Operation of the Large, Public Research Institution?" (master's thesis)

Pennsylvania State University, Graduate School and the College of Education, April 1995).

Dove, Kent E. *Conducting a Successful Capital Campaign: A Comprehensive Guide for Nonprofit Organizations.* San Francisco: Jossey-Bass Inc., 1988.

Dove, Kent E. *Conducting A Successful Capital Campaign: The New, Revised, and Expanded Edition of the Leading Guide to Planning and Implementing a Capital Campaign.* 2d ed. San Francisco: Jossey-Bass, Inc., 1999.

Drozdowski, Mark J. "Not Making the Case." *Chronicle of Higher Education Chronicle Careers* (August 9, 2004).

Drozdowski, Mark J. "A Phantom Menace." *The Chronicle of Higher Education* 50, no. 25 (February 27, 2004): C3.

Edwards, Tamala M. "The Power of the Purse," *Time*, (May 17, 1999).

Epner, Steve. "Surviving Fundraising on the Internet." *Nonprofit World* (March/April 2004): 17.

Epsilon and Barna Research Group, Limited. "The 21st Century Donor; Emerging Trends in a Changing Market." (September 2002).

Fisher, James L. "The Growth of Heartlessness: The Need for Studies on Philanthropy." *The Education Record* (Winter 1986).

Fox, Richard. "Your Partnership with Power People." *CASE Currents* 10, no. 20 (November/December 1984): 43.

Frantzreb, Arthur C. "The Pros and Cons of Feasibility Studies." National Society of Fundraising Executives, Advancing Philanthropy (Winter, 1997–98).

Gardyn, Rebecca. "Faith in Diversity: Religious Groups See Benefits of Hiring People from Other Faiths." *The Chronicle of Philanthropy* (July 24, 2003).

Gearhart, G. David and M. Bezilla. "Fund Raising Success Takes Teamwork." *Fund Raising Management* (March 1991): 42–44, 46.

Giving USA 2004: The Annual Report on Philanthropy for the Year 2003. (The Center on Philanthropy at Indiana University, The American Association of Fund Raising Council, 2004).

Goodale, Toni K. "Is It Feasible?" *Fund Raising Management* (November 2001): 40.

Greenfield, James M. "Fund-Raising Costs and Credibility: What the Public Needs to Know." *NSFRE Journal* (Autumn 1988).

Gundry, Nanci Olson and Peter McKinley. "Advantages of a Decentralized Advancement Research Office." *Connections* (Fall 2002).

Hall, Jeremiah. "When Your Donations Fund Insider Perks." *Christian Science Monitor* (June 21, 2004): 13.

Hall, Margarete Rooney. "Two Approaches, One Goal." *CASE Currents* (April 2002).

Hall, Margarete Rooney. "Fundraising and Public Relations: A Comparison of Programme Concepts and Characteristics." *International Journal of Nonprofit and Voluntary Sector Marketing* 6, no. 4 (November 2002): 368.

Hanson, John H. "Dead Man Walking: Case Statements as Organizational Change Narratives." *Journal of Nonprofit & Public Sector Marketing* 10, no. 2 (2002): 83.

Harrington-Lueker, Donna. "The Lay of the Land; What Factors Affect Giving Today?" *CASE Currents* (September 2004).

Hart, Theodore R. "ePhilanthropy: Using the Internet to Build Support." *International Journal of Nonprofit and Voluntary Sector Marketing* 7, no. 4 (November 2002): 353.

"Highlights of the Foundation Center's 2004 Study International Grantmaking III; an update on U.S. Foundation Trends. The Foundation Center 2004.

Hispanics in Philanthropy. www.hiponline.org

Hoak, Robert. "The Value of the Feasibility Study Best Practices." *On-Philanthropy* (August 8, 2003).

Hogan, Cecilia. "Viewpoint: To Screen or Not to Screen?" *Connections* (Summer 2003): 14.

Joslyn, Heather. "Charity's Glass Ceiling: Salary Gap Persists for Women in Nonprofit Organizations." *Chronicle of Philanthropy—Managing* (March 20, 2003).

Joslyn, Heather. "Young People Fuel Demand for Nonprofit Study, *The Chronicle of Philanthropy* (January 8, 2004).

Kihlstedt, Andrea. *Capital Campaigns: Strategies that Work,* 2nd Edition. Gaithersburg, Maryland: Aspen Publishers, Inc., 2002, 1.

Kirkland Jr., Richard. "Should You Leave It All to the Children?" *Fortune* 114 (September 29, 1986): 18–26.

Klineman, Jeffrey and Elizabeth Schwinn. "Charities' Fast-Track Jobs." *The Chronicle of Philanthropy* (March 18, 2004).

Krit, Robert L. *The Fund-Raising Handbook.* The United States: Scott Foresman Professional Books, 1991.

Kronstadt, Jessica. *Charity, Philanthropy, and Civility in American History.* Edited by Lawrence J. Friedman and Mark D. McGarvie. New York: Cambridge University Press, 2004.

Lawrence, Mary "Lights . . . Camera . . . Action! Screening Prospects for a Capital Campaign." *NEDRA News* (Summer 2003).

Martin, Susan K. "Academic Library Fund-Raising: Organization, Process, and Politics." *Library Trends* 48, no. 3 (Winter 2000).

McGoldrick, William P. "Campaigning in the Nineties," in *Educational Fund Raising: Principles and Practice.* Edited by Michael J. Worth, 144. Phoenix, Arizona: Council for Advancement and Support of Education. Oryx Press, 1993.

Mercer, Joyce. "Footing the Bill for Fund Raising." *The Chronicle of Higher Education* (January 12, 1996).

Minton, Amy. "What Now? Working with Wealth Screening Results: Lessons I Learned." *Connections* (Summer 2003): 8.

Moore, Cassie J. "Nonprofit Organizations Are Hiring Workers at a Faster Pace than Government, Businesses." *The Chronicle of Philanthropy* (June 10, 2004).

Moore, Cassie. "Charities Must Learn to Better Manage Volunteers, Study Finds." *The Chronicle of Philanthropy* (March 18, 2004).

Moran, William J. "An Alternative to the Campaign Feasibility Study." *Fundraising Management* (April 2000): 28.

Native Americans in Philanthropy. www.nativephilanthropy.org

New Nonprofit Almanac and Desk Reference. San Francisco: Jossey-Bass, 2002.

Nichols, Judith E. "Repositioning Fundraising in the 21st Century." *International Journal of Nonprofit and Voluntary Sector Marketing* (May 2004): 163.

Nielsen, Colleen. "Leaving Their Mark." *CASE Currents* (July/August 2003).

Nielsen, Waldemar A. *The Golden Donors, A New Anatomy of the Great Foundations.* New York: Truman Talley Books, E. P. Dutton, 1985.

Oliver, Frank H. "Fellow Beggars: The History of Fund Raising Campaigning in U. S. Higher Education" (dissertation, Columbia University, 1999).

Panas, Jerold. *Making the Case: No Nonsense Guide to Writing the Perfect Case Statement.* Chicago: Institutions Press, 2004.

Panepento, Peter. "Clamoring for Consultants." *The Chronicle of Philanthropy* (March 18, 2004).

Pokrass, Richard J. *CASE Currents*, April, 1986.

Pollack, Rachel H. "Bond Issues." *CASE Currents* (January 2000).

Pulley, John L. "Embracing Performance Pay." *The Chronicle of Higher Education* 49, no. 36 (May16, 2003): A28.

Richards, M. D. and G. R. Sherratt. "Institutional Advancement Strategies and Hard Times." ERIC Report No. 2 (Washington D.C.: American Association of Higher Education, 1981).

Ruderman, Susan Cronin. "Viewpoint: Go Ahead—Skip the Screening." *Connections* (Summer 2003): 15.

Ruffin, Holt. "The Globalization of American Philanthropy." Duke University, October 31, 2003.

Salamon, Lester M. "Nonprofit World Faces Many Dangers." *The Chronicle of Philanthropy* (January 8, 2004).

Schaefer, Susan. "The Challenge of Challenge Gifts." *Grants & Foundation Review* (August 20, 2004).

Schervish, Paul G. and John J. Havens. "Recent Trends and Projections in Wealth and Philanthropy." Social Welfare Research Institution, Boston College, November 1, 2000.

Shaver, Nathan. "Technology in 2005: The Rise of ePhilanthropy." *On-Philanthropy* (December 17, 2004).

Smith, G. T. "The Chief Executive in Advancement." in *Handbook of Institutional Advancement: A Modern Guide to Executive Management, Institutional Relations, Fundraising, Alumni Administration, Government Relations, Publications, Periodicals, and Enrollment Management.* Edited by A. Westley Rowland, 697. San Francisco: Jossey-Bass, Inc., 1986.

Strand, Bobby J. "Building a Donor Information Base." in *Handbook of Institutional Advancement: A Modern Guide to Effective Management, Institutional Relations, Fundraising, Alumni Administration, Government Relations, Publications, Periodicals, and Enrollment Management*. Edited by A. W. Roland, 337. San Francisco: Jossey-Bass, Inc., 1986).

Szabo, Joan. "Funding the Foundation with Fees." *CASE Currents* (September 1997).

Tabios, Divine. "The Why and How of Database Change." *OnPhilanthropy* (October 22, 2004).

Van Til, John, et al. *Critical Issues in American Philanthropy: Strengthening Theory and Practice*. San Francisco: Jossey-Bass Inc., 1990, 4.

"Volunteer Management Capacity in America's Charities and Congregations: A Briefing Report." Washington, D.C.: Urban Institute, 2004.

Wagner, Lilya. "Women in Philanthropy." *OnPhilanthropy,* 2004.

Wallace, Nicole "Building Better Technology." *The Chronicle of Philanthropy* (September 16, 2004).

Walton, R. Christopher. "Rethinking Feasibility Studies." *Fundraising Management* (September 1997): 14.

Watson, Tom. "Philanthropic Landscape: A Fundraiser's View." *OnPhilanthropy* (February 20, 2004).

White, John A. State of the University Address. University of Arkansas, September 24, 2004.

Wilhelm, Ian. "Corporate Giving Takes a Dip, Economic Slump Forces Businesses to Be More Selective." *The Chronicle of Philanthropy* (July 24, 2003).

Williams, Roger L. "Special Cases: A Close-Up Look at Four Group's Progress and Pay." *CASE Currents* (February 1996).

Williams, Roger L. "They Work Hard for the Money." *CASE Currents* (June 1989): 36.

Williams, Roger L. "The Role of Public Relations in Fund Raising." in *Educational Fund Raising: Principles and Practice* (Washington, DC The American Council on Education/Oryx Press, 1993).

Worth, Michael J. Edited by *Educational Fund Raising, Principles and Practice*. Phoenix, Arizona: American Council on Education, Oryx Press, 1993, 18.

Nonprofit Fund Raising Consultants Directory

Barnes & Roche, Inc.
Rosemont Business Campus
Building Three, Suite 302
919 Conestoga Road
Rosemont, Pennsylvania 19010-1375
610-527-3244

Bentz Whaley Flessner
7251 Ohms Lane
Minneapolis, Minnesota
952-921-0111

Brakeley Briscoe Incorporated
51 Locust Avenue, Suite 204
New Canaan, Connecticut 06840
203-972-0282

Campbell and Company
One East Wacker Drive
Suite 3350
Chicago, Illinois 60601
312-644-7100

Cargill Associates
4701 Altamesa Boulevard
Fort Worth, Texas 76133
800-433-2233

Gonser Gerber Tinker Stuhr
400 East Diehl Road, Suite 380
Naperville, Illinois 60563
630-505-1433

Grenzebach Glier & Associates
55 West Wacker Drive
Suite 1500
Chicago, Illinois 60601
312-372-4040

Ketchum Incorporated
Three Gateway Center
Suite 1726
Pittsburgh, Pennsylvania 15222
412-355-2379

Marts and Lundy Incorporated
1200 Wall Street West
Lyndhurst, New Jersey 07071
800-526-9005

Washburn & McGoldrick Incorporated
8 Century Hill, Suite One
Latham, New York 12110
518-783-1949

The Wayland Group
323 Boston Post Road, Suite 3C
Sudbury, Massachusetts 01776
978-443-3224